THE FOUNDATIONS OF KEYNESIAN ANALYSIS

Also edited by Alain Barrère

MONEY, CREDIT AND PRICES IN KEYNESIAN PERSPECTIVE
KEYNESIAN ECONOMIC POLICIES

The Foundations of Keynesian Analysis

Proceedings of a Conference held at the University of Paris I–Panthéon-Sorbonne

Edited by

Alain Barrère

Professor of Economics
University of Paris I–Panthéon-Sorbonne

M
MACMILLAN
PRESS

First published 1988

Published by
THE MACMILLAN PRESS LTD
Houndmills, Basingstoke, Hampshire RG21 2XS
and London
Companies and representatives
throughout the world

Printed in Hong Kong

British Library Cataloguing in Publication Data
The Foundations of Keynesian analysis:
proceedings of a conference held at the
University of Paris–Panthéon-
Sorbonne
1. Economics
I. Barrère, Alain
330.1 HB171
ISBN 0–333–39420–8

Editor's Note

This collection of essays and the two companion volumes, *Money, Credit and Prices in Keynesian Perspective and Keynesian Economic Policies,* were presented at a conference held to commemorate the centenary of John Maynard Keynes at the University of Paris on 12–15 September 1983.

The University of Paris I – Panthéon-Sorbonne and the CNRS – Centre National de la Recherche Scientifique – organised the conference and made this volume possible.

A. B.

Contents

Notes on the Contributors

Antoine d'Autume is Professor of Economics at the University of Lille. His research work is on theoretical macroeconomics and especially disequilibrium theory.

Alain Barrère is Professor of Economics at the University of Paris I, Panthéon-Sorbonne. He has been professor at the University of Toulouse, the Ecole des Hautes Etudes en Sciences Sociales (Paris) and visiting professor at the Federal University of Brazil. He was Dean of the Faculté de Droit et des Sciences Economiques de Paris from 1967 to 1970.

His research is concerned with macroeconomic analysis, especially Keynesian theory, public economy and economic development. He is the author of: *Théorie Economique et Impulsion Keynésienne; Economie et Institutions Financières; Histoire de la Pensée Economique; La Crise n'est pas ce que l'on Croit; Déséquilibres Economiques et Contre-révolution Keynésienne*; and numerous articles.

Jean Cartelier is Professor of Political Economy at the University of Nice. His main publications are concerned with the history of political economy and general economic theory. He is a member of the editorial committee of *Cahiers d'Economie Politique*.

Dudley Dillard is Professor of Economics at the University of Maryland, USA, where he served as Chairman of the Economics Department from 1951 to 1975. He received B.S. and Ph.D. degrees from the University of California, Berkeley and was a visiting scholar at Harvard and a visiting professor at Columbia University. He has been president of the Southern Economic Association and the Association for Evolutionary Economics. His publications include *The Economics of John Maynard Keynes* and *Economic Development of the North Atlantic Community*.

Rodolphe Dos Santos Ferreira is Professor of Economics at the University Louis Pasteur, Strasbourg, France. His research work has been concerned with micro-economic foundations of macro-economic theory and history of economic thought, particularly Marx and Keynes.

Pierangelo Garegnani is Professor of Economics at the University of Rome. He studied Political Sciences at the Collegio Ghislieri of the University of Pavia, obtained his Ph.D. in Economics from the University of Cambridge, and continued his post-doctoral studies at the Massachusetts Institute of Technology.

He has published articles in several Italian and international journals and is the author of *Le Capital dans les Théories de la Répartition.*

Henri Guitton is Emeritus Professor at the University of Paris I, Panthéon-Sorbonne. He has taught economic analysis, statistics and mathematical economics.

His research has been concerned with economic fluctuations with a particular emphasis on time analysis. He has published *Les Fluctuations Economiques; L'Objet de l'Economie Politique; Le Catholicisme Social; A la Recherche du Temps Economique; Anthropie et Gaspillage; De l' Imperfection en Economie*; five textbooks and numerous articles.

Pierre-Yves Hénin is Professor at the University of Paris I, Panthéon-Sorbonne. He is the author or editor of several books on macrodynamics, accumulation and disequilibrium growth, and the disequilibria of an open economy. He is currently working on several topics related to disequilibrium and adjustments in open economies, including labour market adjustments, at both theoretical and empirical levels.

Lord Kaldor was sometime Fellow of King's College, Cambridge, and Emeritus Professor of Economics at the University of Cambridge.

He graduated from the London School of Economics in 1930 and was a member of its academic staff (as Lecturer and then Reader) from 1932 to 1947. He was a Director of the Research and Planning Division of the United Nations Economic Commission for Europe in Geneva from 1947 to 1949. He also acted as an adviser to various governments.

J. A. Kregel is Professor of Monetary Theory and Chairman of the Department of Economics at the University of Groningen, the Netherlands.

Philippe Michel is Professor of Economics and Mathematics at the University of Paris I, Panthéon-Sorbonne. He is now working in several fields: intertemporal equilibrium, disequilibrium growth, time consistent solutions, macro investment functions and Keynesian economics.

Frédéric Poulon is Professor of Economics at the University of Bordeaux. He is the author, or the editor, of several books on Keynesian macro-economics.

Bernard Schmitt is Maître de Recherche at the National Centre for Scientific Research (CNRS) and Professor at the Universities of Dijon and Fribourg. He has made important contributions in monetary analysis.

He is the author of several books which include: *L'Analyse Macro-économique des Revenus; La Pensée de K. Marx* (2 vols with A. Cencini); *La Monnaie Européenne; La France Souveraine de sa Monnaie; Inflation, Chômage et Malformation du Capital.*

Fausto Vicarelli was Professor of Political Economy at the University of Rome. He was an Economic Advisor to the Bank of Italy and a former Professor of the University of Florence. His research work has been concerned with international trade and capital flows, technical progress and Keynesian theory. He is the author of *Keynes: The Instability of Capitalism* and editor of *La controversia keynesiana* and *Keynes's Relevance Today*.

Professor Vicarelli died in a traffic accident at the end of 1986.

Preface: The Keynesian Project

Alain Barrère

Any appraisal of the contemporary significance of the work of John Maynard Keynes would require much more than an analysis of the *General Theory of Employment, Interest and Money* and the many other books and articles which preceded it. Even if we were to add the articles published after 1936, the speeches to the House of Lords, and the preparatory papers for the Bretton-Woods Conference, this would still be insufficient. Certainly, we would have a large number of the necessary elements, particularly if the controversies which Keynes's articles and various other writings provoked were also taken into account; yet all of this would concern only the Keynes of yesterday, perhaps even of the day before yesterday.

Today, Keynes is represented primarily by a return to the original sources and fundamental propositions, which has been made possible by the publication of the Royal Economic Society edition of *The Collected Writings of John Maynard Keynes* (referenced as *CW*, followed by the volume number).

This return to the origins is being pursued in two rather different ways. On the one hand there is the neo-classical–neo-Keynesian synthesis, and on the other the *Keynesian project* of developing Keynes's idea of a monetary production economy proposed by the fundamentalist Keynesians. Both go beyond the sterile debates concerning the appropriate instruments of analysis that have long dominated discussion to propose positive reconsideration of the very foundations of Keynes's analysis. After all these years, economists seem finally to have agreed that fruitful discussion requires the clear delineation of the subject-matter to be analysed prior to consideration of the content of the appropriate tool box.

Today we have a much clearer idea of *Keynes's project*: the interpretation of a monetary production economy, which may be distinguished from the approach of orthodox economics in the same way as monetary differs from real analysis, and analysis of production from that of exchange. The *General Theory* represents the partial realisation of this project in which interest and money represent the complementary contribution given by the *project* as a whole to the analysis of equilibrium at various levels of employment.

A close reading of certain of Keynes's writings had already suggested that the theory of employment belonged to a larger scheme, described by Keynes as the transformation of monetary theory into a theory of output as a whole (*CW*, VII, p. xxii). Indeed, Keynes gives an indication of the magnitude of his intended *project* when he states that 'our method of analysing the economic behaviour of the present under the influence of changing ideas about the future is one which depends on the interaction of supply and demand, and is in this way linked up with our fundamental theory of value' (ibid, pp. xxii–iii). However, it was necessary to wait for the publication of the *Collected Writings*, in particular volumes XIII, XIV, and XXIX, published between 1973 and 1979, to discover an indication of the sources of inspiration, the main themes and the essential foundations, if not the complete exposition, of the project upon which Keynes had embarked. It was then possible to recognise that his projected monetary production economy had been built up in successive stages as the result of the combination of the inspiration of the scientist with the practical experiences of the man of action. The various stages of this evolution are described in Dudley Dillard's contribution in Chapter 2, and in the numerous other contributions which make reference to the *Collected Writings*.

In his process of evolution it can now be seen that Keynes progressed from an *instrument* of knowledge, the theories of money and production, to the *object* of knowledge, the monetary production economy. He did not concern himself with an interpretation of economic activity based on an explanation of the determinants of the demand for money, as one might start from the explanation of the determinants of the demand for real consumption goods; rather he started from the presumption of an economy characterised by the duality of real and monetary phenomena in which the latter exerts a determinant influence over events (production and exchange) occurring in the real sphere. This essential difference was immediately perceived by J. R. Hicks who, shortly after publication of the *General Theory*, described Keynes's conception of the economy as being 'completely out of touch with the classical world' (Hicks, 1937, pp. 110).

What is the basis of this difference? The answer lies in five substitutions and one fundamental option. Keynes substitutes: (i) a monetary economy for a real economy; (ii) a production economy for an exchange economy; (iii) an enterpreneur economy for a consumer economy; (iv) variations in production and employment for given quantities and revealed preferences; (v) a world of non-probabilistic uncertainty, which therefore requires the necessity of forming often-disappointed expectations, for a world of certainty where expectations are practically and necessarily confirmed.

A fundamental option faces economic agents at the beginning of each period: it concerns the decision of whether an asset or an available surplus is to be set aside in a reserve to increase *total accumulated wealth*, or to be invested to *increase current wealth*, i.e. expand current income.

THE REAL EXCHANGE ECONOMY AND THE MONETARY PRODUCTION ECONOMY

In order to give precision to the essential differences between these two types of economy, Keynes uses a method similar to Schumpeter's abstract construction of a steady state circular flow to demonstrate the dynamic character of economic evolution. We thus find in *CW*, vol. XIII the distinction between a co-operative, 'neutral', or 'real exchange economy', characterised by real wages, the equality between output and aggregate demand, and the permanency of full employment contrasted with the 'entrepreneur' or 'monetary' economy with 'non-neutral' money, money-wages, variable income and employment, all organised by entrepreneurs whose decisions determine productive activity.

We know that these two frameworks were not reproduced in the final version of the *General Theory*, but the first prepares and explains what becomes chapter 1 of the *General Theory* describing the postulates of classical economics which reproduce the characteristics of a real exchange or barter economy where the presence of neutral money has no independent influence on the exchange of real values. The framework of the entrepreneur economy presents the essence of a monetary production economy by introducing the entrepreneur, credit money, money-wages and expectations; all four are necessary to obtain increased production and employment in accordance with the expectations of aggregate expenditures that evoke the hope of maximum monetary profit.

In Chapter 2 of this volume and chapter 10 of *Keynesian Economic Policies*, Dudley Dillard and Marie-Hélène Devillers follow and explain in more detail the evolution of Keynes's thought, from his first writings on money to the distinction between a *real economy* and a *monetary production economy*. Their contributions make explicit the role of money in determining production and employment and demonstrate why the volume of the effective product differs from that of the potential product.

THE GENERAL THEORY AND THE 'SPECIAL' THEORY

Keynes's pretensions to a 'general' theory aroused strong critical reaction. In the *General Theory*, he gives arguments which he believes justify his position. Aggregate analysis considers the operation of the system as a whole, thus avoiding the error of extending to the *whole* propositions which can only be demonstrated for one part of the system considered in isolation. The general level of prices, and individual prices, are both determined in a similar fashion by supply and demand. This links their determination to the fundamental theory of value, generalised so as to cover both real values and monetary values, and to eliminate the dichotomy between cost and utility theory and the quantity theory of money. 'We are thus led to a more general theory, which includes the classical theory with which we are familiar, as a special case (*CW*, VII, p. xxiii). Expectations about the monetary values of assets held over time and the behaviour of consumers and holders of money are subject to change because individuals lack any firm knowledge of the evolution of future events. Finally, the variations in the level of output and employment show the equilibrium positions for various levels of unemployment representing the 'norm', as against full employment which must thus be considered as a special case.

Keynes's conception of aggregate economic analysis and his demonstration of less than full employment equilibrium gave rise to heated discussions. But, in retrospect, it is indeed surprising to note the extent to which these discussions were based on simple misunderstandings of Keynes's positions, and orthodox reactions were due to the fact that the arguments almost always concerned with the analytical framework employed, rather than the foundations of the classical analysis which Keynes had called into question.

Such discussion seems completely outmoded in the contemporary environment, which is more directly concerned to produce final realisation of the synthesis between neoclassical and Keynesian interpretations on the one hand, and to emphasise the generality of the now clearly specified Keynesian project, rather than just the theory of employment, on the other. It is thus no longer a question of identifying the specific differences between the two approaches, but rather of a joint examination to discover how the development of each one has contributed to our understanding of the economic system.

The distinction between *neoclassical synthesis Keynesianism*, and the *generalisation of Keynesianism* which stems from the *Keynesian project*, furnishes the framework for discussion in this introduction to the contributions to the contemporary development of Keynes's ideas that are collected in this book. I would like to stress that this distinction should not be interpreted as a criterion capable of classifying the authors themselves into two schools. Such a division would not only violate the freedom of choice of each author to classify his own work, it could also be challenged as the most suitable general method of classifying economists. Yet, by identifying two of the major poles of attraction of modern economic research, it has the advantage of making the distinction between the already existing 'neoclassical synthesis' approach and what I have called the *project of generalisation* which has recently emerged from the series of writings attempting to determine the generality of Keynes's entire contribution to economics.

I NEOCLASSICAL SYNTHESIS KEYNESIANISM

The expression 'neoclassical synthesis Keynesianism' is itself not devoid of ambiguity. For some, its dominant element is an attempt to integrate Keynes's essential contributions into the neoclassical framework by amending them in such a way that they are distorted beyond recognition. For others, it suggests the position that the development of the *General Theory* was based on elements which were so vague and imprecise as to require a neo-Keynesianism which allowed resolution of certain ambiguities present in the traditional interpretation.

There is also the problem that the connotation of the label 'Keynesianism' encompasses a much wider range of ideas than its original reference to the 1936 book, and the widespread belief that the introduction of certain of Keynes's essential ideas into the neoclassical system has brought about their reinterpretation in a way which has been clearly beneficial to economics. Indeed, this is one of the more evident benefits that is expected of the process of synthesis.

Finally it may be maintained that even if the Keynes of 1936 and of the *Collected Writings* is not faithfully represented in the neoclassical synthesis, it still represents Keynesianism as it is perceived by the majority of economists after nearly fifty years of continuous controversy.

The real question at issue, however, is to adopt a position which allows us to go beyond sterile discussion and complicitous silence in order to produce fruitful confrontation emphasising positive critical aspects. A good example may be found in Lord Kaldor's review (Chapter 7) of some of the themes expressed by Edmond Malinvaud, who himself reconsiders the conception of the labour market (chapter 2 of *Keynesian Economic Policies*) as does Gérard Grellet (chapter 3 of *Keynesian Economic Policies*) although from a different perspective.

The *IS–LM* Interpretation

What a curious destiny the *IS–LM* diagram has had. It is still today considered by most textbooks as the most suitable pedagogical presentation of the Keynesian system, even though its author conceived of it as a *pedagogical presentation of the neoclassical system which was to ease comparison with the Keynesian system*. The confusion is such that it can only be dissipated by letting its author speak for himself.

When, in 1937, J. R. Hicks wrote his famous article 'Mr Keynes and the Classics: A suggested Interpretation' (Hicks, 1937/1982), his estimation of the *General Theory* was rather critical. He accuses Keynes of attempting to compare his own approach with a conception of classical economics which is identified with the writings of Pigou, especially his *Theory of Unemployment*. According to Hicks, the ideas developed in that book are just as alien to the ordinary classical economist as those developed by Keynes himself. Hicks notes in particular Pigou's exaggerated emphasis on the analysis of variables in real terms, in particular the use of commodity-wages, and the elimination of the analysis of a range of monetary problems. It was this that allowed Keynes to assert that there is no existing classical theory of money-wages and of employment. Although Hicks himself admits this point as it applies to the usual presentation of the textbooks, he rejects it with reference to classical theory itself. In his view a correction was necessary to give a correct idea of classical theory; thus he proposed a model of the 'typical classical theory', i.e., without the deformations of Pigou's theory. It was only on the basis of a comparison between the results of this typical classical theory and Keynes's conclusions that a satisfactory judgement of Keynes's contribution could be reached. That this was Hicks's intention can be seen by reference to the statement of the author himself: 'We may hope to be able to isolate Mr Keynes's innovation, and so to discover what are the real issues in dispute. Since our purpose is comparison, *I shall try to set out my typical classical theory in a form similar to that in which Mr Keynes sets out his own theory* (Hicks, ibid, pp. 102–3, italics supplied). Hicks's intention is clear: *IS–LM* is a presentation of *classical theory* in Keynesian form, it is *not* an exposition of *Keynes's theory* itself.

This process of substitution by which *IS–LM* came to represent Keynes's theory, with consequences that can still be seen today, took place imperceptibly, starting with the development of Hicks's original diagram by Alvin Hansen which subsequently appeared in his pedagogical work *A Guide to Keynes*. It was then taken up by the textbooks where it evolved from a Keynesian formulation of classical theory into a neoclassical vision of Keynesian theory and finally became the generally accepted presentation of Keynes's theory.

The interpretation that has been made of the correspondence between Keynes and Hicks on this subject (*CW*, XIV) is no less curious: a blanket approval of the entire *IS–LM* framework has been constructed on the basis of one restrictive sentence (cf. J. A. Kregel, Chapter 11, who draws attention to this fallacy of composition). In this respect, mention must be made of the reservations expressed by Hicks himself, in particular in his 1982 article, *IS–LM*–an Explanation (Hicks, 1982), concerning abuse of his *IS–LM* framework. In this article, which unfortunately seems to have passed unobserved by a majority of economists, Hicks has fundamentally 'reconsidered his position on the interpretative capacity of his initial model' (cf. Fausto Vicarelli, Chapter 5).

For the present, we shall limit our comments to two observations. It is not our purpose here to present a critique of *IS–LM* analysis (it has been done by several authors), but rather to attempt to discover what it offers to the contemporary analyst. The present book offers two answers to this question. The first comes from J. A. Kregel (Chapter 11) who draws on the correspondence between Keynes and Hicks published in volume XIV of the *Collected Writings* to identify Keynes's criticism of Hicks's 1937 article, in particular Hicks's erroneous conception of the interest rate, and more generally, the conception of the nature and role of money. Kregel also points out the profound modifications that would have to be made to the *IS–LM* schema for it to become a correct representation of Keynes's theory. The author of Chapter 11 takes the opportunity to use effective demand and liquidity preference to show that the distance separating the Keynesian and Hicksian interpretations becomes even greater when the relations between money, the money rate of interest, and money prices are made more explicit.

Kregel's cirtique to the *IS–LM* diagram can be summarised in four points (cf. Chapter 11):

(1) The money market and the loans market are not perfect substitutes as determinants of the rate of interest in Keynes's theory.
(2) Keynes's analysis of the demand for money is not a substitute for the quantity theory.
(3) In order to make the *IS–LM* framework acceptable, money must be considered as the real factor and the rate of interest as the monetary factor, rather than money as a monetary factor and the rate of interest as a real factor.
(4) We have to recognise Keynes's refusal to attribute to the quantity of money a direct and proportional action on prices and the rate of interest.

The second answer is given by Pierre-Yves Hénin and Philippe Michel (Chapter 4). From the perspective of the neoclassical synthesis, they choose *IS–LM* as a *reference model* to undertake a reconstruction of the macroeconomic conception of equilibrium in the presence of rationing. Before elaborating this position, we have to see how the elements of the synthesis have led up to it.

The Elements of the Neoclassical Synthesis

The primary intention of a synthesis is to establish a logical and coherent interpretation based on elements of diverse origin and inspiration. We should not therefore be surprised to discover that there are a variety of paths leading to the Keynesianism represented by the neoclassical synthesis.

In an attempt to keep our discussion of a complex process as simple as possible we shall organise discussion around three questions:

(1) Which type of Keynesianism is to be integrated into the neoclassical framework?
(2) Which neoclassical system will be used as the 'general framework'?
(3) What are the points of reference between the two approaches upon which the synthesis is to be constructed?

The Type of Keynesianism to be Integrated

It is not so much the Keynes of the *General Theory* that has to be integrated into the neoclassical approach as the 'Keynesianism' which has emerged from the discussions of the last forty years, and which has reduced Keynes to an 'hydraulic flow mechanism'. From an instrument used in support of economic policy, it eventually came to be considered as the 'standard macroeconomics', which may be compared to Keynes's work as 'ready-to-wear' is to *haute couture*.

Thus it is Keynesian *macro* analysis which has to be integrated into neoclassical theory. Since neoclassical theory is founded on the analysis of the maximising behaviour of individuals and firms, the first problem to be resolved concerns the level of aggregation, i.e., the microeconomic foundations of macroeconomics. It is this problem, as will be seen later, that characterises the dominant theory.

The second element of the Keynesianism to be integrated is the dominance of quantity adjustments over price adjustments, justified by the fact that quantity signals have greater information potential in conditions in which prices are not perfectly flexible. Recognition of the role of quantity adjustments is one of the foundations of the importance of expectations, which in themselves represent a very difficult problem when they are integrated into the discussion of the determination of equilibrium. This difficulty can only be resolved by assuming that expectations are always verified, for otherwise it is impossible to determine equilibrium, unless we admit that it is either consistent with rationing or an ideal state which is almost never realised.

Unemployment equilibrium, the most important of the Keynesian propostions, is expressed as the rationing of supply in the labour market. The neoclassical synthesis attempts to propose an homogeneous explanation of the various situations of unemployment: Keynesian unemployment, defined by a lack of employment opportunities; classical unemployment, due to an unsatisfactory return to capital; inflationary unemployment, and so forth.

Two important points need to be considered in this regard. No role is given to effective demand in these analyses, and money plays only a secondary role. If the economy under consideration is a real economy, *in stricto sensu*, then money-liquidity and money as a store of wealth cannot play any active role.

The Neoclassical Frame of Reference

Certain critical concepts are retained from the Keynesian counter-revolution suggested by Clower and Leijonhufvud,[1] in particular imperfect information, the rejection of Walras's law, the disequilibrating role of a numeraire money (assuring transactions which permit relations between markets). From the neoclassical system the market, and its essential role in allocating resources according to aggregated individual preferences is preserved. But the analysis of the market undergoes a profound modification: optimisation under constraint is defined relative to the finance constraint which introduces the dual decision hypothesis based on the contraposition between notional and effective demand (in Clower's sense). The financing constraint and rationing therefore appear as two of the principal elements, which, together with 'false' prices, modify the structure of the Walrasian analysis of the market mechanism.

The Basic Points of References for the Synthesis

The first point of reference with Keynes's theory is the explanation of involuntary unemployment. Keynes's explanation in terms of effective demand is replaced with a condition of disequilibrium resulting from the operation of rationing in a constrained labour market. Such analysis may be extended from the labour market to disequilibrium conditions in other markets to produce a generalised interpretation of an aggregate economy in conditions of disequilibrium.

A certain dissatisfaction with these results, expressed in a number of studies, generated attempts to further develop this approach which suggested the necessity of a return to the notion of equilibrium, although subject to a series of qualifications to specify its precise meaning in various situations and conditions: short and long term, fixed and flexible prices, quantity disequilibrium, alternative constraint specifications, propagation or neutralisation of rationing, etc. The result was to call into question both the conceptions of quantity and price disequilibria and of an equilibrium which necessarily requires the equalisation of quantities by means of variations in prices. In a way, this was a logical inevitability: once Walras's law had been questioned, the argument was followed to its logical conclusion – the rejection of the strict definition of Walrasian equilibrium. This opened the way to the concept of a non-Walrasian equilibrium with short-side quantity rationing which could be extended easily to the interpretation of the various specifications of unemployment, inflation and a number of other conditions which had up to that point only been capable of analysis within the Keynesian system.

The Keynesian Compromise

A compromise is not a synthesis; it is based on transactions and mutual concessions, while synthesis attempts to reconstitute a unique theoretical framework from elements considered to be unrelated or at least independent from each other. It is none the less useful to give some attention to the 'Keynesian compromise' investigated by Pierangelo Garegnani (Chapter 10), for even if most economists would reject this description, an equally large number do seem to fit this category, although possibly involuntarily, when one considers the textbook expositions of the Keynesian system.

According to Garegnani, the origin of the 'Keynesian compromise' is to be found in the very theoretical structure that Keynes himself created, in the sense that it contains a highly original theory of aggregate income and a theory of investment and interest that retains particular elements which can be traced to traditional methods of thought. In Garegnani's view any compromise is characterised by two factors: a tendency simultaneously to produce divergent interpretations and a tendency to frequent changes in interpretation.

The most obvious of a number of examples that might be given of such divergent interpretation is the assumption of the downward rigidity of wages, which is considered necessary to explain unemployment in the Keynesian interpretative literature based on the traditional point of view. However, Keynes rejects the possibility that the flexibility of wages might determine the amount of employment, because in his theory it depends on investment which is an independent variable. Garegnani suggests that Keynes's formulation of his theory of investment and interest was less radical than traditional, and for this reason he even considered it as provisional. Thus Keynes's 'struggle to escape' was not as vigorous in these areas as it was for other subjects which he considered to be of more essential importance. It is for this reason that the traditional approach to the theory of interest and investment was able to re-establish a position of dominance which allowed its supporters to advance anti-Keynesian critiques and reinforce their previous beliefs, which Keynes had called into question, in an even stronger form.

The instability of the 'Keynesian compromise' is thus caused by the existence of these two opposing positions. It is expressed in the attempts made by the neoclassical theory to encompass Keynes's theory as a special case of traditional theory on the ground that Keynes's 'innovation' in fact was nothing more than excessive emphasis on a few particular factors of secondary importance on which agreement had already been reached. Thus it was once again possible to identify the essential role played by downward rigidity of wages which provided justification for the renewed application of monetary policies.

But the instability of the compromise started to have adverse effects in the 1950s when the development of the critique of the traditional conception of capital called into question the generality of the monotonically decreasing functional relation between the rate of interest and the demand for investment. Everything was thus in place for the recognition of Keynes's innovation in the area of the theory of aggregate income. In Chapter 10, Garegnani proposes his own solution to this conflict. But new conflicting themes will certainly arise to offer another 'compromise' as the possible 'third way' or a third pole of attraction for post Keynesian research.

The synthesis which is currently being attempted obviously will encounter the difficulties associated with any enterprise of this kind: will anyone be satisfied by a position in which each of the synthesised elements is of necessity altered in its very essentials? Will it succeed in convincing each of the particular approaches of its contribution to the synthesis when there is the clear risk that none of them will recognise any element similar to its own position? This is why we must appreciate the prudence shown by the *neoclassical synthesis Keynesians* in admitting that non-Walrasian equilibria are not necessarily Keynesian equilibria just because they are brought about by adjustment of quantities. Their main preoccupation remains to show that the Keynesian positions may be integrated into a neoclassical structure which is suitably extended to accommodate Keynesian problems.

But in addition to these difficulties of a methodological, and thus non-negligible, nature, a conceptual problem of much more difficult resolution remains. The *IS–LM* scheme represents Hicks's attempt to apply the Walrasian analysis of *real* exchange to the markets which characterise a *monetary* economy, i.e., the goods market, money market, the loans market, but no labour market. The essential concern of *neoclassical synthesis Keynesianism* is to renew Hicks's approach in the hope that the application of non-Walrasian equilibrium to these same markets will permit the resolution of this problem that has thus far remained without a general solution. But how can one explain the decision to hold money within a system represented by a *real* conception of the economy? It would seem impossible unless the essential difference between the non-Walrasian and Walrasian conceptions of equilibrium is discovered to be the determination of quantities by factors such as uncertainty, expectations and money in the former replacing the exchange of given quantities in the latter.

The process of synthesis that is now underway has benefited from a wide range of contributions, in particular in the works of a number of authors who have developed the original insights of James Tobin, such as R. J. Barro and H. I. Grossman, J. P. Benassy, E. Malinvaud, P. Y. Hénin, C. Fourgeaud, and A. d'Autume (cf. the bibliographies at the end of Chapters 3 and 4).

II THE GENERALITY OF KEYNESIANISM

It is now some time since Leontief (1948) pointed out that if generality is assessed on the basis of the existence of a general and unique proposition, then the theory of choice, which permeates the entire neoclassical system, offers a much greater degree of generality than the Keynesian system. The Keynesian system does have, however, a rather different advantage for, being based on a number of distinct postulates derived from observation of the real world, it is applicable to a larger number of different situations and thus offers a larger number of practical solutions.

This position seems to be confirmed in the large number of different themes that it is possible to identify in the experimental foundations of the *Keynesian project whose development constitutes the basis of the generalisation of Keynesianism.* Indeed, the arguments referred to above that in the past have been used to justify the generality of the *General Theory*, today appear outdated as more general and more fundamental principles are now available which refer to the aggregate behaviour of the system which Keynes identified by means of direct observation, from lessons of past experience, and from the emergence of institutional phenomena in contemporary societies.

The generality of the *Keynesian project*, conceived as something much larger than Keynes's 1936 work, is based on a set of general principles, postulates and assumptions characterising a monetary production economy:

- the entrepreneur economy is based on a fundamental decision to act to increase current income over the long run; in this sense, it is a wealth-producing economy;
- entrepreneurs, by determining effective demand, decide the expansion of wealth and the volume of employment at any point in time;

– individuals make use of real goods by acting to satisfy a rational preference for money;
– the operation of markets is circumscribed by macroeconomic factors.

These characteristics can be summarised in four principles:

(1) the principle of expansion of current wealth;
(2) the principle of effective demand;
(3) the principle of rational preference for money;
(4) the principle of macroeconomic foundations of the market.

1. The Fundamental Decision to Expand Current Wealth

Keynes defines wealth as the *power* to consume a particular good at an undetermined time in an undetermined place[2]. In this way, it becomes a part of his general conception of economic activity whose ultimate aim is consumption. The expansion of wealth is the object of economic activity for both individuals and nations; it is an activity that occurs over time, with effective or potential results which are not only immediate, but also occur in the future and are therefore subject to uncertainty which is beyond conceptualisation in terms of probability (cf. 'The General Theory of Employment', *CW*, XIV, pp. 112–13). This explains the common tendency for all economic agents to attempt to preserve this power over future consumption as a protection against insecurity. But this cannot make agents forget their present, short-term preoccupations, and therefore their power to consume goods from day to day: the general preference for wealth will thus determine both the orientation and the nature of economic activity according to the fundamental decision facing agents concerning the disposition of their wealth. On what elements is it based?

When economic agents have an asset or a surplus at their disposal they can choose between two different actions: they can either *accumulate* by adding this surplus to their existing stock of wealth, or *invest* in order to increase current wealth in future periods, i.e., to generate an income that 'comes in' regularly.

The fundamental decision thus concerns the choice between accumulating acquired wealth to ensure security, or investing current wealth to increase future income, with its attendant uncertainty. While the choice that is made depends in the last instance on individual decisions, it is also influenced by common opinion which may exhibit a preference for either a static or a dynamic conception of wealth. According to Keynes, it is the static conception which has been historically dominant, producing a tendency to save natural wealth which was stronger than the urge to invest in new productive capital: saving was sign of the will to be protected against insecurity due to ignorance of the future and reluctance to run the risk of investment required by the entrepreneurial spirit:

> The desire of the individual to augment his personal wealth by abstaining from consumption has usually been stronger than the inducement to the entrepreneur to augment the national wealth by employing labour on the construction of durable assets. . . . The weakness of the inducement to invest has been at all times the key to the economic problem. (*CW*, VII, p. 348)

The entrepreneur economy, on the other hand, is based on a dynamic conception of the increase of resources and wealth. In the presence of an active incentive to invest, entrepreneurs borrow directly from savers or their agents or engage bank credit, opening new perspectives for the use of the surplus since it multiplies the means of rendering it more productive and diminishes the reluctance to bear risk. In this way, the surplus in an entrepreneur economy can be divided between accumulation and investment in order to yield the greatest advantages in terms of both industrial and financial wealth.

The representation of the conditions determining the fundamental decision is then in part reflected not only in common opinion but also in the scientific conceptions of the problem. These conceptions survived long after the disappearance of the world that engendered them because it was particularly difficult for economic doctrine to abandon the static conception of wealth. It was persistently affirmed that saving determines investment, in the sense that the interest rate and the volume of investment are spontaneously established at their optimal levels through mechanisms which are dominated by agents' decisions to save. These ideas resulted in the limitation of the active role of money, and contributed to the development and extension of the quantitativist's fears which had emerged from Jean Bodin's earlier perspicacity. Although there were contrary opinions, as well as differences and divergences of form, the preference for real wealth and the suspicion of money became the two basic presumptions of classical thought. Even when the surge of industrial and financial activity brought the determinant role of the entrepreneur and the banks to the forefront of attention, the dynamic conception of wealth and resources was still interpreted in terms of the real conception of wealth. It was necessary to wait until 1912 for Schumpeter to claim the overriding importance of credit. And just as Keynes would add that it was the increase in production that led to an increase in saving, the diversification of the various forms of holding wealth occurred simultaneously with the changes in the attitude towards money, which appeared ever more frequently in the form of credit, as a phenomenon if not new at least renovated, evolving with the nature of wealth itself.

The variety of the means of holding and storing wealth in a real and immobile form now became widespread with the use of commodities which were no longer limited to land and bricks, and in a liquid form with the detention of money with various degrees of liquidity. The former was still preferred on the presumption that it was safe from depreciation in value (which was, however, far from being generally true) and because it could also produce a flow of additional wealth in the form of industrial investment which makes the physical assets appear productive and profitable and thus the object of accumulation. These two advantages are thought to be absent from liquid assets because money is neither productive nor exempt from depreciation when its quantity exceeds the quantity required to circulate existing goods.

However, liquid wealth presents other advantages which make the various forms of money a common means of holding wealth. Money presents a threefold advantage. Because of the liquidity property, which it possesses *par excellence*, it is possible to obtain any good at any place and at any time, i.e., it is a store of wealth under the Keynesian definition. Moreover, compared to the accumulation of real assets, it possesses the advantage of being continuously available for speculation on variations in the values of other goods, of being transferred without loss of value over time, and of being invested in financial assets of various term at the pleasure of agents. In a word, its liquidity property gives it the possibility of exerting control at any time over combinations of goods which cannot be rationally and certainly predetermined in the real economy. Finally, because the cost of holding money is practically zero and because its production and substitution elasticities are negligible, money exhibits a characteristic scarcity which makes it universally desirable.

The primary impact of this evolution is on the accumulation of wealth itself. The individual now has to choose how he will distribute his wealth between real, immobile forms, and money forms of varying liquidity, but which is always available.

Now the fundamental decision between increasing total accumulated wealth or current wealth takes on a new and often more complex form compared to the long historical tradition which none the less still exists, although veiled in the conception of a real economy. The essential factors determining the decision to adopt the dynamic conception and increase current wealth are all linked either to the investment of money to create physical or financial assets with expected profitability, or money in its various liquid forms being lent at interest, or the pure and simple hoarding of liquidity. These various possibilities create a continuum of different stores of value which allow passage from one form to another without discontinuity between them. In this way, the paralysing dichotomy between real and monetary forms is eliminated, the simultaneous recognition of both forms allowing diversification of the elements bearing on the fundamental decision.

However, a fact of major importance still remains to be explained. Why is the emergence of the preference for money as a store of value linked to the predominance of the decision in favour of increasing current wealth?

2. Effective Demand and the Expansion of Current Wealth

In reality, the idea of effective demand represents not a single aspect of the economy, but the interpretation of four different aspects.

Determination of the Level of Output and Employment

The first aspect is the use of effective demand, as in the *General Theory*, to explain the determinants of the level of income and employment. It is based on an aggregate supply function linking specific expected values of the former to unique values of the latter, and thus combines the flows of expected investment expenditures and consumption expenditures resulting from the interaction of the fundamental variables. The employment function, the inverse of the aggregate supply function measured in wage units, plays an important role because it explains the level of utilisation of the labour force in either the entire economy, or across individual firms. It thus shows the consequences of variations of effective demand on the distribution of employment between industries.

This is the conception of effective demand which provides the foundation of the theory of output and employment. It does, however, lead to ambiguity (as explained in more detail in Chapter 1, section 2, below) when it is interpreted, as Keynes seemed to do, as representing the limit to possible situations of equilibrium.

The Macroeconomic Determinants of the Theory of Prices

The second aspect of effective demand concerns its role as an instrument of analysis in price theory. The analysis in terms of effective demand makes necessary the specification of the flows of income and expenditure in order to explain their origins and means of adjustment. It also requires specification of the action of expectations and money in the formation and determination of prices which are used in the description of the circular flow and of specific markets. Further, it refers directly to the distinction between expected prices which constitute the aggregate supply and demand curves, and the actual prices which are established in the markets as the circuit of income and expenditure flows adjusts by means of price changes, or adjusts in ways that disappoint expectations. We are not at this stage concerned with the formulation of expectations and the decisions that are based on them, but rather by their confirmation or disappointment and the consequences this will have on actual prices. The analysis must of necessity confront the analysis of the consequences of decisions made in recognition of the fact that they may be disappointed. This underlines, in particular, the importance of the relation between realised effective demand and variations in the money supply which will produce both variations in the output and in actual market prices. We are thus concerned with the macroecomomic foundations of the market, but it is a rather different type of market from that analyse by Walras, as will be seen more clearly below.

General Equilibrium of Monetary Values

The first two aspects that we have discussed must be seen as taking place successively. The first, the theory of employment, employs effective demand as a framework for the analysis of real quantities, production and employment in a monetary production economy. The second, the theory of prices, uses effective demand as the guiding principle for the interpretation of the expected adjustment of monetary flows through the operation of the circular flow and the equalisation of expected prices and actual market prices established by the necessity of the realisation of the circular flow process. It is thus possible to see how the confirmation (or disappointment) of *expectations* adjust (or fail to adjust) the flows of production *expenditures* and income expenditures which produce the equality (or inequality) of *savings* and *investments* and consequently the equality (or inequality) of *expected prices* and *actual money prices*.

We thus describe a general equilibrium of monetary values or a general equilibrium theory of a monetary production economy which is distinct from the general equilibrium of a real exchange economy; it presents a coherent and unified interpretation of the theory of output and prices in which money plays a determinant role from the very beginning, from the formation of the production decisions to the formation of supply and demand for output and the resulting market transactions. In this way we establish, as will be described in more detail below (Chapter 1, section 1), the macroeconomic foundations of the general equilibrium of monetary values and the principle of the monetary conditions of production.

The Expansion of Current Wealth

The fourth aspect suggested by effective demand leads to another improvement of the *General Theory* in the sense that it enlarges the field of analysis from the theory of income to the theory of production by integrating the capital cycle: investment–disinvestment–replacement, going beyond the simple considerations of user costs and recasting the terms of the discussion of the question of the determination of the scale of output with expanding productive capacity. Here effective demand moves from the consideration of net to gross values and analysis is extended to consider effects in future periods. In this type of analysis the variable to be determined is no longer net income, but gross national, or domestic, product (GNP or GDP). It is therefore necessary to substitute gross effective demand for net effective demand in order to pass from a situation of increasing income and employment with given equipment, and the analysis of the problem of the degree of utilisation of existing productive capacity, to analyse an increase in gross national product due to an expansion of fixed and circulating capital. The analysis thus also shifts from short-term to long-term (Chapter 1, section 3).

We now have the entirety of the *Keynesian project* as it relates to the fundamental decision concerning an increase in current wealth, together with the analysis of accumulated wealth held in forms which differ radically from those which have been adopted during a long historical past. The *Keynesian project* may now be perceived in its full generality, for money, already an essential part of the formation and the use of effective demand, can now be integrated into the general economic process leading from real production to monetary exchange.

3. Is the Preference for Money Rational?

If, as Joseph Schumpeter said, 'all that is essential leads to the world of goods', why should there be a preference for holding money, and is this preference rational?

With hindsight, it has become evident that the controversies concerning the demand for money, prior to the publication of the *Collected Writings*, were mainly concerned with the determination of the interest rate by means of the state of liquidity preference itself. Although this is an important attribute of money, it does not exhaust all its attributes, in particular the fact that it serves as a store of value because of its negligible carrying costs and negligible production and substitution elasticities. Moreover, the argument which attributed Keynes's explanation of unemployment to downward rigidity in nominal wages led to the development of the idea of 'monetary illusion' which only wage-earners seemed to suffer.

To highlight one element of the generality of the *Keynesian project* requires the demonstration that the preference for money is not illusory, but rational, because: (i) money is, as we have seen, not only liquidity, but also a store of value held in a liquid form; (ii) part of its importance is derived from the fundamental decision taken in an entrepreneur economy in favour of increasing current wealth. It is this second aspect that bears further consideration. This can best be achieved by a prior discussion of two arguments.

The Path from Monetary to Real Values

The act of acquisition of real goods always takes place via the conversion of monetary into real values, since individuals do not have direct access to real goods except in the case of own production. Such direct acquisition of real values becomes irrelevant as soon as we come to consider the acquisition of the economy's aggregate output by the entire population of consumers and producers.

In order to show that one cannot acquire the use of real values except from the prior possession of money, and that the simple hypothesis of a numeraire good is not sufficient to satisfy this requirement, reference can be made to the example of the payment of wages in real terms, an example which may also be extended to the consideration of real interest, real prices, real profits, etc.

In an entrepreneur economy where the wage is paid in money, neither the worker nor the entrepreneur can make direct estimates of either the good-wages and the subsistence minimum which are the constituent elements of the classical real wage, or Pigou's conception of wage-goods which has already been criticised by Hicks. It is only possible to establish a relation between the nominal wage bill on the one hand and the general level of absolute prices determined by the quantity of money on the other. A measure composed of two monetary magnitudes, the second of which refers to past prices, is thus obtained. In fact, the latter is represented by a simple index of the purchasing power of money. This may be satisfactory for the policy purposes of trade unions and governments, but the economist needs more than a rudimentary measure; he needs a concept capable of defining an instrument which is sufficiently precise to allow the analysis of equilibrium in the labour market on the basis of the two basic postulates of classical economics. To discover such a concept it is necessary to look behind the veil of money, but without the concept of goods-wages and wage-goods he finds a conceptual void.

This is especially important once the attempt is made to go beyond the analysis of the level of real output that is compatible with the equilibrium of the individual firm in terms of workers' real remuneration to identify the role of real wages in the determination of the equilibrium level of aggregate output and employment.

The Liquidity Condition

In the real exchange economy the equilibrium of real values produces a system of real relative prices. In such conditions all goods are perfectly liquid because the value of any good in terms of the value of the others is guaranteed. It is only for reasons of convenience and as an appeal to reality that money is introduced, but its role is purely banal since its only role is as a numeraire, and as a means of exchange renders it neutral, incapable of any effect on real values.

The extension of the condition of liquidity to the economy as a whole in the *Keynesian project* allows the formulation of effective demand, the level of output and employment necessary to ensure the expansion of current wealth, in particular by means of investment in financial and physical assets. Not only are aggregate supply and demand prices pushed to the maximum levels compatible with the expectation of maximum profits, but the demand for credit which will be added to financial reserves and the quantity of money already in circulation to insure finance for the new production is determined with reference to these levels. The path leading from monetary values towards real values thus raises the question of monetary illusion, while the liquidity condition poses the difficult problem of the relations between debt, credit and the rate of interest.

'Monetary Illusion' or a Rational Preference for Money?

Traditional theory does not seem to have been concerned to resolve the above mentioned confusion between the measure and the concept of real values for it bases its representation of the labour market on the behaviour of wage-earners with respect to real wages. Faced with Keynes's proposition that 'the demand of labour is for a minimum moneywage and not for a minimum real wage' (*CW*, VII, p. 8), traditional theory responds that labour suffers from 'monetary illusion', suggesting that workers are so naive as to place sole attention on the monetary aspects of the wage contract, rather than on amount of necessary wage goods it implies. The source of this position is founded on tradition and its inspiration lies in rejoinder. The tradition is classical ricardianism which views the worker's wage as a real wage composed of wage-goods (or their equivalent in a monetary value equivalent to the subsistence minimum). The answer consists of the demonstration that the defence of a minimum nominal wage[3] produces the downward rigidity of real wages which prevents the elimination of unemployment, a particular condition which Keynes inappropriately generalised to reach the conclusion that unemployment was a common, even usual situation. The answer is, then, that Keynes's theory of employment is founded on the assumption of monetary illusion.

The debates in the 1940s and 1950s on this point were so numerous that it is impossible to mention them all here; instead we shall limit discussion to those which attempt to relax the assumption of monetary illusion, although without completely rejecting it, as being of greatest relevance to our discussion.

Leontief's homogeneity postulate (Leontief, 1936; Hams, 1948) states that when money wages and the price level of wage goods vary in the same proportion, real wages do not change so that the volume of employment is unaffected. If we add a utility function expressed in money terms to the labour supply curve, also expressed in money, the *nominal* wage rate becomes a choice variable for the wage-earner and may produce behaviour which differs from that adopted in a real economy. Consider two situations that are alike with respect to real wages, but with the nominal wage and the level of prices twice as high in the first: in traditional theory there is no difference between the two situations, while in Keynes's theory there will be a preference for the first because it satisfies a preference for larger money magnitudes.

The reasons for this choice are analysed by Tobin who was unconvinced by the postulate of homogeneity. Tobin demonstrates a limit to the applicability of money illusion by identifying conditions in which it is more advantageous for wage-earners to receive rigid *nominal* wage than flexible wages which adjust to price decreases to preserve stable real wages (Tobin, 1948). He suggests a number of possible cases: the wage-earner is a net debtor; his payment commitments are expressed in money (taxes, insurance premiums); he expects stable prices to increase his nominal savings, or falling prices to increase the real value of his future saving; he defends his existing nominal wage to preserve his wage differential relative to other groups of wage-earners. In these various cases, a tendency for nominal wages to increase improves the position of the wage-earner and it is not irrational to prefer increasing nominal wages in order to ensure stable real income.

These arguments refer exclusively to the applicability of the hypothesis of monetary illusion to the labour supply function. Tobin notes that this assumption is never raised with reference to the other functions of Keynes's system and that it is difficult to understand why behaviour should so suddenly change when the wage-earner becomes a consumer, or why it should not apply to the owners of natural resources, and financial and capital assets. The supposed answer would run as follows: if Keynes had assumed that the owners of factors other than labour also suffered money illusion, the prices of these factors would also be downward rigid, in which case the propensity to consume could not be a function of real income and Keynes's entire system would be called into question. We are thus led to the necessity of considering that through the effect of expectations, substitution and saving, the nominal wage rate is as much a determinant of employment as the real wage rate.

There is always a certain ambiguity present in such positions, for while they assume a real exchange economy where the 'supply of labour' is a function of wage variations, Keynes's system (as shown by Gérard Grellet, chapter 3, *Keynesian Economic Policies*) does not consider the wage as a price, nor that the volume of employment is determined by a 'labour market', but rather by effective demand. The determination of income thus takes on much greater importance.

The attribution of money illusion to Keynes's theory is used by traditional theory mainly to show that the cause of unemployment is downward rigidity of real wages.

In the *Keynesian project*, labour's concern over the monetary aspects of the wage contract is not incoherent and certainly not irrational; it is only one manifestation of the preference for money, for the franc 'in itself' or the dollar 'in itself' are at one and the same time liquidity, store of value and purchasing power, three fundamentally associated characteristics which give money its own utility. Lerner has suggested the notion of the 'marginal efficiency of holding money' or the increase in utility gained by the acquisition of an additional unit of money. In this respect it is important to note that the acquisition of the real by starting from the money, the liquidity condition, and the rejection of the notion of monetary illusion, all lead to the preference for money, which can only be fully understood within the framework of the fundamental decision in favour of expanding current wealth which is determined by effective demand.

The Keynesian intention to generalise the preference for money thus arises together with effective demand. It has sometimes been said that it has been presented as a theory of the demand for money. But if it is money demanded, it cannot be banal in its influence on the system. As liquidity, purchasing power and a store of value, money acts through effective demand as the means of obtaining current wealth, which as income returns periodically, and 'comes in' to ensure expenditure and saving of each period. It thus determines the amount of aggregate money-income, which represents an increase in demand, which maximises entrepreneurs' expectations of profit. But entrepreneurs do not attempt to maximise the rate, but rather the *mass* of money-profits, by maximising their proceeds and therefore the level of aggregate expenditure financed by money-incomes, i.e., in an entrepreneur economy, mainly by money-wages.

The marginal efficiency of money (Minsky), the marginal efficiency of holding money (Lerner), the marginal utility of money, and other notions of the same type are useful instruments for the analysis of the rational preference for money exhibited by entrepreneurs, wage-earners (as consumers), and expressed in the maximisation of money wages or profits. Dillard (Chapter 2) describes the mechanisms by which the various categories of agents seek to maximise their net wealth, throwing light on the significance of chapter 17 of the *General Theory*.

There is still an implicit question raised by the critique of monetary illusion which remains to be answered: are individuals so conscious of their preference for money that they become insensitive to their real income? The answer is obviously negative, but the essential point is that real wages, as well as real profits, are not determined simply by establishing a direct relation between nominal wages or profits and the general level of prices as the theory of real exchange presumes for lack of any other possible explanation.

As Grellet demonstrates in chapter 3 of *Keynesian Economic Policies*, formation of income depends on three elements:

(1) on money-wages and total profits comprised in aggregate supply price;
(2) on the level of effective demand and thus the level of employment and its distribution between production of wage goods and investment goods;
(3) on the level of output.

Neither wage-earners nor entrepreneurs as groups can determine their own real income from their received or expected money-income. Recognition of this aspect opens a new approach to the theory of distribution in which the traditional theories can be presented as particular cases of a more general interpretation.

4. The Macroeconomic Foundations of the Market

The proposition that a study of the macroeconomic foundations is necessary to a full understanding of the operation of markets is not simply a counterproposal to the traditional pursuit of the microeconomic foundations of macroeconomics. The microfoundations problem is unique to the traditional theory, and stems from the attempt to integrate Keynes's ideas by extending the traditional analysis from the individual and the firm to the aggregate economy. This process requires prior identification of the variables to be aggregated as well as a way of making them homogeneous so that they can be summed. The microeconomic foundations of macroeconomics seem to have been the result of dissatisfaction with the analysis of 'representative' units, a method derived from Marshall's representative firm. The limits of a microfoundations based on the summation of specific homogeneous units to derive a *total* conception is quickly seen in the fact that it provides little more than a technical solution due more to an arithmetical operation than a set of propositions concerning the analytical coherence of an organic *whole*. This *total* is not a wholistic concept; it lacks an organising element, be it finality, inspiration, motivation or a working hypothesis. 'A cathedral is not just an aggregation of stones.'

Macroeconomics is conceived as the discovery and expression of the forces resulting from aggregate behaviour expressed in tendencies, habits, preferences, psychological choices of various categories of agents, groups, socio-economical classes because of the common characteristics, feelings and interests of the various members composing the groups. The propensities represent this direct knowledge of the whole. They are measured by functional relations established on the basis of the behaviour of a group facing an economic event, for example the behaviour of consumers as a whole in determining their spending as a proportion of their income, or the behaviour of entrepreneurs making their investment decisions according to an 'expectation of profit' common to the entire group.

These two different approaches to the resolution of the relation between microeconomic and macroeconomic phenomena are specific to each type of analysis; each has its own advantages and inadequacies and implies different answers, but neither necessarily precludes the other.

The Insertion of Macroeconomic Foundations in the Theory of the Market

It is at the level of the endowments of traders that we discover the macroeconomic foundations of the market process. The influence of macroeconomic phenomena on traders' endowments is evident: in the real exchange economy endowments are unknown unless permanent full employment of factors and resources is assumed; indeed, they are already a part of the market process to the extent that they are given and their production is assumed to occur outside the framework of analysis.

The exchange of equivalent real values determines a system of relative real prices, but it cannot establish the level of absolute prices because nominal prices only appear in relation to the quantity of money which varies independently of the market process, as Ricardo's money rain. Money only appears at the moment transactions take place; it can thus influence the pattern of demand, but it cannot affect the quantities supplied which are given. It is thus unnecessary to enquire whether or not money modifies the conditions of production, since production is not considered at this stage of the analysis. The level of total activity is then only determined if we assume perfect competition and full employment; the adjustments necessary to determine it can only take place at some other time and may produce a different equilibrium position than the one assumed. To summarise, the budget endowments of consumers may vary, while the goods endowments of the suppliers are perfectly inelastic.

By combining the monetary conditions of production and of exchange the *Keynesian project* determines the budgetary and monetary endowments of the consumers and the goods endowments of the suppliers at the same time as it establishes the level of absolute prices and the level of aggregate economic activity. Here production not only requires the use of real resources, it also requires the use of money in such a way that recognition of the effect of money on the production process determines the quantities produced at the same time as it determines the level of activity via the level of produced output. This level is itself established by the level of effective demand which determines the maximum expectation of profit by confronting expected demand and supply, thereby creating the conditions for the realisation of supply and demand on the market. Production thus determines the monetary conditions of exchange and the formation of prices.

The Articulation of the Relation Between the Circular Flow and the Market

Most interpretations of Keynesian theory mention the adjustments which take place in the evolution of the circular flow of incomes and expenditures, but give only minor, and sometimes even negligible, consideration to adjustments realised via the market. They thus emphasise one aspect of the analysis while ignoring the other, forgetting that the fundamental element of the system is effective demand realised through the simultaneous and co-ordinated functioning of the circular flow and the market, which only become instruments of analysis because they are the 'battlefields' where the flows of expenditures meet prices.

The activity of exchange is not the only operation that occurs within the completion of the circular flow, although it is obvious that most of them are market operations. Inflows and outflows take place between all the various decision-making centres, but the initial impulse arises in the market as the result of the actions of agents concerning their endowments. Goods, services, capital and money are exchanged in the markets where the flows start the journeys which constitute the circular flow; they are thus the location of the adjustments that take place in the aggregate flows. I shall call Keynesian a market of this type; it differs from a Walrasian market whose macroeconomic foundations are created by means of interaction with the circuit.

The Keynesian Market

The non-Walrasian disequilibrium and equilibrium theories have already shown the possibility of the existence of other types of market than the Walrasian market. The discussion of the theory of Keynesian prices in section III of *Money, Credit and Prices in Keynesian Perspective* below highlights their specific aspects, in addition to providing a simple presentation of the way they function and adjust. As stressed by Grellet in chapter 3 of *Keynesian Economic Policies*, the supply and demand curves cannot be considered as independent, and agents are ignorant of the real terms of exchange, which only appear *ex post*, but they do entertain expectations about them.

To express the concept of a Keynesian market in a more systematic way, we can say that equalisation of expected aggregate monetary supply and demand is implicit in the decisions of entrepreneurs as expressed in effective demand. This expected equalisation simultaneously creates the money value of output and the money-income necessary to buy the output at the actual prices which entrepreneurs believe will confirm the expected prices they have adopted as their supply prices. It is thus through the action of effective demand that entrepreneurs alone create the necessary conditions for market adjustment. This differs from the Walrasian market where each agent contributes to the determination of the conditions of exchange. In the Keynesian market entrepreneurs create the monetary conditions of production and determine the monetary conditions of exchange to the extent that their expectations are confirmed by consumers' behaviour. This is a point of capital importance since individuals conserve freedom to spend their income in any way they choose. In the Keynesian market, money-prices are formed directly without the necessity to equate real values which only appear *ex post*; these money prices are neither given nor fixed, with the obvious consequences.

The Coherence of the Theories of Production and Prices Based on Effective Demand

In a monetary production economy, two co-ordinated elements, effective demand and the market, explain the formation of actual money-prices. The former determines the level of expenditures on employment and production which inject an amount of liquidity into the circular flow corresponding to aggregate supply prices. The latter expresses the way factors of production spend the money they receive as income from entrepreneurs' expenditure as demand for the quantities of output decided by entrepreneurs. This shows clearly that expected money demand will just equal the expected value of output, which maximises profits at actual prices, which equal expected prices if entrepreneurs' expectations are confirmed.

This descriptive discussion of the structural coherence of the circular flow and of the market process based on money-liquidity which accounts for the formation of *money-* prices is extended in Kregel's already-mentioned conceptual analysis (Chapter 11, sections 4 and 5) which examines the previously mentioned adjustments in more detail.

He rightly stresses that 'Keynes's theory replaced not just Say's Law, but Say's Law *and* the Quantity Theory which formed a unified whole', and concludes that:

> One of the most important tasks of Keynesian monetary theorists must be the pursuit of Keynes's theory of the determination of money prices within the theory of liquidity preference, and his theory of price adjustment within the theory of the income adjustment process of the multiplier; both sides of the income adjustment coin should carry equal importance.

Adjustment by Means of Variations in Prices and Quantities

There are a number of lessons that can be drawn from the analysis of the macroeconomic foundations of Keynesian markets and prices. Market prices are *money*-prices, not *nominal* prices, because they are directly determined by entrepreneurs' production decisions, which in turn lead to money-expenditures on factors of production which represent the money-incomes that will be used in the market to form aggregate demand prices. The transactions that lead to the appearance of actual prices closes a sequence of confrontations between supply and demand, intermediated by money, which take place throughout the production and distribution process. Money prices appear to be the result of the various decisions taken with reference to the components of factor costs, user costs, the cost of risk, which are sanctioned by final purchase transaction, where these various elements are not so much confronted as progressively reconciled during the course of the series of stages which starts with the expectation leading to the production decision, followed by the expenditure on factors and the creation of incomes and products, and concluding in the market with the formation of actual prices.

The direct formation of *money*-prices is a result of the fact that the amount of money injected into the circular flow is equal to the aggregate supply price, and constitutes aggregate money-incomes which will determine aggregate demand price as they are spend on output. The absolute level of prices is thus determined, while the system of expected relative money-prices is implicitly contained in effective demand in the anticipation that the expected prices will be ratified by actual market prices. By contrast, the *nominal* prices of traditional theory are determined by a process that takes place in three separate stages, without any relation between the first two and the third, and which requires the combination of a number of heterogeneous elements: (i) the system of real relative prices is determined at the level of exchange equilibrium; (ii) the transactions which transform them, without disturbance, into relative *nominal* prices take place with transactions completed with a neutral money or a numeraire; (iii) a confrontation between the total of transactions and the quantity of money, which exists for unknown reasons, leads to the appearance of *the general level of nominal prices*.

The macroeconomic approach to the foundations of the market, on the other hand, starts with an identification of the elements necessary for an integration of the theories of value and of money; its essential principle is that it is the monetary conditions of production of use values which determine, along with other factors, the monetary conditions of the formation of exchange values (cf. Chapter 1, section 1).

There are a number of important consequences that follow from this approach:

- it is to the advantage of entrepreneurs that actual market prices should correspond to their expected prices since their expectations of maximum profits are based on these prices;
- actual prices have to adjust to expected prices which are implicit in supply prices if the expectation of maximum profits is to be confirmed;
- the adjustment of actual prices and expected prices is 'preconditioned', since the aggregate demand price is just equal to aggregate supply price when expectations are confirmed;
- even though 'preconditioned', Keynesian prices are not given, since the equalisation does not take place if expectations are not confirmed;
- the 'pre-conditioning' depends on adjustments that take place in the circular flow, counterbalanced by the realisation or the non-realisation of $I = S$ *and* on the equalisation or non-equalisation of actual and expected prices in the *market*. Consequently the adjustment is not necessarily achieved by means of quantities alone, but simultaneously by prices and quantities represented by variations in stocks which indirectly act to offset the deficiency to bring about the equality of $S = I$, and by investment and involuntary saving;
- the variations in the quantity of money act in two ways, the first on effective demand (supply elasticity), the second on money-incomes (demand elasticity), so that the variations of actual money-prices are not proportional to variations in the quantity of money.

The possibility of adjustment being realised partly through quantities and partly through prices has an influence on profits since realised money-profits will not equal expected profits. Entrepreneurs can unilaterally determine the quantities produced, but they cannot really determine the quantities sold or the selling prices because consumers are not simply price 'takers'. As a result of their preference for money consumers will prefer the lowest possible money expenditure, independently of their perceptions about real prices. The location of general adjustment is thus neither only the circular flow nor only the market, but the combination of the market and the circular flow, articulated in effective demand and money. It is at the heart of this combination that the variations of money flows associating quantities and prices take place and where the operation of adjustment is constrained by four conditions:

(1) the confirmation of expectations;
(2) the compensation of the circular flows of money adjusting the money value of aggregate supply and demand;
(3) the equality of saving and investment which sanctions this compensation at the completion of the circuit;
(4) the equalisation of actual and expected prices.

It should be pointed out that the prices of investment goods are established by a different process with its origin in the determination of the values of capital assets in financial markets. It should also be pointed out that large capital installations, requiring large investment expenditures, are often subject to direct negotiations between the client and the producer to contract particular specifications of the equipment, conditions of delivery and prices; discussion of such specific factors are very different from the classical *tâtonnement* process.

III THE DEVELOPMENT OF THE KEYNESIAN PROJECT

The identification of the basic foundations of the generality of the *Keynesian project* in the four principles briefly outlined in this introduction (decision in favour of the expansion of current wealth, the determination of this expansion by entrepreneurs' formulation of effective demand, agents rational preference for money, and the macroeconomic determination of markets) suggests that a great deal of work still separates the realisation of this project from the initial steps found in the *General Theory*. It is possible, however, to survey the broad lines of the developments which will be necessary for the completion of the generalisation of Keynesian macroeconomics, such as it appears today, in both a national context and with reference to the multinational communities of different levels of development.

The first element of such a programme must be concerned with the determination of the immediate objective of the expansion of wealth on the one hand, and the dimension of the economic space in which this objective will be pursued on the other. The objective cannot be reduced simply to the attainment of the 'limiting point of all the possible positions of equilibrium' representing full employment in the domestic economy as given by the full utilisation of the labour force and the available productive capacity. As I have tried to show (cf. Chapter 1, section 2) this conception of equilibrium lends itself to ambiguity. In fact it places an arbitrary limit on the expansion of the system. Such a limit may be surpassed in two ways. The first concerns the combination of productive factors. The long period of exceptional growth which characterised the 1948–73 period has shown how the redistribution of employment among labour surplus and deficit nations by means of immigration rolled back the limits of full employment in countries experiencing rapid growth. The second refers to the research and development of highly productive equipment which has produced both a rapid increase in productivity and the substitution of capital for labour. The result has been a shift in the composition of costs of production from wage costs to capital costs, a shift which has increased the financial costs of the replacement of a capital stock in continual expansion. Such considerations take us beyond the simple theory of employment.

The conditions determining the formulation of the concept of effective demand are thus themselves modified. Entrepreneurs are forced to extend the formulation of their expectations to the introduction and the future replacement of their plant and equipment, as well as to the creation of sufficient financial resources which are reserved for capital expenditures and are thus no longer available to finance the consumption and savings of households. It is thus necessary to take account of gross values in the formulation of expectations; the determination of gross output by gross effective demand replaces the determination of net factor incomes by net effective demand. The analysis thus comes up against the divergence which I have explained in Chapter 1, section 3, between the expansion of production and the lesser expansion of income and consumption. Effective demand is now no longer formulated only in respect of net magnitudes: it is extended to encompass the phenomena of liquidity and its multiplication, the creation and replacement of capital, and its operation through time (cf. Chapters 7–12).

The determination of the economic space within which the expansion of current wealth must take place leads to a regeneration of the role of economic policy. The questions posed by the disposition of financial resources highlight the problem of indebtedness characteristic of the modern international economy. Indeed, finance, adjustment and regulation are inseparable, for the question at issue is not limited to the provision of the resources needed by the expansion of revenue and of the capital that labour needs to put it to work. It is necessary to influence the adjustment of aggregate money values injected into the circular flow in order to make certain the equality of saving and investment, and that markets operate so as to assure that actual prices have the greatest possibility of achieving their expected levels (cf.*Money, Credit and Prices in Keynesian Perspective*). The multinational economic system thus appears as a 'closed' system surpassing the limits of any particular national economy, encompassing the economic space exploited by multinational enterprises and the financial space determined by the international markets for investment, lending and foreign exchange. These relations evoke the difficulties of transfers and of payments between surplus and deficit countries which no longer take place in terms of flows of excess labour, as has been noted above, but in terms of flows of financial resources. The resolution of the adjustment problems in the international monetary economy may thus be expressed in terms of the necessary reduction of disequilibrium, or the introduction of regulation on a global level, both of which represent the search for an acceptable principle of adjustment of financial and monetary resources (cf. *parts I and II of Keynesian Economic Policies*).

Economic policies are thus seen to be circumscribed by organisational forms dominant in the contemporary monetary economy (cf. Boyer, chapter 7, *Keynesian Economic Policies*) on the one hand, and by norms capable of influencing a transnational macroeconomy (cf. De Brunhoff, chapter 8, *Keynesian Economic Policies*), on the other. Since the disequilibria concern employment, production and liquidity, their control presupposes the simultaneous control of quantities and the determination of multiple criteria to form the basis of the definition of a principle of regulation (cf. Devillers, chapter 10, and Ducros, chapter 11, *Keynesian Economic Policies*).

It is certainly one of Keynes's great merits that he foresaw that any system of international payments established in a transnational macroeconomy represents more than a simple technical solution, and must create multilateral regulations which facilitate the utilisation of the financial resources of the surplus countries so necessary to the 'economic world in which we live'. This world exhibits two major defects which concern not only individuals whose employment is badly insured, but also concerns the arbitrary and inequitable distribution of wealth and income between nations.

Notes

1. For a study of the entire range of this point of view and its significance with respect to Keynes's theory, see Barrère (1983).
2. We know that for Adam Smith it was the power to command labour.
3. In neoclassical theory this is a *nominal* wage, the expression in terms of neutral money of the real wage, and not a 'monetary wage' or money-wage.

References

Barrère, A. (1983) *Déséquilibres economiques et contre-révolution keynésienne*, 2nd edn (Paris: Editions Economica).
Harris, S. (1948) *The New Economics: Keynes' Influence on Theory and Public Policy* (New York: Knopf).
Hicks, J. R. (1937) 'Mr Keynes and the Classics, A Suggested Interpretation', reprinted in Hicks (1982, pp. 100–15).
Hicks, J. R. (1980) 'IS-LM – an Interpretation', reprinted in Hicks (1982, pp. 318–31).
Hicks, J. R. (1982) *Money, Interest and Wages* (Oxford: Blackwell).
Keynes, J. M. (1971–86) *The Collected Writings of John Maynard Keynes* (*CW*) volumes I–XXIX (London: Macmillan, for the Royal Economic Society).
—(1973) *The General Theory of Employment, Interest and Money* (*CW*, VII).
Leontief, W. (1936) 'The Fundamental Assumptions of Mr Keynes Monetary Theory of Employment', *Quarterly Journal of Economics*, November.
—— (1948) 'Postulates: Keynes' General Theory and the Classicists', in Harris (1948).
Schumpeter, J. (1912) *The Theory of Economic Development*, English translation, R. Opie (New York: Oxford University Press, 1961).
Tobin, J. (1948) 'Money Wages Rates and Employment', in Harris (1948).

Introduction

Alain Barrère

The foundations of Keynesian analysis which will be examined in this book can be grouped in three parts.

PART I: DEVELOPMENT OF FUNDAMENTAL ANALYSIS

1. The Monetary Production Economy

In the opening chapter, Alain Barrère builds on the conception of the 'Keynesian project' to introduce three essential points of continuity between the *General Theory* and Keynes's more ambitious general Project: the monetary conditions of production, the extension of the field of application of employment equilibrium, and the expansion of output over time. In Chapter 2, Dudley Dillard shows the place of the theory of employment in the evolution of Keynes's thought in order to highlight the general framework of the monetary economy in which Keynes's employment analysis is developed.

2. Macroeconomic Equilibria

The second section in Part I is opened by Antoine d'Autume, who supports his argument that the non-Walrasian equilibrium theory may be considered an adequate representation of the logical conclusions of traditional Keynesian analysis by elaborating two lines of thought: the inclusion of investment and the accumulation of capital, and international exchange, within the disequilibrium framework. He is thus able to trace the foundations of investment behaviour in disequilibrium under a sales constraint, discussing the diversity of models which may be formed on the basis of their initial assumptions. He shows how a dynamic approach may be obtained as a succession of non-Walrasian equilibria, and discusses the possible interpretations of the diverse stationary states. Then, turning to an examination of the potential applications of non-Walrasian equilibria, he analyses several current problems presented in terms of disequilibria in international exchange: employment, devaluation, the oil shock.

The chapter by Pierre-Yves Hénin and Philippe Michel seeks to show how it is possible to attain a reformulation of the concept of macroeconomic equilibrium with rationing by using Hicks's conception of temporary equilibrium to generalise the *IS–LM* curves. The analysis builds on the identification of the various macroeconomic configurations that may result from different conditions prevailing in the labour and consumption goods markets. The result is a typology of macroeconomic configurations: Keynesian unemployment, Classical unemployment, inflation, underconsumption. The generalisation of the *IS–LM* scheme to encompass disequilibrium conditions rests on a distinct derivation of the *IS–LM* curves for each configuration, in order to produce an intersection representing the constrained equilibria which then possess an original definition that demonstrates the diversity of the possible constraints (given their maintained hypotheses). One of the most interesting of the many contributions of this analysis is that its reinterpretation of the *IS–LM* scheme makes it more representative of the Keynesian theory of employment than it was in its original simplified form, and at the same time more appropriate for the interpretation of the neo-Walrasian equilibria. It thus joins d'Autume's analysis in elaborating the Keynesian synthesis.

3. The Foundations of the General Theory

Equilibrium and Probability

Can the analysis of the functioning of the economic system in which we really live be carried out with the help of the neoclassical conception of equilibrium so often used to reinterpret the *General Theory*? Keynes's ideas are foreign to this notion of equilibrium because he analyses the economics of uncertain decision-making determined by short- and long-term expectations, which is incompatible with Walrasian equilibrium. This is the point of departure chosen by Fausto Vicarelli (Chapter 5) for his comparison between Keynes's foundations and those of neoclassical theory.

He finds that the importance of expectations in Keynes's thought has not been adequately expressed in the neoclassical synthesis, nor by the Rational Expectations School, nor by the Cambridge tradition. In his view, it is unfortunate that the *General Theory* did not refer explicitly to the principles of logical probability which suggest a linkage of probability to logic rather than to mathematics and the possibility that theoretical knowledge may be established by construction on the basis of the knowledge of facts. The probabilities used relate to the degree of our conviction which makes up part of our human baggage and in which confidence and speculation play an important role in taking decisions. Thus the criticism of lack of objectivity made of analyses based on expectations is without conviction, because 'on the basis of the knowledge of certain propositions based on evidence, it is possible to construct a knowledge of other non-observable propositions by means of a logical relation between the first and the second'.

On the basis of this interpretation of probability and expectations in an uncertain world, Vicarelli investigates the significance of Keynesian equilibrium. The traditional conception of equilibrium would not be able to capture this significance because it cannot represent the behaviour of entrepreneurs who are required to anticipate the future. Attempts have been made in terms of sequential models, or models in which expectations are always satisfied, but this simply eliminates the problem of uncertainty without resolving it. It is thus necessary to return to the concept of probability and attempt to move, as Keynes did, towards a conception of a virtual equilibrium which explains the confrontation of expected and realised results, producing the formulation of a new state of expectations.

In this respect it is of crucial importance not to confuse short- and long-term expectations with the short and long period of Marshall, for Keynes did not construct a short-period analysis, but a combination of decisions based on short- and long-term expectations. The exogenous character of expectations – that is, the dependence of equilibrium on long-term expectations and liquidity preference – shows that Keynes did not reject long-term analysis. Rather he considered it within the context of the formation of average opinion.

Keynes's Heterodoxy

The essence of Keynes's work is often considered to be his novel analysis of traditional themes in economic analysis. However, attempts to reintegrate Keynes within the framework of the dominant theory suggest that his most important innovations were elsewhere, in his original reflections on themes considered outside the realm of traditional economic science. Attempting this diagnostic, Jean Cartelier (Chapter 6) suggests that the rupture brought about by the *General Theory* can be seen in three points: the use of wage-units and money, effective demand,

and the absence of adjustment. On these points Keynes based a heterodoxy with respect to the dominant theory, but not necessarily in opposition to it, given that the new non-*tâtonnement* schemes worked out within the general equilibrium framework are not incompatible with the heterodox position which also faces a number of unresolved analytical problems. This position is supported with the construction of a scheme using the three cited points which is used to analyse one of heterodoxy's non-resolved problems: the determination of the rate of interest.

The framework to be based on the new givens proposed by the *General Theory* will then be that of the Entrepreneur economy, in which the entrepreneur decides the initial values of employment, money and expenditure to take into consideration without any prior objective co-ordination, producing effective demand as determined by the equalisation of the marginal efficiency of capital, and the rate of interest and the equalisation of the own-rates of interest. Entrepreneurs anticipate the return and the aggregate cost; short-term expectations determine current production from given capacity, while long-term expectations concern the eventual expansion of productive capacity. From the ensemble of these actions initiated by effective demand springs the possibility of the initiation of productive activity. But at this stage nothing has yet been established concerning the process of adjustment. This is linked to agents' expenditure on output in the market, that is, to the confrontation of expectations and realisations and the creation of aggregate income as divided between consumption and savings, the latter being either another name for investment or another name for the entrepreneurs' deficit financing. Thus the savings made by factors, or what is the same thing, the entrepreneurs' financial deficit, indicate that there is no adjustment in the circular flow of incomes. Here one has to part company with Keynes. But will not the deficit on one side be balanced by the surplus on the other? The answer is to be found in the appearance of a new factor, the formation of finance capital, whose manner of creation should be the object of further study, a study upon which Schmitt has already commenced. It also suggests the problem of the determination of the rate of interest.

For Cartelier, there is no general rate of interest for any level of effective demand, but as many as one for each entrepreneur's personal preference for liquidity. Are these capable of determining the rate of interest? The answer seems to be negative, but it is linked to a series of reflections on money itself which acts to transform the surplus in money (with respect to the entrepreneur's deficits) into an asset surplus, all of which confirms that the identity between deficit and surplus must be considered within the context of the formation of finance capital.

PART II: EFFECTIVE DEMAND AND TIME

Increasing Effective Demand and Long-Term Growth

Is the continued expansion of effective demand capable of bringing about long-term steady growth? It is generally accepted that effective demand constitutes the essential element of the process by which available resources are committed to the expansion of current wealth. But we must not forget an additional element. Effective demand determines the proportion of the available resources that it appears profitable to use for this purpose. This is pointed out by Lord Kaldor, who adds that the effective demand required to justify entrepreneurs' decisions is the sum of an endogenous component – the demand for consumption whose variations are proportional to factor costs – and an exogenous component – the demand for investment financed by capital, considered as given in the short period. Effective demand expresses the equilibrium level of output and employment at which the output anticipated by entrepreneurs is just equal to the amount they consider to be just sufficient to justify their expenditures in producing the corresponding output.

To the two constraints identified by the Keynesian synthesis as producing Classical and Keynesian unemployment, Lord Kaldor (Chapter 7) adds a third: the economy's propensity to import relative to exports. The latter play the role of the exogenous component, while imports, investment and the consumption of domestic output constitute the endogenous component. In a situation of steady growth where all the components grow at a constant rate (which is not necessarily the same for all) the third constraint takes on crucial importance.

The model, constructed on the basis of that set out by Harrod, gives an explanation of differences in growth rates between developed countries (excepting Japan) in the post-war period. The essential question is whether the third constraint operating at the level of supply possesses, in the long run, a role equivalent to that which is played in static conditions by the constraints set out by Malinvaud for equilibrium with rationing. Now, it is evident that productive capacity does not increase at the same rate in all sectors, and that Classical unemployment may appear in some, at the same time as there is Keynesian unemployment in others as a result of complementarity which is no less important than substitutability. It is foreign trade which adjusts to reduce the difference that is likely to arise between the aggregate potential output on the supply side and the output required on the demand side: thus the appearance of the constraint on the capacity to export which determines the limits on the capacity to import. With the aid of numerous examples, Lord Kaldor shows that according to the type of output the external constraint will influence the level of productive capacity rather than labour, and that the effect of each of these constraints is different in the short and the long term so that it is difficult to envisage a long-run balanced growth path, either for a single country or for the world as a whole. The example of the 1950s and 1960s and the disequilibria which followed underline the policy errors and the difficulties provoked by the rise in imports relative to the capacity to export.

The Definition of the Short Period by Reference to the Duration of the Circuit

Keynes's preoccupation with short-period analysis suggests an unresolved question: Is it theoretically possible to determine the temporal duration of the short period? What is the evolution of real time which it covers? Frédéric Poulon (Chapter 8) proposes an answer to this question based on the time necessary for the circulation of money flows, considered as the duration of the circuit. His ingenious demonstration is undertaken in three stages.

In the first stage, the short period refers to a monetary cycle which encompasses the succession of money flows during the period. These flows are those which the decisions underlying effective demand introduce into the circular flow. In the second stage, the time necessary for the completion of this monetary circulation can be evaluated by reference to two extreme limits: circulation starts when demand is made to financial intermediaries for an amount of credit determined by expectations; it ends when this credit constitutes households' savings. In the interval, money circulates between the constituent poles of the circuit, according to a representative scheme of successive appropriations with money as the objective: production expenditures, creation of incomes, accumulation of capital, consumption expenditures, until the formation of household savings which can be captured by the entrepreneurs on financial markets. The capture marks the end of the monetary circulation which corresponds to the time required to validate the entrepreneurs' original expectations. This is clearly the Keynesian short period whose duration (calculated on the basis of an appropriate model) appears to be about one year. In addition to furnishing a numerical estimate, the duration of the circuit sheds new light on the instruments of Keynesian analysis, the multiplier and the savings investment equilibrium conditions, whose interpretation underwent modification between the *Treatise* and the *General Theory*.

The Paradox of the Identity of Aggregate Supply and Demand in the Long Period

The relation between effective demand and time leads Bernard Schmitt (Chapter 9) to propose what I shall call the paradox of the identity, because the subtle development of his basic conceptions reconciles what initially appears to be contradictory. A paradox because entrepreneurs, gambling that their expectations of aggregate supply and aggregate demand prices will be confirmed in the behaviour of other agents, are making a gamble that is useless against a non-probabilistic future, because time acts on a different level from that in which the process of adjustment takes place. But these adjustments which seem impossible initially, are internalised within the identity itself. The entire problem consists in knowing to what extent real behaviour is reflected by the significance of concepts. Let us try to capture both the logic and the paradox in a short argument.

Supply and demand go together: that is, they are in a relation which is neither one of causality (Ricardo), nor of interdependence (Walras), but of identity (Keynes). Only this identity gives logical coherence, not only to Keynesian analysis, but to economic science itself because it provides the central concept: *supply and demand are necessarily monetary*. Supply is monetary because it is defined by the money payments to factors; demand is also monetary because the factors receive output, not in real terms, but in money in the form of money-income: supply is instantaneously demand since the expenditure of these incomes simply delivers the physical possession of the new output to those who already own it. There can thus be no question of an advance by entrepreneurs to the factors, but the appropriation of the output by the beneficiaries of the distribution of factor incomes. This signifies that money and output are created simultaneously in the act of production, such that the factors receive the product in money and become, by this fact, owners of the physical product: money is the form or the receptacle and output is instantaneously the content. It is thus necessary to understand that the intermediation of money is equivalent to an *instantaneous* demand for output by those who produce it, and that if money does not intervene when output is supplied its producers will demand it in physical form. It is not possible for output that is supplied not to be demanded and vice versa, because it is impossible to demand without money and all money is by association an output. In summary, supply contains the output in the money distributed to factors; in the act of demand output is instantaneously transferred in money to the factors and the supply–demand identity persists in time until the distribution of output in its physical form. The Keynesian logic is thus founded on the identity of money and output established by the identity of two events: the creation and the destruction of national income, which are complementary aspects of one and the same movement. This identity does not preclude the possibility that firms earn a positive proportion of current output which is subtracted in the form of money. One thus rediscovers both an adjustment between *I* and *S* and the definition of profit, *I-S*, which opens the way to the definition of inflation and of crisis: without inflation, unemployment is zero.

PART III: EFFECTIVE DEMAND AND THE PROCESS OF PRODUCTION

After the examination of the operation of effective demand in time, we come up against the problem of the various factors which are put into motion by effective demand in order to produce output. Three questions are pertinent in this context. They concern the role of interest in the determination of investment and thus in the accumulation of capital (P. Garegnani), the role of the multiplier and liquidity preference in the income adjustment process (J. A. Kregel), and the microeconomic foundations of the aggregate supply function (R. dos Santos Ferreira and P. Michel).

Capital and Interest: The Keynesian Compromise

It is within the perspective of the Keynesian compromise, already referred to, that Pierangelo Garegnani (Chapter 10) confronts the much discussed question: Can variations in the rate of interest adjust investment to full employment savings, taking account of the Keynesian hypothesis of wage rigidity, considered by orthodox economists as the obstacle to the realisation of full employment?

The origin of the problem, which is analysed in all its complexity by Garegnani, is Keynes's affirmation that it is the level of income and not the rate of interest which ensures equality between saving and investment. Since the orthodox theory considers that it is wage flexibility which insures full employment, the S = I relation should imply that investment adjusts to full employment savings. Therefore, in the orthodox view, Keynes's challenge to the principle of full employment in terms of insufficient effective demand must be based on the downward rigidity of wages–thus the source of the problem under discussion. The basis of the analysis is Wicksell, who argued that the demand for loan capital and the supply of savings are strictly identical at the 'natural' rate of interest. Comparison of the two positions leads to a double result: the origin of the difference between Keynes and the orthodox economists must be sought in the theory of interest; the nature of the difference resides in Keynes's rejection of the equalisation of the demand and supply of full employment savings by means of the rate of interest, rather than in his desire to impose his own theory.

The discussion centres on an examination of the Keynesian critique of traditional theory which is supposed to be based on two points: it suffers from indeterminacy in the sense that the only possible conceivable supply of savings is that corresponding to full employment; it ignores the effects engenderd by the store-of-value role of money, while it is by virtue of this role of money that the demand for money depends on the rate of interest. Garegnani considers these criticisms to rest on such weak foundations that he suggests they have been solely responsible for the dominance of the thesis that wage rigidity is the sole obstacle to full employment. The traditional approach is thus reinforced, at least as it applies to the long period and the accumulation of capital.

However, it still remains to be proven that the average level of investment varies inversely with the rate of interest in the long period in such a way that the level of investment is sufficient to permanently absorb full employment saving. If this proposition cannot be logically supported then the conclusions put forward by Keynesian theory could be supported for the long period, independently of any propositions concerning the influence of expectations on the rate of interest, or the role of liquidity preference. Now the criticisms of the orthodox conception of capital and distribution highlights the weakness of the analytical foundations of the inverse relation between the amount of investment and the rate of interest. Garegnani thus suggests a return to the equalisation of savings and investment by means of aggregate income in the long period, producing the Keynesian compromise.

The Multiplier and Liquidity Preference

In the course of the section in this Introduction consecrated to the development of the 'Keynesian synthesis', I presented the criticism levelled by Kregel (Chapter 11) with respect to Hicks's representation of Keynes's theory by means of the *IS–LM* schema. It thus only remains to examine the other aspect of his contribution which suggests (in sections 4 and 5 of Chapter 11) the transformations that must be carried out on Hicks's presentation in order to arrive at a 'correct representation of Keynes's theory'. This transformation rests on the inseparable relation which is established by effective demand between the multiplier and money prices explained by means of liquidity preference.

Considered in its generality, the 'Keynesian project' substitutes effective demand for Say's Law, and liquidity preference linked to the income multiplier, for the quantity theory of money. The essential distinction between Keynes and the representation that Hicks gives of him, rests in the relation between money, the money rate of interest and money prices; the multiplier cannot be separated from liquidity preference because they are 'two sides of the same coin'.

Kregel bases his representation on Hicks's system of three equations to underline the differences in interpretation and the possibilities for similarities. Rather than adopt the structure of effective demand in terms of aggregate supply and demand, Hicks's approach is based on demand formulated with respect to a given level of physical output. For Keynes, the expectations of increased profits lead entrepreneurs to formulate their demand for investment, while the multiplier acts to adjust the level of income to the point at which savings equal investment, and prices move to the level at which receipts produce anticipated profits. Thus, an increase in effective demand increases revenue until the marginal efficiency of capital equals the rate of interest as determined on the money markets. Differences remain between Hicks and Keynes, both on the nature of the rate of interest, which for the latter is a monetary phenomenon, and on prices, which Keynes considered as money prices.

Thus it is possible to stress that, for numerous economists, the Keynes of yesterday is that of the multiplier income adjustment process formulated in the Hicksian context. The Keynes of today should be one of adjustment by means of the rate of interest in determining the general level of prices and of income in adjusting relative prices. That is to say that the Keynesian theory of the determination of monetary prices is based on the theory of liquidity preference and the interrelation of the price adjustment process and the income adjustment process based on the multiplier.

The Macroeconomic Foundations of the Aggregate Supply Function

The distinction that Keynes proposed between the theory of the firm or the individual industry and the theory of output and employment as a whole is considered by Rodolphe dos Santos Ferreira and Philippe Michel (Chapter 12) as an essential dichotomy, constituting a very important positive component of the *General Theory*. It is, in fact, founded on two distinct objectives of analysis, rather than on different methods of analysis, for was the distinction not treated as a simple aspect of a methodological dichotomy: microeconomics/macroeconomics?

However, they propose to investigate the microeconomic foundations that the analysis of entrepreneurs' decisions and anticipations gives to the aggregate demand function expressed, in this case, as an extension of Marshallian analysis because of the light that it sheds on supply conditions. With reference to the opposition between the assimilation of the Keynesian aggregate supply function within a function of total variable costs (Patinkin), on the one hand, and the position that the function is a simple extension of the Marshallian supply function (D. H. Robertson, and Sidney Weintraub), on the other; they show how it is possible to accommodate both positions within a dualist conception of the principle of effective demand.

In the *General Theory* each individual entrepreneur determines the level of employment and output by maximising his profits in a given state of long- and short-term expectations; but it is these expectations that should also influence demand conditions which play the major role in the determination of the current level of output. The second aspect of dualism is constituted by the existence of an equilibrium level of employment, determined by the realisation of entrepreneurs' expectations in the market. The authors seek to show that it is possible to find a place for both of these aspects in a dualist conception of effective demand. To do this they are led to the introduction of two stages of analysis within the dualist interpretation of effective demand: the determination of the *current level* of employment and the determination of the *equilibrium level* of employment, leading to a critique of Say's Law.

On this basis they pronounce two results. The first concerns the attention that Keynes gave to the microeconomic foundations of his analysis, showing the aggregation procedure that permits the passage from an analysis of the individual entrepreneur to propositions of an aggregate economic character; the second is that the Keynesian revolution is largely based on Marshallian tradition.

Can I make a simple remark about this brilliant presentation? In a competitive regime without individual monopolists, the decisions of the individual (non-monopolist) entrepreneur are neither independent nor autonomous, in the sense that each entrepreneur has to decide his level of output in function of his anticipation of *aggregate* demand. For it is not he alone, but the ensemble of entrepreneurs, who, through their common decisions, create the incomes and thus the expenditures of their own clients; they cannot expect to increase their sales unless they also expect the aggregate level of incomes to increase. The consequence is that each individual entrepreneur will find it in his interest to decide the current level of output and employment that he undertakes in conformity with the decisions of the same order taken by all other entrepreneurs together, or at least to the extent that they can be foreseen. This should facilitate the aggregation procedure, but does it not also radically alter the analysis of the microeconomic foundations of the aggregate supply function?

Part I
Development of Fundamental Analysis

Section I
The Monetary Production Economy

1 The Foundations of a Monetary Production Economy

Alain Barrère

The simple inversion of John Stuart Mill's famous dictum that in economics there is nothing more insignificant than money cannot be considered as a satisfactory characterisation of a monetary production economy. Money is not more significant than goods, nor is it less important. The formulation of abstract models in which monetary theory is given the position of importance formerly reserved for the analysis of goods is thus equally unacceptable. The generality of Keynes's theory involves an analysis dealing with commodities as well as money and production as well as exchanges.

THE REAL–MONETARY DUALITY

The monetary production economy, arising from a dual approach to economic phenomena, is based on the observation that money as well as goods play an integral part in the modern economy. It consists of an integration of both real and monetary phenomena into an inseparable whole. On this basis it is possible to formulate four propositions which form the basis of the subsequent discussion:

(1) Recognition of two types of phenomena: real and monetary, each with its own specific nature and action.
(2) These two phenomena are interrelated from the very beginning of the economic process, that is, from the beginning of the production process, given the fact that it is necessary to produce goods before exchanging them. Now, production requires the intervention of money because producing supposes an option between conserving acquired wealth and investing it to create additional wealth. It follows that money plays part of its role even before it acts as a means of effecting transactions in the process of exchange.

(3) Money is neither the garment nor the reflection of real phenomena. Extending Schumpeter's assessment of interest to all monetary phenomena we could say that the monetary form is not the exterior appearance of phenomena which are in essence real, but the direct expression of their own essence.[1]

(4) Economic events concerning money are not simple reflections of events taking place in the realm of real goods: monetary events set up and arrange real events, because in the modern economy agents exercise their control over goods by means of a process which starts from money to reach the real.[2]

This interpretation highlights the diversity of agents' behaviour with respect to goods and to money, and reveals the existence of a diversified economy composed of entrepreneurs, investors, consumers, savers, hoarders, each differing in their access to money, to credit and to debt, and each differing in the way they speculate over time; all, however, run the same risks of uncertainty and all must take decisions in the present on the basis of 'future values' which can only be determined on the basis of their expectations. A link is thus necessary between current decisions and the results that are expected from the use values which will be received in the uncertain future.

This 'subtle' link is provided by money, whose essential characteristics allow the transfer of value over time and thus serve as a support for expectations of future values, even though these future values remain unknown. In this respect one of the determinant decisions involves the choice between the preservation of wealth in forms offering varying degrees of liquidity and the investment of money in productive equipment expected to yield future profits. What are the factors which influence this choice?

MONEY, LIQUIDITY AND UNCERTAINTY

In a monetary economy, money is the instrument, *par excellence*, which possesses the attribute of liquidity: that is, the attribute which gives to the holder of the instrument the power to dispose of his wealth with the maximum of convenience and security in any place and at any time. If it is difficult to accept the idea of absolute liquidity, then money is the economic category which possesses liquidity in the highest degree. Money's liquidity is not, however, fixed but varies according to time and circumstance and differs for different types of monetary instruments.

In addition, the fact that the carrying costs associated with the holding of money are practically zero makes money the privileged instrument for the preservation of wealth in a liquid form: that is, the preferred instrument for holding 'the potentiality to consume an unspecified article at an unspecified time'.[3] But why should one want to hold wealth in this liquid form, when, in contrast to holding wealth in financial assets, holding money yields a zero return, the money-liquidity being neither an asset nor a good? The answer to this question lies in our attitude to the non-probabilistic future, which we can only attempt to foresee and anticipate. Time, uncertainty and expectations are inseparable.

Keynes contrasts the economics of uncertainty which results from our tendency to preoccupy ourselves with the future consequences of our present activities despite the fact that we have no absolute or precise knowledge of the future, with the economics of the present, of the revealed, which leads to the certainty of equilibrium. In the economy of certainty variations in the conditions of equilibrium are not necessarily excluded, but their quantitative changes are considered subject to the laws of probability and thus calculable; expectations can thus be treated as if they could be, in principle, exact and realised. The uncertainty of the future is thereby reduced to the quasi-certainty of the present.

The existence of non-probabilistic uncertainty engenders instability, because it requires us not only to consider the absence of our knowledge of the quantitative consequences of an event, but the impossibility of making any precise estimate of the likelihood of the occurrence of the event itself, or the conditions which might provoke it, much less its exact consequences. Even consideration of current events produces doubt and disquietude, for we cannot avoid reaching a decision and taking action. Thus we are led to employ rudimentary palliative techniques to help us face the consequences of the future 'we do not know', although they cannot protect us from risk and error, and at the same time we have to act even if we rapidly change our opinions as well as our decisions. In contrast to the rationality of the perfectly informed neoclassical agent stands the conventional judgement of the Keynesian agent who, possessing certain information only for past events, must formulate expectations of the future and confront the incompatibilities of the present. Thus, he seeks to reassure himself of his decisions by adopting behaviour similar to that of his fellows. Nevertheless, this does not eliminate his disquietude and he continues to search for a way to guarantee himself against the hazards inherent in the noncontrollable future, by giving major importance to those activities which permit him to increase his wealth and to accumulate. These are the outlines of the economics of uncertainty,[4] which is by nature monetary because money permits one to exercise that control over goods at the desired moment which seems impossible to organise in advance with rationality and security. The possession of money is conservation and accumulation of wealth and, therefore, compensation for uncertainty.

Even though money yields no return, but compensates for uncertainty, it will only be given up in exchange for a premium which offsets the advantages that are lost by lending it out. The size of this liquidity premium which is required to induce agents to hold wealth in a less liquid form (non-money debts) depends on the degree of confidence of the holder of money in his own speculations; variations of this degree of confidence constitute one of the elements determining fluctuations in the size of the premium demanded. We know that the adjustment, at the margin, of the demand for money to hold, and of the quantity available for this purpose, led Keynes from money's liquidity premium, the highest of all assets, to the money-rate of interest which he considered the price of money in terms of money and for this reason the most significant of all rates of interest.

UNCERTAINTY AND THE VARIABILITY OF PRODUCTION

Why should production, rather than exchange, be associated with uncertainty and money? There are a number of reasons, the first of which is of a purely logical nature. It is only possible to exchange something that has already been produced, even when it is assumed that only exchangeable goods are produced. The second reason follows from the fact that since the quantity of factors employed is not given, but variable, an explanation of the factors which determine the decisions concerning the employment and production of factors is indispensable. Before affecting exchange and the market, uncertainty has a determining influence on the conditions of production, since the desire to conserve and accumulate wealth in the form of money competes with the decision to invest wealth in productive assets. As a consequence, monetary conditions of production determine the endowments of factors which, as will be seen below, themselves constitute one of the determinant elements of the mechanism of price formation.

Finally, there is a third reason which combines and extends the first two. When traditional theory assumes given quantities of already produced and available goods, it is obviously the determination of the exchange values of goods which predominates the analysis. The real exchange values result from the Walrasian condition of liquidity: in equilibrium, but only in equilibrium, the exchange value of each good against every other good is established; all goods possess absolute liquidity in such conditions and a system of real prices can be established spontaneously through barter exchange. But, starting from the problem of the determination of the total output destined to supply markets in which the level of demand must be anticipated in advance, not only must the hypothesis of real exchange in which goods buy goods be abandoned, but the assumption that goods producc goods without reference to time and money must be given up. Not only does production require the passage of time, it is linked to the choice between the current employment of available resources and placement in reserves which conserve wealth and allow the redistribution of satisfaction by means of the transfer of value through time. It is thus necessary to dispose of an instrument which links the future to the present and permits the uncertain calculations relating to present and future needs, and of the advantages that one might expect from the satisfaction of the one or the other. We are thus led back to the money-liquidity which allows financing in anticipation, not only of production, but also of the expenditures that agents will make in the exchange process. It is thus necessary to further investigate (in section I below) the monetary conditions of production which are determinant, notably in the field analysis to which Keynes addressed himself, the theory of employment (section II), and which must be extended (in section III) to the analysis of the growth of production.

I THE MONETARY CONDITIONS OF PRODUCTION

The basic proposition that lies behind the analysis of this section is that the rhythm and volume of current production are subject to variations produced by monetary factors. The justification for this proposition results from examination of the four stages of the production process: the choice between the production of assets and conserving wealth as money; the advance of money to finance production; the determination of the volume of production; and the determination of the absolute level of prices.

A. The Choice Between Production of Assets and Holding Money

Consider a wealth owner who, subject to certain conditions, is willing to forgo holding his wealth in the form of money. He has a choice between two possible courses of action: he may lend money at the prevailing rate of interest, that is, he may substitute money for another financial asset; or he may buy a productive asset which may take the form of an investment in a capital good if he is an entrepreneur or a share representing the value of a capital good in which case he becomes a financial investor. At the level of the economy as a whole, equilibrium will tend to be established at the margin between the advantages offered by each of the two possibilities through variations in the prices of the two types of investment, until their discounted future returns offer to the wealth-owner the prospect of a return that is equal to the rate of interest he would receive from lending his money. In this way the rate of interest enters, along with a number of other factors, into the determination of the price of assets. Among these other factors are the discounted future yields of the assets and the variation in their capital values which are also subject to the uncertainties and sudden changes in expectations produced by the impossibility of any knowledge of the future; the forecast of future yields are thus subject to frequent reassessment. The price of physical capital assets is thus also ultimately subject, taking account of their costs of production, to the same sort of fluctuations produced by the combination of expectations which act jointly on the factors that determine them: discounted future yields, the rate of interest, costs of production, and expected capital values. Thus we have not only the enumeration of the monetary conditions of prodution of physical assets, but at the same time the monetary conditions for the purchase of capital goods and thus the monetary conditions of aggregate production.

Entrepreneurs in the investment good sector will decide to produce new capital goods when the price at which they expect to sell them exceeds their costs of production. These prices are primarily determined by variations in the rate of interest and the expected future yields of the capital goods over their expected productive lives. Thus, if the combined effect of the level of the rate of interest and the discounted future yields produces a rise in the selling price of capital goods above their cost of production, the volume of production will increase while the volume of production will be reduced when prices show a downward tendency. Thus the volume and rhythm of investment will also be subject to sudden and appreciable variations, since they depend on the variable evaluations which investors must make concerning the future evolution of interest rates on money loans and the expected return from holding financial assets and capital goods. There is no reason to expect that a change in the evaluation of the future value of one of these factors should be offset by an offsetting change in the other direction of the other; rather they have a tendency to move cumulatively because of the interdependence which exists between the price of money, shares, physical capital goods and financial assets. Thus fluctuations in expenditure on investment subject the economy to a regime of variability of production resulting from changes in the opinions of 'decision makers' with respect to expected future conditions. These changes will manifest themselves in movements of the monetary variables: the rate of interest representing the price of money's liquidity property and the expected future value of returns to investment measured in money. However, the variability which is thus produced is circumscribed by variations in the level of effective demand which is also subject to determination by monetary phenomena.

B. Effective Demand and Money-Advances

The essence of the monetary production economy resides in the concept of effective demand, which expresses the expectations concerning the consituents of the curves of aggregate demand and supply prices which are linked;[5] that is, it expresses the complex of elements which determine their expected monetary value and fix the volume of employment and production. Because effective demand is itself an expected monetary magnitude it is not the same thing as the level of demand actually exercised on goods markets. It is thus effective demand and not the circular flow of income which is unique to the monetary production economy, because it is the former that sets in motion the monetary advances on production which compose the money flows which are observed in the circular flow.

These elementary propositions concerning the circuit of outflows and inflows which constitute the circular flow would be purely formal if they did not bring to light the important relationship between the money advances actually *expended* in initiating production and the expenditures of incomes *expected* in the categories of consumption and saving which determines the volume of production that it is profitable for entrepreneurs to undertake. The necessity of making advances on income, which is inherent in the principle of effective demand, turns out to be of capital importance because it expands our understanding of a number of concepts, such as money wages, savings, the division of incomes between savings and consumption, and finally the level of absolute prices. The following sections will attempt to demonstrate how.

1. Monetary Advances on Production

Investment expenditures are subject to the procedure already described, consisting of the decision between holding wealth in a more or less liquid form and using it to produce new physical assets. In the investment goods sector, expenditures between entrepreneurs are settled by means of recourse to bank credit or out of retained earnings. These expenditures in fact consist of money expended in advance of the anticipated savings to be created in the course of the circular flow. With respect to employment, expenditures on wages consist of money advanced in anticipation of the money to be received from the output to be produced, and constitutes an important element in the distinction between a real and a monetary economy.

In a 'real-wage economy' labour's remuneration is expressed in physical terms, full employment being assured when the wage is equal to the marginal product of labour and the utility of the wage is equal to the marginal disutility of the volume of employment. Labour is itself considered as a produced good which is exchanged on a market against other goods at a price which is expressed by the wage. The real-wage economy presumes that the labour market is identical to the market for any other good and that money is neutral.

In the Ricardian system, workers are paid in terms of wage-goods advanced by the entrepreneur out of his stock of capital, the advances are in terms of physical goods and the analysis is eased by the assumption that there is only one produced good in the economy, such as Ricardo's wheat. Wheat is thus produced by inputs of wheat and, by extending the argument, commodities are produced by commodities.

It is not possible to represent the modern economy by means of a single produced good and no money. The worker cannot be paid with a share of the output that he helps to produce, for example by means of a piece of a machine which he has constructed. He can only receive his wages in terms of money whose liquidity allows him to obtain whatever goods he desires, whatever the time and place.

The money-wage is thus not an advance from capital, but an advance on the monetary value to be realised from the sale of output to be produced, an advance of income on an anticipated use value which is an expression of the very logic of the operation of finance by means of credit. One of the basic uses of money is the payment of wages and as such not only provides current financing of production, but also financing of the anticipated monetary expenditure which will buy it. An important distinction between nominal and monetary values thus emerges. The labourer is paid a *nominal* wage in a monetised real exchange economy: that is, the real exchange value of labour already determined by the play of supply and demand in the labour market is expressed in terms of neutral money. The wage advanced in a monetary production economy is a *monetary* wage, in the sense that it does not represent a previously established real wage multiplied by the level of prices, but rather the income in terms of money-liquidity attributed to a unit of labour time employed in production.

Aggregate expenditure on wages thus does not depend on the volume of employment determined in the labour market by the equalisation of the real wage and the marginal productivity of labour, but on the relation between the volume of production determined by effective demand and the quantity of labour necessary to produce it, given techniques of production and the existing productive capacity. As a consequence, the quantity of labour that finds employment will be determined by effective demand, while the level of money-wages, established by collective bargaining and convention between workers and entrepreneurs, is independently determined. It is thus not the real wage which determines the volume of employment, but the volume of employment which reveals the magnitude of the real wage.

The differential distribution of power among the various agents in the modern economy can thus be clearly recognised: holders of money who determine its use; banks which grant credit; workers who negotiate money-wages and above all entrepreneurs who, by initiating effective demand determine the volume of output and employment and advance money-income, in particular the wage incomes corresponding to the volume of labour that they engage in production.

There is then no place for the labour market in the Keynesian system: this market is a theoretical fiction only necessary for the construction of the ideal schema of a real exchange economy, and is nothing more.[6]

2. The Expected Expenditure of Anticipated Incomes

We now come to the decision of how incomes will be spent and thus of the division of aggregate income between the well-known headings of consumption and saving in conformity with the standards of behaviour commonly found in communities with a high standard of living. Let us start the discussion by making the origin of this division more precise:

consumption must be considered prior to saving, which is simply the excess of aggregate money incomes over expenditures on consumption. This part of Keynes's original proposition, which is often invoked, defines the *magnitude* of the sums available to be saved. But there is a second part of the propostion defining the *act* of saving which must not be forgotten: it is impossible to save without acquiring an asset in one or another of the forms, cash, a debt or capital goods (cf. *General Theory*, chapter 7, section V). If saving takes the form of the acquisition of a newly produced asset, then it is investment; if it represents the acquisition of an already existing asset sold by someone who is 'dis-saving', it is simply the reinvestment of funds. In both cases, saving is created by the transformation of liquidity which takes place with the purchase of financial or physical assets. If the magnitude of the difference between income and consumption is unaffected, or is only partially affected, by the purchase of assets, saving cannot be said to take place, but rather the hoarding of all, or part, of that difference held in a liquid form. Hoarding is the conservation of money, which has the highest degree of liquidity; it is the negation of expenditure.

In a situation of increased aggregate income we must discover how the additional income will be divided between consumption and saving. The answer is simple: if each increases absolutely, the proportion which determines the division of the increase in income between the two is, in principle, the same as that which prevailed before the increase. The reason for this simple response is easily seen. It is the increase in output which determines the *size* of the increase in income to be divided between consumption and saving. Since both increase, neither one can increase by more than total income increases. This leads to the formulation of the 'psychological law' that when income increases, consumption expenditure increases by a lesser amount. This 'law', so often disputed, is nevertheless indisputable in principle. Consideration of the opposite hypothesis should furnish a sufficiently convincing argument.

Let us suppose that the community increases its consumption by the same amount as the increase in income. This would imply consuming the entire increase and that, as the community becomes richer, it ceases to save. This is not only illogical, it contradicts the observed behaviour of rich societies. Now consider the opposite case: the community saves the entire increase in income. It is difficult to understand why an economy would increase saving in order to increase investment if consumption does not increase when income rises. It is thus evident that the only point that is subject to dispute is the magnitude and the stability of the proportion in which income is divided between consumption and saving; the division itself is evident.

In fact, the stability of the average propensity to consume is logically necessary for the stability of Keynes's system, and the variations of the marginal propensity may constitute one of a number of factors causing instability. But the stability of the average propensity itself implies that the increase in income is divided between saving and consumption in the same proportion that prevailed before the increase. It is this proportion which exercises a direct action on the determination of the volume and the structure of production.

C. The Determination of the Volume of Production

We thus come to the principal question in our analysis, the relation between the expenditures *advanced* by entrepreneurs in the investment good sector and the expenditures *expected* by entrepreneurs operating in the consumption goods sector. It is this relation which determines the volume of production and the associated level of employment.

1. The Two-Sector Economy

The modern economy does not produce one single good, even if we often employ the artifice of aggregation, nor is it composed of a single productive sector. In reality there is a close link between the output of the investment goods and the consumption goods sectors: expenditures for the output of consumption goods in any period is a function of expenditures for the production of investment goods in the same period. It follows that the levels of production and aggregate employment are influenced by variations in the decisions to produce investment goods, which are in turn subject to fluctuations in the rate of interest and the expected rates of return on investment in capital assets, both of which are monetary phenomena. This is an example of a principle that we have already discussed above: monetary events elicit and determine real events.

We have already seen how the amount of investment expenditures was governed by the relation liquidity–interest–discounted expected yields on investment, in the sense that entrepreneurs who employ investment goods will demand additional capital goods as long as their discounted expected future yields exceed the rate of interest. It is this relation which, in respect to effective demand, determines the amount of expenditure on investment undertaken during the period.

Entrepreneurs who produce consumption goods have no incentive to produce and sell a quantity of output whose cost exceeds the proportion of aggregate income that the community reserves for consumption; but they do have an incentive to produce up to the point where the total cost is equal to this amount.

2. The Relation Between the Production of Consumption and Investment Goods

It follows from these observations that entrepreneurs in the consumption sector will be led to produce a volume of output whose cost of production relative to the cost of production of the investment sector's output is in the same proportion as the division of income between consumption and saving. Consumption output should thus have costs which are a multiple of the costs of production of investment goods. For example, if the community currently spends nine-tenths of its income on consumption goods, entrepreneurs in this sector will have an incentive to establish the volume and the cost of the goods that they produce such that the aggregate supply price of their output equals nine-tenths of aggregate incomes, i.e. to nine times the cost of investment goods (the example is Keynes's, given in 'The General Theory of Employment', *Quarterly Journal of Economics*, February 1937). This relation lies behind the determination of the volume of production and employment by expenditures on investment; it relates the propensity to consume and the multiplier, and produces the *ex post* equalisation of saving and investment, subject to the two fundamental equilibrium conditions: the realisation of entrepreneurs' expectations and stability of the propensity to consume. As a result of this relation, the expenditure on investment may be financed by means of credit, since saving will cover the bank advances, or by the purchase of shares representing the value of the assets created. It is in this sense that the amount of savings may be said to be determined by the amount of investment expenditures.

Here we again see the confirmation of the basic principle of the monetary production economy: employment and production are real phenomena whose magnitude and variation are produced and determined by the magnitude and variation of monetary phenomena.

3. The Equilibrium of Output, Employment and Income

The level of output does not necessarily reach equilibrium at full employment of available resources or, in particular, full employment of labour. For full employment to be achieved, effective demand must be sufficient to produce a demand for labour equal to the volume of labourers willing and able to work for the prevailing wage as determined by collective bargains. If effective demand is insufficient to employ the entire labour force willing to work at the prevailing wage, but the entrepreneurs' expectations are realised, the equilibrium that is established will be a less than full employment equilibrium. If expectations are not realised, in particular if consumption, saving and hoarding do not correspond to the anticipated magnitudes, the circular flow is not confirmed and disequilibrium of the monetary variables and prices with unemployment is established. But the level of employment is not affected within the period, since it is determined at the beginning of the period in order to produce the volume of output determined by effective demand. For the same reason this volume of output is itself unchanged. What do change, on the other hand, are the conditions of sale: that is, the level of prices and the quantities sold, with the resulting repercussion on the volume of stocks. A level of sales less than the volume of output produced leads to an increase in stocks represented as involuntary investment.

D. The Absolute Level of Prices

From the point of view of a real-exchange economy, Keynes's theory is interpreted as having substituted quantity adjustments for price adjustments; prices are considered to be rigid or even fixed. Such quantity adjustment could, at best, only take place over a number of periods since, as we have just pointed out, the level of employment and quantities produced are given within the period. Even subject to this correction such an interpretation cannot be accepted, because the absolute prices that are the object of Keynesian theory are not distinguished by flexibility or rigidity, but by a distinction between their anticipated and realised levels. The whole point is to determine when and how these two levels will be made consistent. A short explanation of this point should be sufficient.[7]

It is well known that exchange is the point of departure of traditional theory; there is no explanation of the source, and above all, the size of the agents' budget allocations. As a consequence the level of absolute prices is also indeterminate, except by reference to the quantity theory of money.

The orginality of the Keynesian theory of prices[8] is the influence of advances of income on agents' budget allocations; on this basis it becomes possible to form anticipations, based on the interdependent curves of aggregate supply and demand, about the absolute level of prices, in the expectation that they will be confirmed by the actual price level which will be formed in the market. The theory of prices thus becomes the product of the evolution of money-income flows in the circuit and of the market produced by the level of effective demand. This process deserves more detailed explanation.

The action of effective demand injects income advances into the circuit corresponding to the factor costs and the minimum expected profit, which together constitute the aggregate supply price and represent agents' money incomes. In addition, the conclusion of the production process ultimately determines the distribution of products among the future suppliers. It is in this way that the allocation of the money-incomes of potential buyers and the allocation of the product of the eventual sellers are determined. Since the aggregate supply price also expresses the amount of money-incomes distributed and the total price at which the goods produced should be sold, it also represents the money-incomes which will be used to buy them, and the expected prices at which they must be sold in order to justify their production. These two aggregate money-values are evidently equal, since they are but two different aspects of the same money sum.

The fact that the curve of aggregate demand prices is intersected in one, and only one, point by the curve of aggregate supply prices, expresses that the entrepreneur-sellers expect that the aggregate monetary demand that the buyers will exercise in the market on the purchase of the corresponding output will be equal to its aggregate supply price. In other words, they expect that the actual level of prices that will be established in the market will be equal to the price level incorporated in effective demand. Evidently, this can only be the case if the expected incomes which constitute the aggregate demand price are confirmed by the expenditure of money-incomes, that is by the expenditure of the buyers' budget allocations. In the event that expectations are not confirmed the actual prices observed on the market will differ from the expected prices. Now, the equalisation of aggregate supply price and aggregate demand price signifies the completion of the circular flow of incomes through the equalisation of the outflow of expenditures and the inflow of receipts, that is, by the expenditure of the money incomes advanced on the purchase of consumption goods and for saving (the purchase of assets) covering the costs of production of the currently produced consumption and investment goods. As a consequence, the confirmation of the aggregate of expectation which constitutes effective demand leads to a *monetary equilibrium* understood as a *general equilibrium of monetary values* characterised by the reconstitution of the incomes advanced in by means of the circular flow, the equalisation of saving and investment, the stability of the level of hoarding, and the equalisation of expected prices and actually realised prices.

Prices in Keynesian theory cannot then be fixed; if expectations are too optimistic or too pessimistic actual prices will diverge from expected prices by a factor which depends on the influence of the error on the behaviour of demand. One possible explanation of the widespread belief in the assumption of fixed prices to Keynes's theory is the extensive use in traditional theory of correct expectations of future conditions which may be fully described by a probability distribution. We have already noted that Keynes's view concerning future events was precisely the contrary.

On the other hand, it is important to underline that actual prices are subject to conditioning and prior regulation, because the sum of the budget allocations advanced and distributed to individuals as income is equal to the aggregate supply price of output. This is why the realisation of expenditure expectations assures the equalisation of the actual price level and the expected price level. Prices are not fixed, but are determined by the expenditure of income in the market.

We thus reach the last of our considerations of the monetary conditions of production: the monetary conditions of production of use values (production of goods) determines the monetary conditions of the formation of exchange values (actual prices). We must now turn to an examination of the application of the principles of analysis which we have just briefly set out.

II ANALYSIS OF THE ECONOMICS OF EMPLOYMENT

While the *General Theory* laid the foundation of a monetary production economy, its immediate objective was to provide a theory of employment, without proceeding to a complete theory of output *as a whole*, or the theory of capital necessarily linked to it. The analysis is thus limited, not only by its objectives, but also by the instruments which are employed and the use that is made of them in achieving those objectives.

The time framework of the analysis is Marshall's short period. This is particularly evident in the assumptions of a given quantity of fixed capital, given techniques of production and a labour force of given quantity and quality. While Keynes recognised that these factors vary, he simply noted that his analysis did not take their variation into consideration. These given factors completely determine certain relations which are themselves independent of such variations (in particular the employment and aggregate supply functions), so that it is the basic independent variables which uniquely determine the dependent variables, employment and output, 'in the sense that there is a unique correlation between the two' (*General Theory*, p. 246). The Keynesian theory of employment is primarily concerned with the determination of the utilisation of a variable fraction of the available labour force, given the quantity of fixed capital and the techniques of production embodied in it, variations in investment and circulating capital only modifying the degree of capacity utilisation of the given equipment.

The possible theoretical developments of this point of departure may be indicated by the question: Is the nature of full- and less-than-full-employment equilibrium similar in the sense that each follows consistently from its particular criteria and may be explained in terms of the operation of the same variables?

A. The Ambiguities of the General Theory of Employment

Keynes presents his work as a unified, general theory of all the different possible positions of employment equilibrium, with the implicit understanding that the normal equilibrium position of the economy is at less than full employment which must be considered as 'a limiting point of the possible positions of equilibrium' (*General Theory*, p. 3). The question that emerges from this description is whether the two general conditions represented in the normal and limiting cases represent two positions of an inherently different nature, which Keynes seems to imply when he suggests that the applicability of the classical theory is limited to the case of full employment. However, Keynes's position is ambiguous, for it implies that the classical interpretation is but a special case of his more general interpretation, yet it retains a specific, if limited, applicability. The same explanation of the determinants of equilibrium would then apply to all possible levels of employment except at the limiting point where the classical explanation retains validity.

In other words, does the full-employment economy have the same characteristics as the less-than-full-employment economy? Keynes appears to answer this question in the negative, for example when he suggests that certain propositions, such as 'the crude quantity theory', are valid in conditions of full employment. But his analytical support for such propositions is so superficial that the following question has remained unresolved: Is the only difference between full employment and unemployment equilibrium the quantity of labour employed, with similar adjustment mechanisms and determinant variables; or on the contrary, does the attainment of full employment represent a qualitative structural barrier which introduces a different adjustment mechanism which operates with variables of a different type and nature because employment, having attained its maximum value, can no longer increase and thus becomes given rather than variable?

The question is of even greater importance, because it leads directly to the consideration of whether it is useful to direct the analysis solely to the levels of employment and growth, at the expense of more important factors such as the transformations which may come about in certain structural elements, changes in the evolution of productive processes (productive combination of factors), in the rhythm of accumulation, or in the substitution of capital for labour displacing part of productive expenditures from wages towards equipment.

In fact, these observations pose the question of the structural similarity of full-employment and under-full-employment economies. Keynes himself gives an indication when he writes: 'It follows that an increase in the quantity of money will have no effect whatever on prices, so long as there is any unemployment, and that employment will increase in exact proportion to any increase in effective demand brought about by an increase in the quantity of money' (*General Theory*, p. 295), a passage which is often quoted as a rehabilitation of the quantity theory. But this would require the insertion of at least two additional conditions: supply must have become perfectly inelastic, and effective demand must vary in the same proportion as the quantity of money; conditions which do not bear any close resemblance to situations of unemployment where the second condition is in any case inapplicable.

In summary, full employment conditions remain within the confines of the structural framework applicable to the study of variations in the level of employment, that is, within the Marshallian definition of the short period. Within this framework, the characteristic of an economy in conditions of full employment is, by its very definition, the full utilisation of the total available labour force, i.e., a fixed amount of employment, similar to the given quantities of productive equipment and techniques, so that the employment function, the aggregate supply function and the combination of productive factors all remain unchanged. The level of full employment can thus be considered as a structural constraint which sets the upper limit on increases in national income. Two consequences follow from this, one concerning real quantities, the other the nature of money.

In terms of real quantities, i.e., the level of employment and production actually achieved, additional productive activity cannot increase the level of output; it can only substitute previously existing activity. The economy is thus in a condition where variations do not concern the volume, but rather the internal structure, of production; to the extent that the economy is able to adapt to the new conditions it must transfer productive activities, either between the investment and consumption sectors, or within each of them. The analysis thus faces one of the major concerns of the dominant theory: the problem of the substitution and the optimal allocation of a given volume of resources within the framework of a given volume of production.

In such conditions would it be necessary to abandon the analysis of the monetary production economy, limited to conditions of unemployment, and adopt the analysis of a real exchange economy, better suited to the analysis of a full-employment economy? A positive response to this question would have two consequences:

(1) The possibility, when full employment conditions prevail, of direct and immediate identification of real prices on the basis of nominal prices: That is, variations in nominal prices may be translated directly into variations in the same direction and the same proportion in real prices, which serve to assure the maintenance of equilibrium quantities and prices and the realisation of the optimal distribution of resources. Now, Keynes has shown unequivocally that it is not possible to derive the variations in real prices from variations in nominal prices.
(2) The fact that the very nature of money changes so that it has only a neutral impact on the economy, transforming, without deforming, the equivalent real values exchanged into nominal terms.

In effect, the variations taking place in the system of nominal relative prices should produce sufficient changes in the system of real relative prices to bring about the necessary reorientation of activities, of factors and of resources, through the operation of substitution, to achieve an optimal allocation. Now, since only nominal prices can be directly observed, it must be the influence that the action of variations in supply and demand exert on that which brings about the necessary adjustment in real prices. Thus, it must be presumed that money only expresses the nominal equivalent of the real exchange values without deforming them: that is, it is necessary that money be neutral.

But, the adoption of the assumption of neutral money contradicts the conception of money's liquidity, and implies the abandonment of any influence of anticipations on current decisions concerning the transfer of productive activities. The implication of this line of reasoning is, then, that unless we consciously consider the question of the significance of the renunciation of speculation of future conditions, the acceptance of full employment as equivalent to conditions of a given volume of production in fact goes much further and leads to the identification, even if unintended, of a full-employment economy with a stationary, real economy.

B. The Conception of a Fully Employed Economy

Is Keynes's conception of full employment the same as the Classics'? Despite the common criterion of the absence of unemployment, the full employment situation is very different, depending on whether it is considered as a condition complete in itself, as in the traditional theory, or as the limit of a series of successive situations of diminishing unemployment which is eventually attained as a desired goal of policy, as in Keynesian thought.

According to the dominant theory, full employment is the normal state of affairs, customarily occurring in the real-exchange economy. There is no such thing as approaching full employment; the economy does not approach full employment because it does not depart from it; it is permanently installed there and unemployment is considered as being nothing more than an accident which the natural forces of the system move quickly to correct if they are permitted full liberty of action. Full employment is the only possible state for a real-exchange economic system.

On the other hand, according to the logic of Keynes's argument, full-employment and less-than-full-employment equilibrium are two different states of affairs, corresponding to two different types of economy even though one is the end point of the progress of the other. While it is possible for the economy to remain for long periods of time in conditions of less-than-full-employment equilibrium, one of the objectives of the *General Theory* is to demonstrate the possibility of moving out of this condition towards higher and higher levels of employment in order to ultimately achieve the limiting position of full-employment equilibrium–'limiting position' because in comparison with the full-employment equilibirum of the real-exchange economy, the equilibrium that is established is precarious and imperfect.

The explanation of the reasons for the precariousness and the imperfections of this limiting position, also reveals the reasons that lead to the consideration of the full-employment and the unemployment economy as constituting two different types of monetary production economy, without making the implicit identification of a monetary production economy with a real exchange economy when the position of full employment prevails, so that 'the classical theory comes into its own again from this point onwards'.[9]

C. The Monetary Production Economy and Full Employment

It is sometimes said that the dominant theory is built on the sensitivity of relative prices, while the Keynesian theory is based on the sensitivity of the absolute level of prices. This proposition can be interpreted in the following way.

In a situation of less than full employment, it is effective demand which determines the volume of production and assures the adjustment of aggregate money values as agents seek to validate their expectations. It is thus the absolute level of money prices which constitutes the expression of equilibrium in the supply and demand for output, because it equalises the money values of aggregate supply (cost) and of demand (expenditure) at the level of aggregate income that determines employment (employment function).

An increase in effective demand leads to an increase in production expenditures which produce three specific types of increase as a consequence: an increase in the volume of production, an increase in the level of money wages as the economy approaches full employment, and an increase in costs due to decreasing returns. Thus, as production increases, the absolute level of all prices tends to increase more than in proportion to the increase in the volume of production, and inflationary tensions appear as full employment is approached.

As a consequence, the economy enters conditions of full employment on the wave of a series of increases in money-wages and absolute money-prices. Not only are absolute prices subject to an upward trend which exists prior to the establishment of conditions of full employment, but this upward movement persists even when the limit of employment is attained. In effect, in situations of full employment, the increase in the wage bill distributed to the labour force stimulates expenditure on consumption goods and thus encourages entrepreneurs to increase effective demand. But, when the amount of aggregate money-income distributed increases without production being able to expand to meet it, nominal income diverges from the volume of production which remains stable and the causes of the increase in the level of absolute money-prices will persist. It is in this way that the differences between an under-full-employment and a full-employment economy appear in terms of their particular processes and the contents of the equilibrium established.

In conditions of less than full employment, the increase in effective demand produces an increase in employment and in the level of output. The variations in aggregate money-income, by confirming expectations, establish the equilibrium of aggregate supply and demand by means of equalisation of the actual level of absolute prices to their expected level, which will remain stable until the economy approaches full employment.

In conditions of full employment, on the other hand, an increase in the amount of expected receipts has, by definition, no effect on the level of employment and output while aggregate money-income continues to increase under the influence of the increase in aggregate supply prices, reflecting increases in wages and production costs (decreasing returns). The only influence towards adjustment produced by national income would be the equalisation of actual prices to the anticipated level, but both will be increasing.

We thus come back to Keynes's proposition, but without having to appeal to the support of the quantity theory of money: in conditions of unemployment an increase in effective demand produces an increase in employment and production; in conditions of full employment the increase in effective demand brings about an increase in absolute and relative prices with a constant volume of production.

The conclusion is not encouraging: as soon as the economy reaches full employment any hopes of price stability and additional growth must be abandoned, a conclusion which is as unacceptable as it is artificial. This is because it is based on three analytical hypotheses implicit in the use of the Marshallian short period: the given stock of capital, the given techniques of production, and constant productivity which assures the constancy of the employment and aggregate supply functions. These hypotheses necessarily lead to the interpretation of the effect of variations of investment on employment of labour, because the framework of analysis neutralises the action of investment on the level of utilisation of the capital stock. It is thus to the role of capital that we must extend the field of analysis of the monetary production economy.

III THE FOUNDATIONS OF A GROWING PRODUCTION ECONOMY

It is inappropriate to eliminate the effects on the level of employment and output, of the process which assures the maintenance of the stock of capital, even owing to the Marshallian methodology of short-period long-period analysis. Indeed, there are two, not one, principal elements which act to produce the influence of expectation and speculation on current decisions to hire labour and produce output. The first is money, to which Keynes gives the preponderant role already examined; the second is 'the existence of durable equipment which links the economy of the future to the economy of the present' because it is created in function of the returns expected over its lifetime. Keynes simply mentions this factor without providing any analytical support, except in the discussion of user cost and the discounted returns to capital.

It is this second point which we propose to elucidate briefly under two headings: the transformation of user costs into a determining variable, and the cost of depreciation and replacement in terms of its consequences on the relative expansion of gross output and net income. The discussion retains the limits of this exposition and is restricted to an examination of the foundations of the problem.

An ambiguity implicit in the *General Theory* will serve as our point of departure. Effective demand is defined as a net monetary magnitude comprising the sum of the cost of factors and profit in terms of money, excluding user cost. However, when Keynes discusses the determination of output at the level of the firm, he makes it clear that user cost should be included in the determination of the supply price of output, even though it is excluded from the level of effective demand which determines the aggregate level of production at the point of maximum net profit without taking account of depreciation of capital, or its financing comprised in gross profits. Thus the ambiguity. Is there any methodological reason why the analysis at the firm level should so differ from the analysis of the economy as a whole? In fact, the ambiguity arises from the concepts employed in the analysis.

At first sight it appears logical to reason in terms of aggregate supply price net of user costs, since effective demand corresponds to aggregate income. User cost does not form part of aggregate income because it represents the consumption of capital; it is not a cost which provides income. But this argument is only logical in appearance, and conceals a contradiction. In effect, Keynes points out that while aggregate supply price is defined net of user costs, 'the aggregate sums paid by the purchasers are, of course, *gross* of user cost' (*General Theory*, p. 24, n. 2), so that aggregate demand prices should also be gross of user costs. Now, since the two curves of aggregate demand and supply prices are interdependent it is difficult to understand why the first expresses net magnitudes and the second gross magnitudes. Consistency would seem to require that user cost be subtracted from aggregate income and considered as a part of the capital account. The circular flow of money values would then comprise two distinct circuits: one expressing the income circuit which only includes the cost of factors and net profits of the entrepreneur-consumer, the other expressing the capital account enclosing the gross profits. These profits represent the equivalent of the costs of the use of the capital stock and must assure that the existing capital stock is maintained intact. This interpretation opens up a line of analysis which is completely ignored in the *General Theory*–that of the gross product circuit, which encompasses the well-known circuit of aggregate net income as well as the capital circuit whose analysis remains to be completed.

For the income circuit, in which user cost is in fact neutralised, effective demand is a net magnitude. For the product circuit, effective demand is a gross magnitude; it thus provides a link between the income circuit and the capital circuit and integrates the factors determining the creation and the utilisation of money incomes for consumption and saving on one hand, and the influence of user cost, in its expanded role as the variable which integrates the costs of depreciation and the maintenance of capital, on the other. It is to the analysis of this new variable that we now turn.

A. Disinvestment and Capital Replacement as Variable Costs

In the framework of the present exposition it is only possible to present a summary study of the variable costs of disinvestment and replacement of capital. It will be limited to the examination of the most significant aspect, but it should be clear that there are any number of others which give the concept the necessary degree of generality and diversity.[10]

1. The Hypotheses and the Givens

The analysis will require expansion of Keynes's excessively restrictive set of basic hyptotheses, placing ourselves in a situation characterised by the accumulation of fixed capital equipment, continuous capital-using technical progress, a replacement rate for equipment sufficiently high to allow rapid introduction of the improved techniques, a clear tendency to substitute capital for labour, sustained growth inducing the expansion of productive equipment in the major manufacturing sectors, and latent generalised inflation of the prices of consumption and production goods.

These hypotheses, which are in themselves just as limiting but in a rather different manner, generally correspond to the particular conditions which prevailed during the strong and sustained growth of the 1950s and 1960s.[11] It is thus evident that hypotheses such as capital-using technical progress or appreciable increases in the prices of consumption and production goods will have to be carefully applied in the analysis of particular situations which are much more diversified.

The givens rest on the difference between net and gross values at the aggregate level: it is necessary to distinguish between gross national product, which comprises all costs of production including those produced through utilisation of the capital stock, on the one hand, and net income composed of the costs of production paid to factors and net profits, which must be divided into expenditures on consumption and household savings, on the other. The difference between gross product and net income is thus determined by the real and monetary consequences of the various aspects making up the cycle and the circuit of capital, as well as the monetary effects of the capital account of the public finances which do not affect distribution, and the balance of foreign trade. Only the consequences related to the cycle of capital will be discussed here.

By the *cycle* of capital we shall mean the repetitive process composed of three phases: investment, disinvestment, replacement. In each period, the cycle produces a *circuit* of capital, made up of an outflow of monetary expenditures corresponding to the user cost of capital which is reflected in the gross aggregate supply price, and an inflow represented by that part of aggregate receipts set aside to provide the financial provision for the effect of amortisation on the capital account, in prospect of the replacement of depreciated equipment. The income *cycle* is also composed of three phases: production–distribution–consumption, related to the fact that it concerns monetary incomes which may be spent without diminishing aggregate income because expenditures always return periodically as income in some sector. The income circuit associated with this cycle is the classical Keynesian circular flow.

2. The Gross Product Circuit and the Combination of Factors of Production

Our object in analysing the capital circuit is not to provide an answer to the problem of the relation between the growth of investment and the growth of revenue, as in the so-called Harrod–Domar models; rather it is to establish the relations of reproduction linking capital and income and to extend them to the explanation and interpretation of the divergence of gross product and net income. It is thus necessary to analyse the process which divides the circuit of gross product into those which reproduce capital and those which create income, that is between the costs of current production (costs of productive capital) and the current satisfaction of needs (consumption, savings). This process also covers modifications in the combination of the productive factors, labour and capital, and is thus determined by the employment and aggregate supply functions which are now considered as variable. Ultimately, it becomes necessary to set out the analysis in terms of a framework of a sequence of periods, each of which is assumed to be equal to the average duration of the stock of capital equipment, in order to isolate the effects of the variable representing the cost of disinvestment and replacement.

Although user cost, disinvestment and replacement are all mentioned in various places in the *General Theory*, Keynes does not integrate them into his analysis which is uniquely concerned with the influence of net effective demand on the combined variation of employment and income independent of variations in fixed capital.[12] However, a new investment implies maintenance costs over its life and amortisation costs to cover its replacement, which produce a divergence between the relative expansion of gross product and net income. In addition, the employment function is modified when the new investment embodies technical progress, for this will imply substitution of capital for labour, and thus a shift in the composition of current costs of production from wages to capital costs. As a consequence, the combination of productive factors, as well as the structure of the processes of production, will be subject to the influence of factors which lie outside the analytical framework of the *General Theory*. These factors will not only have effects on the volume of employment, but also on the relation Keynes posits between employment and income, 'in the sense that there is a unique correlation between the two' (*General Theory*, p. 246). A major portion of the theory of employment must then be considered subject to revision, to account for the implications of the use and replacement of the capital stock.

3. Disinvestment and Replacement of Capital

The costs associated with the use of the capital stock are those which result from the necessity of maintaining capital account balance. When depreciation in the value of the equipment due to use and the passage of time is entered on one side of the balance sheet, an entry must be made on the other representing the financial provision set aside for the replacement of the capital so destroyed. The financial provisions necessary to cover these costs are accumulated over the life of the equipment through deductions from the gross receipts from the sale of output. They must be sufficient to cover two elements: the full costs of replacing the capital goods, and a replacement 'overload'.

The disinvestment costs comprise all costs brought about by the transformation of fixed and working capital into liquid capital, that is, into final products ready for sale. It is composed of the sum of user costs and maintenance costs. User costs represent the reduction in the value of equipment caused by its operation to produce output; it is the counterpart of capital's contribution to the value of output. Maintenance cost is linked to the preservation of the productive capacity of the capital stock, including the costs of repairs, carrying costs for stocks, and such amounts as may be required to make good the effects of disuse, technological obsolescence and monetary depreciation. It is not only the counterpart of capital's productive contribution, it also represents the costs required to maintain the value of the capital stock over time.

Disinvestment costs thus represent the entirety of anticipated costs and are much more than a simple bookkeeping calculation; their significance goes beyond the idea of amortisation, in the sense that they must assure the maintenance of capital values which, in their absence, would continuously diminish as a result of the physical deterioration of the equipment as well as depreciation caused by the passage of time. In the first place, they must assure that the value of amounts accumulated over past periods remains sufficient, and they must be concerned with the expected values of the future provisions so that at the end of its working life the monetary value of the capital equipment has been reconstituted in a manner which assures its replacement without impoverishment of the economy.

The second element of capital costs is what we have called the 'surcharge' (overload) on replacement overcost. In order to guarantee the replacement of capital a supplement must be added to the expected replacement costs to cover any anticipated increases in the prices of new equipment. Such increases may result from the fact that replacements are seldom identical, but will encompass (by hypothesis) the latest capital-using improvements in technique, or there may have been increases in prices due to inflationary conditions. As these elements are uncertain there will be a tendency, in the name of financial prudence, to overestimate the amount of the margin required to meet such costs, in order to give the operation the maximum of security. Thus the origin of the 'overload' on expected replacement costs.

It is therefore necessary to add to the current value of the original cost of the equipment to be replaced a series of money-values, some known, others anticipated, but all linked to the necessity of reconstituting the value of capital in the next period in order to calculate the full anticipated replacement cost, and thus the required financial provision to cover the acquisition of the new equipment.

It therefore emerges that since the replacement cost of capital equipment comprises both the expectation of the sum of full replacement costs and the 'overload' on these costs, it will, given the set of hypotheses mentioned above, exceed the original investment expenditure on the capital due to be replaced.

There is an additional dimension to capital costs which emerges when the discussion is expanded from consideration of a given type of capital good to the expansion and development of the aggregate productive structure of the whole economy which occurs in the presence of sustained growth. In fact, on the aggregate level the excess of the cost of replacement over original investment expenditure will be increased by the impact of a rate of accumulation which exceeds the rate of increase of total product. Aggregate replacement costs will then have a tendency to increase due to the pressure of growth.

In an expansion of the aggregate economy over a series of periods the replacement of productive capacity is assured by means of a series of partial renewals of equipment taking place within different branches and sectors. The incorporation of technical progress thus takes place gradually, progressively expanding into all sectors of production. Since the original investments have been made at dates and for periods which may differ widely, the process of replacement and diffusion can only be extended to the entire economy over a sequence of periods. The consequence of the combination of these two movements is a progressive increase in aggregate replacement costs which increase the capital costs that must be deducted from gross national product. This increase becomes more accentuated if, as is likely, the progressive integration of technical progress speeds up the rate of turnover of capital equipment and if the innovations are capital-using. This would lead to conditions similar to those observed between 1948 and 1973: an increasing rhythm of accumulation making necessary a continual increase in aggregate investment, bringing about an even more rapid increase in aggregate replacement costs.

And, not only does the weight of capital costs on the national economy increase, but there will also be an impact which extends into future periods, since the financial provisions planned over the entire useful life of the equipment created will tend to be increased at the same time.

If the level of output increases, the annual financial provision for capital costs can be spread over a greater number of units of output whose market price increases because the inflationary increase in prices raises the costs of replacement for capital equipment at the same time. But if the rhythm of accumulation exceeds growth by more than a certain proportion, then distribution of capital costs over output leads to their taking on a higher and higher proportion of unit costs, and this increase in capital costs per unit of output becomes more accentuated if the growth rate happens to decline. In this case recession would feed inflation and reduce the profitability of employing capital. Here we return to the problem of the relative rates of expansion in gross product and net income.

B. Income Growth Lagging Behind Growth of Product

These inclusive capital replacement costs should be considered as costs which do not generate income, in Lundberg's sense, because they do not create income during the period in which they occur. Any resulting expenditures will only take place in periods subsequent to that in which the financial provision for the replacement investment takes place. However, it is not this temporal lag in expenditure which is the most significant aspect, but the fact that replacement cost does not represent the remuneration of a factor and is simply the counterpart of the maintenance of capital's value, something of a different nature from income. This is why the financial provision for capital costs which must be subtracted from gross product is logically entered in the capital account while it is waiting to be used, and is available for neither consumption nor for household savings. We thus arrive at the first consequence of our analysis: the effect of the financial provision for disinvestment in the capital account creates a margin between gross product and net income. A second consequence then follows immediately.

The supply price of output must be sufficient to cover replacement costs in order for the financial provision to be recovered at the level of output where aggregate demand equals the supply price. This is the principle underlying the inflow and outflow of gross product that is generated by gross effective demand. But how can we be sure that capital costs will be fully included in aggregate supply prices? Keynes, within the logic of the short period, would have responded, by a compensating amount of investment. But when it is a question of the growth and expansion of the economy, we have to take account of the fact that the capital stock will be composed of equipment of different ages which will have to be replaced at different times. As a consequence we will observe a current flow of renewal investment which represents in any period the annual replacement cost set aside to assure the renewal of ancient generations of capital. Thus, during each period a fraction of the financial provision built up over past periods is taken from reserves to be integrated into the aggregate expenditures on gross investment and thus entering aggregate supply price. The failure of these costs to generate income is thereby attenuated. It is not, however, entirely neutralised, because of the fact that the annual expenditures for replacement investment are calculated on the basis of current prices, while current financial provision for replacement is calculated on the basis of anticipated future prices, i.e. taking into account the tendency for replacement costs to rise in future periods. The possibility of supplementary investment in compensation of the effects of capital replacements is thus not excluded, nor are its effects, among them the tendency to cause replacement costs to increase in future periods.

Gross effective demand determines the volume of gross product which, at the stage of its realisation on the market, will be divided between the reproduction costs of capital and the satisfaction of current needs by expenditure of the remaining disposable net income in such a way that net income equals gross product less the amount of aggregate replacement cost which is entered on capital account. But, since the amount of the annual financial provision for capital costs is greater than the current amount of replacement investment, capital costs immobilise a part of the money incomes which should have been available to assure the required expenditure on consumption and household savings.

That is, first, that capital replacements costs increase at the expense of income, and thus that growth modifies the distribution of income, and second, that the cost of replacement is the autonomous variable which governs the relation between the relative increase of gross product and net income.

However, these effects may be provisionally and in part neutralised by a sufficiently rapid rate of expansion in which a part of the multiplier effect of investment on growth takes up the reduction in income caused by the effects of the financial provision for replacements. But the failure of the rising replacement cost to generate increases in income will act as a brake on the multiplier effect of investment. Thus when growth proceeds too rapidly and too long it will have programmed into future periods requirements for replacement provisions whose excess will be more and more difficult to offset by means of the compensatory investment that becomes more and more necessary. Such conditions verify the pertinence of Keynes's remark: 'Each time we secure to-day's equilibrium by increased investment we are aggravating the difficulty of securing equilibrium to-morrow' (*General Theory*, p. 105).

It thus becomes obvious that the *level* of net effective demand is less than gross effective demand, that the increase in net revenue is inferior to the increase in gross product, and that the disposable income of consumer-savers is less than 'Keynesian revenue'. The result is an impediment to the increase in consumption corresponding to the effects of the substitution of capital for labour which reduces the volume of employment.

It thus becomes possible to formulate a 'law' of the lower growth of net income relative to gross product: *When product increases, income and consumption increase, but income increases less than product, and consumption less than income.*

The consequences of this 'law' often pass unnoticed, because the divergence of the behaviour of gross product and net income is masked by the fact that growth is normally measured exclusively in terms of gross product. But this practice deprives us of a point of reference for a consequence of greatest importance: the appearance of over-investment, one of the determinants of crisis which signals the fall in the profitability of capital and the reduction in the volume of employment.

C. Over-investment

Over-investment is defined as follows in the *General Theory:* 'a state of affairs where every kind of capital-good is so abundant that there is no new investment which is expected, even in conditions of full employment, to earn in the course of its life more than its replacement cost'.[13]

Over-investment is the result of a process which emerges from the tensions created between the requirements of growth and those of the profitability of the capital stock which no longer appears, rightly or wrongly, sufficient to cover the costs of replacement and produce a net profit.

In this context, replacement costs take on the aspect of an autonomous variable whose value is determined by expectations, because its movements are determined by changes in entrepreneurs' expectations relative to the expected discounted values of user costs, of maintenance costs and of the replacement overcost. As these variations are subject to diverse influences, some of them contradictory (above all when the hypotheses presumed for this discussion are amended), the forces which lead to increases in replacement costs should be qualified as tendencies, whether they affect capital as a whole or a particular type of capital good.

The replacement cost of aggregate capital gives us an explanation of why a shift in part of production costs from labour to capital brings about a reduction in the amount of disposable income available for consumption, and influences distribution. As a result of the reduced rate of growth of future expenditure on consumption, expected profitability will not be achieved. To this downward movement of profitability we must also add the tendency for replacement costs to increase. After a lag which will depend on the level of accumulation, conditions will develop in which new investment no longer appears capable of covering its replacement costs over its useful life. Conditions of over-investment then prevail, and even those entrepreneurs who possess adequate financial means are no longer willing to invest in the creation of new capital goods.

The replacement costs of particular types of capital provides an explanation of the spread of conditions of over-investment and the progressive decline of growth accompanied by the appearance of unemployment in successive sectors of industry. When conditions of rapid growth with substitution of capital for labour appear in a particular industry, the replacement costs of the corresponding type of capital good may reach a level which is equal or superior to 'the returns expected from the capital-asset during its life', according to the criterion used by Keynes in his definition of the marginal efficiency of capital. New net investment is then brought to a halt in the particular industry concerned, for it has attained the conditions of over-investment.

We are thus able to eliminate a number of ambiguities associated with the limitation of the level of investment by means of the liquidity trap, which, it is often said, was created to provide an explanation for the collapse of investment incentives. But the essential point is the elimination of the limit to the growth of production brought about by full employment as defined by reference to the utilisation of a given amount of fixed capital. The integration into the analysis of variations in the volume of equipment incorporating technical progress increases the productivity of labour and the productivity of productive capacity as a whole, and thereby shifts out the 'limiting point of the possible positions of equilibrium' to the point where over-investment threatens. Since variations in employment and income are no longer strictly related to one another, variations in the volume and the productivity of equipment will also intervene to modify the combination of productive factors and provide flexibility to the employment and the aggregate supply functions. Of course, this does not mean that the growth of output can go on without limit, but rather that the limit is not uniquely situated at the level of full employment: it concerns the relation between the expansion of capital equipment of increasing productivity and variations in the level of employment. The analytical questions thus opened will then extend into the sphere of the relation between gross product and net income, and ultimately reach the question of the division of productive effort between provision of the costs of current production and the satisfaction of current needs. We are thus led to the threshold of the problems of distribution.

* * *

Keynes's contribution to the science of economics is often considered as the revolutionary revival of macroeconomics. Since the publication of his *Collected Writings*, which have confirmed and amplified the intuitions and implicit assumptions underlying the *General Theory* and certain of his prior works, notably the *Treatise on Money*, this judgement can be confirmed and reinforced. Today there can be no doubt that Keynes's essential contribution lies in the foundations of monetary production macroeconomics, their application to the determination of the level of employment and the groundwork for a more complete interpretation of production itself.

It is in his proposal of this line of approach that we discover the originality of his message: his conception of the modern economy as one in which monetary phenomena elicit and condition real phenomena without eliminating them leads to the identification of production, rather than exchange, as the most essential of all economic activity. Even the direction of his analysis is the inverse of the traditional approach, from the monetary to the real, from production to exchange. This is more than an optional choice of methodology; rather it represents the results of close observation of the functioning of the economy and the behaviour of the agents who operate in it. These agents do not have access to real values except through monetary values, they cannot exchange without having first produced, and they hold money, despite the frequent and undesirable surprises it may bring with it, because it is the least deficient means of preserving purchasing power over present and future goods.

Notes

1. J. Schumpeter, *The Theory of Economic Development* (Oxford University Press, 1961): 'this money form is not shell but kernel' (p.184).
2. The third and fourth propositions, which represent what we shall consider as the very foundation of Keynes's approach, are linked to positions put forward by Schumpeter in *The Theory of Economic Development*: 'Everything which is essential is born in the world of goods.' 'Use value is the cause of the exchange value of goods.' 'Value appears first as use value.' 'To advance credit against future goods, to finance evolution, this is the principal function of the money market and of capital'; and by Francois Perroux in the Introduction, pp. 112–13, to the French edition of Schumpeter's book: 'Rather than reflecting the events that take place in the goods sphere, [money] initiates them.'
3. This is Keynes's definition of wealth given in the *General Theory*, p. 211 (all references are to the Royal Economic Society Edition).
4. Initiated by F. H. Knight, followed by Keynes, and developed in the works of Paul Davidson and Hyman Minsky.
5. The market supply and demand curves of neoclassical theory are independent because they express the individual preferences of the exchanging agents. In effective demand, aggregate demand prices depend on the expectation of the receipts arising from the expenditure of the incomes represented in aggregate supply price. It is in this respect that the two curves representing the behaviour of these two 'prices' are interrelated.
6. Cf. G. Grellet, 'Money-Wages and Distribution', in chapter 3 of *Keynesian Economic Policies*, and the detailed criticism of the notion of the labour market in A. Barrère, *La crise n'est pas ce que l'on croit* (Editions Economica, Paris, 1981) pp. 83–8.
7. A detailed study of the Keynesian theory of the price level is given in A. Barrère, *Déséquilibres économiques et contre-révolution keynésienne* (Editions Economica, Paris, 2nd edn, 1983) pp. 264–95.
8. The study of prices in Keynes's work has been approached in a number of different ways, and in particular by S. Weintraub, P. Davidson and E. Smolensky, P. Garegnani, and most recently by S. Parrinello, 'The price level implicit in Keynes' effective demand', *Journal of Post Keynesian Economics*, no. 1 (1980).
9. Keynes writes in the *General Theory*, p. 378: 'But if our central controls succeed in establishing an aggregate volume of output corresponding to full employment as nearly as practicable, the classical theory comes into its own again from this point onwards.'

10. I have presented more detailed analysis of this point in three different works published by Editions Economica: *Controverses sur le système keynésien* (1976); *Déséquilibres économiques et contre-révolution keynésienne* (2nd edn, 1983); *La crise n'est pas ce que l'on croit* (1981).
11. R. Marjolin writes, *Banque*, Feb. 1981, p. 135: 'The rate of increase of the capital stock divided by the number of hours worked by the labour force during the period 1950–70 was three times higher than it had been during the preceding eighty years.'
12. Keynes recognised that he should have integrated user cost into effective demand. See the correspondence with H. Townshend published in vol. XXIX, pp. 245–7 of the *Collected Writings* (London, 1979).
13. *General Theory,* chapter 22, section 3. Over-investment should be distinguished from excess capacity.

2 Effective Demand and the Monetary Theory of Employment

Dudley Dillard

I INTRODUCTION

One test of a great theory is its ability to survive many refutations. Based on this criterion, John Maynard Keynes is not dead, in the long run. The title of this chapter contains three main elements that are, I believe, basic to the vitality of Keynes's theory: money, (un)employment, and effective demand. Keynes is largely responsible for restoring each of them to the mainstream of economic theory, and they seem destined to be part of the principles of economics for some time to come.

Thirty-five years ago I published a book on the economics of John Maynard Keynes, with the subtitle, 'The Theory of a Monetary Economy' (Dillard, 1948). This remains, I think, the appropriate emphasis for a general interpretation of his work. Evidence from the *Collected Writings* (Keynes, 1971–86) is consistent with this theme. All three of Keynes's major books in economics are about money: the *Tract* (1924), the *Treatise* (1930), and the *General Theory* (1936). Keynes's career as an economist unfolds as one of progressively subtle insights into the nature of money as the key institution of modern capitalism (Dillard, 1954, p. 30).

For reasons that defy common sense, money occupies virtually no place in the principles of classical and neoclassical economics. John Stuart Mill's incredible statement that nothing could be more insignificant in the economy than money, illustrates this point. Like God in Unitarian theology, money is there but it doesn't do anything. This anti-monetary tradition I refer to as the Barter Illusion. The capitalist economy is presumed to work as if it were a barter economy in which goods exchange for goods and wage-earners barter their services for subsistence. Keynes's economics may be viewed as an assault on the Barter Illusion. He integrated money into general economic theory in a way that general theorists can ignore only at their peril.

Unemployment has been with us since the dawn of capitalism, yet orthodox economic theory hardly knew the word until recent times. Economic principles from Ricardo through Marshall and beyond were primarily the theory of production and distribution of a *given* output. Certainly the introduction of involuntary unemployment and the acceptance of total output as a variable changes the logic of the principles of economics. Recent attempts to take the sting out of unemployment by making it appear as a voluntary part of the search for better jobs will not cause involuntary unemployment as a problem to disappear. Use of the search process to wash out involuntary unemployment reminds one of Lord Acton's statement that the 'worst use of theory is to make men insensitive to fact' (Acton, 1886, p. 40). Perhaps it is unfortunate for our discipline that some of our colleagues have not been able to write about involuntary unemployment as a personal experience! In the United States today more than ten million people are involuntarily unemployed, and perhaps an equal number have withdrawn from the labour force or are denied the opportunity of self-fulfilment because of the constricted demand for labour in the fields of their choice. The current American Administration has raised the 'inflation-threshhold' rate of unemployment to the range of 6 to 7 per cent, and the numbers are rising. Is this too high a price to pay for an economic system? Limited employment opportunities in the United States, as in other advanced capitalist countries, have led in recent decades to a vast welfare system for the appeasement of those who, for one reason or another, cannot cope within the free-enterprise system. The time has come for Gunnar Myrdal, or his surrogate, to write another book about another *American Dilemma*. A substantial minority of Americans of all races are destined to remain outside the economic system until the problem of unemployment is conquered. Sigmund Freud taught that the two fulfilling needs of people are love and work. Fulfilment in one is difficult without fulfilment in the other. Unemployment is a profound human problem as well as a grievous economic one.

Finally, the principle of effective demand, which Malthus debated with Ricardo and was, as Keynes says, the most important issue in political economy for a quarter of a century and which for a century thereafter dwelled furtively only in the underworlds of Karl Marx and John A. Hobson, was restored by Keynes. It seems likely to remain part of the corpus of economic theory. In place of the proposition that supply creates its own demand, Keynes prefers the principle that expenditure creates its own income (*CW*, XXIX: pp. 80–1). Effective demand is the centrepiece of Keynes's theory of a monetary economy.

II FRUSTRATION OF POTENTIAL IN A MONETARY ECONOMY

One can select almost at random from among Keynes's early economic writings and find the genesis of the idea of a monetary economy. For example, in a 1923 article on 'Currency Policy and Unemployment', in referring to the interval of time between the beginning of production and the end of the production process, he wrote:

> During this interval the business world is entering into liabilities in terms of *money* – borrowing money and paying out in money for wages and other expenses of production – in the expectation of recouping this outlay by disposing of the product for *money* at a later date. . . . Whether it likes it or not, the technique of production under a regime of money-contract forces the business world always to carry a big speculative position; and if they are reluctant to carry this position, the productive process must be brought to a standstill.
>
> (*CW*, XIX: p. 114, Keynes's emphasis)

Now this is the argument of *A Tract on Monetary Reform*, but it is well within the framework of a money-dominated system of production. At this stage of his career Keynes emphasised monetary policy as the key to general economic reform. The problem being confronted was the trade cycle, and Keynes saw its solution in a managed currency. In his later career his emphasis shifted from monetary policy to fiscal policy, and the analysis from prices to output as a whole. In both periods, however, money was the focus of attention.

Pervading Keynes's economics is a spirit of frustration associated with the great discrepancy between potential output and what is actually produced. The key to this discrepancy is the properties of money, which tends to constrict production. The conflict between the private money-making interests of entrepreneurs and the social, goods-producing interests of consumers bears a resemblance to Thorstein Veblen's dichotomy between making money and making goods, or between pecuniary and industrial employments. This is the central theme of Veblen's theory of capitalism (Dillard, 1980). Likewise, Karl Marx in *Capital* integrates money into a theory of capitalist production and contrasts the restrictive nature of monetary production with the great potentialities of advanced industrial technology (Dillard, forthcoming). All three theories may appropriately be described as monetary theories of production. By contrast, classical and neoclassical economics, which minimise the role of money, have little to say about the discrepancy between potential and actual production.

Keynes's Preface to *Essays in Persuasion* illustrates his frustration with the existing economic organisation:

> the central thesis throughout – the profound conviction that the economic problem, as one may call it for short, the problem of want and poverty and the economic struggle between classes and nations, is nothing but a frightful muddle, a transitory and *unnecessary* muddle. For the western world already has the resources and the technique, if we could create the organisation to use them, capable of reducing the economic problem . . . to a position of secondary importance.
>
> (*CW*, IX, p. xviii, Keynes's emphasis)

The same central message appears in the opening paragraphs of *The Means to Prosperity*, published on the eve of the World Economic Conference in the spring of 1933. The means to prosperity are not to be found, Keynes says, in hard work, frugality, abstinence, endurance, and invention:

> In fact, our predicament is notoriously of a another kind. It comes from some failure in the immaterial devices of the mind, in the working of the motives which should lead us to the decisions and the acts of will, necessary to put in movement . . . I call attention to the nature of the problem, because it points to the nature of the remedy. It is appropriate to the case that the remedy should be found in something which can fairly be called a *device*.
>
> (*CW*, IX, pp. 335–6, Keynes's emphasis)

In hundreds of passages Keynes expresses his profound conviction that production is obstructed by the narrow accounting of a monetary economy. Let one more passage suffice:

> The whole conduct of life was made into a sort of parody of the accountant's nightmare. Instead of using their vastly increased material and technical resources to build a wonder-city, they built slums; and they thought it right and advisable to build slums because slums, on the test of private enterprise, 'paid', whereas the wonder-city would, they thought, have been an act of foolish extravagance, which would, in the imbecile idiom of the financial fashion, have 'mortgaged the future', though how the construction today of great and glorious works can impoverish the future no man can see until his mind is beset by false analogies from an irrelevant accountancy.
>
> (*CW*, XXI, p. 241)

To Keynes, the failure to achieve abundance lay in the accounting system associated with monetary production. This accounting system failed to reconcile private and public interests. The economic problem of want and poverty was at bottom a 'frightful and unnecesaary muddle'. The remedies lie in right thinking and in devices such as monetary and fiscal policy. Consistently Keynes's proposed reforms aimed at 'bringing production and consumption into a fruitful union' (*CW* XXVII, p. 194).

For the book that was to become the *General Theory*, Keynes's initial (1932) title was 'The Monetary Theory of Production' (*CW*, XXIX, p. 49). This was changed (1933) to 'The Monetary Theory of Employment' (*CW*, XXIX, p. 62) and then (December 1933) 'The General Theory of Employment' (*CW*, XXIX, p. 63; *CW*, XIII, p. 421) before becoming (1934) *The General Theory of Employment, Interest and Money* (*CW*, XIII, p. 423). The title of Keynes's Cambridge course of lectures, which changed from 'The Pure Theory of Money' to 'The Monetary Theory of Production' in the autumn of 1932, became 'The General Theory of Employment' in the later years of preparation of the *General Theory* (*CW*, XIII, pp. 343, 411–12).

The original title for the book perhaps best describes its contents because it is a theory of production (or output) with a monetary explanation of deficiencies and fluctuations in output. 'The Monetary Theory of Employment' means virtually the same thing but is at once more limited in scope and more focused on the problem of unemployment. Adequacy of production *per se* is not the problem of advanced industrial countries. American farmers can produce enough to feed half the world and have surpluses left over, but the American economy cannot provide enough jobs for its workers. Modern industry can produce so abundantly that business enterprises form monopolistic combinations to restrict output and obviate the market so that businesses can remain profitable. A maximum profit economy is not a maximum employment economy. The trouble spot is limited employment opportunities.

III EARLY MODELS OF THE MONETARY THEORY OF EMPLOYMENT

The early drafts of the *General Theory* give a clearer picture of the relation of money to unemployment than does the published version. Keynes's barebones model for the monetary theory of employment conceives of an economic organisation of society with two classes:

entrepreneurs possessing the means of employment (capital assets) and money for purchasing materials and for paying wages; and a class of workers seeking employment. (*CW*, XXIX, pp. 63–4). Access of the means of production to the workers depends on monetary calculations by the entrepreneurs, who estimate whether they can produce physical output and sell it for an amount of money in excess of the money costs of wages, materials, and the user cost of the capital equipment, that is, the cost of using the capital equipment as compared with leaving it idle. Entrepreneurs are dealing throughout in money terms, since the firm, in Keynes's words, 'has no object in the world except to end up with more money than it started with. That is the essential characteristic of an entrepreneur [monetary] economy' (*CW*, XXIX, p. 89). Entrepreneurs rather than consumers dominate decision-making in a monetary economy. This marks another sharp departure by Keynes from the classical system of theory.

In the early drafts Keynes wrestled with the question of why a monetary economy has involuntary unemployment and a non-monetary economy does not. All this is by way of distinguishing between his monetary theory and the classical theory. He contrasts two types of economic societies, one involving unemployment and the other without unemployment. Economic systems with involuntary unemployment are variously labelled monetary, entrepreneur, and money-wage economies. Those without involuntary unemployment are referred to as barter (but not without money as a medium of exchange), co-operative, and real-wage economies. A barter or co-operative non-monetary economy resembles a collective economy in which a predetermined share of aggregate output is distributed directly to the factors of production (*CW*, XXIX, pp. 76–7). A co-operative economy may use money as an instrument for distributing its output but the purpose of the economy is never to maximise a monetary return. In these circumstances all workers will be employed so long as the utility of their output exceeds the marginal disutility of their labour. In other words, the second classical postulate holds in a co-operative economy. In a monetary or entrepreneur economy, on the other hand, 'the volume of output which will yield maximum value of product in excess of real cost may be "unprofitable" ' (*CW*, XXIX, p. 67).

Where does classical economics fit into these classifications? It is a hybrid between the entrepreneur (monetary) economy and the co-operative economy. Keynes calls it a neutral entrepreneur or neutral monetary economy (*CW*, XXIX, p. 78). The classical model is a limiting case of an entrepreneur, monetary economy. Workers are hired by entrepreneurs for money but with an arrangement 'where there is a mechanism of some kind to ensure that the exchange value of the money incomes of the factors is always equal in the aggregate to the proportion of current output which would have been the factor's share in a co-operative economy' (*CW*, XXIX, p. 78).

Money in the classical model is a temporary convenience used by the factors to purchase the whole of current output from entrepreneurs within the accounting period. The classical neutral entrepreneur economy works as if it were a co-operative economy. Classical theory represents the limiting case of an entrepreneur economy, the case in which money is neutral. This, argues Keynes, is not the kind of world in which we actually live. It is not true that workers will be hired so long as the marginal utility of their output exceeds the marginal disutility of employment. In the real-world monetary economy there is a 'failure of organization which prevents a man from producing something, the equivalent of which he would value more highly than the effort it would cost him' (*CW*, XXIX, p. 78). By accepting the second postulate, classical theory rules out the possibility of involuntary unemployment. It accepts Say's law that supply creates its own demand.

Fluctuations in effective demand are the reason why output that would be produced in a co-operative economy may be unprofitable in a monetary economy (*CW*, XXIX, p. 80). Except for minor flurries, effective demand does not fluctuate in a co-operative or neutral economy. Output will always tend to be at the level corresponding to full employment. 'But in an entrepreneur economy the fluctuations of cyclical demand may be the dominating factor in determining employment; and in this book, therefore, we shall be mainly concerned with analyzing the causes and consequences of fluctuations in effective demand' (*CW*, XXIX, p. 80). Effective demand enters on the ground floor in the construction of Keynes's model.

In these early drafts, in which Keynes was struggling to get a handle on the classical theory of employment and to discern the analytical differences of the classical model from his emerging theory, clearly money makes the difference between the two. This is the main point we wish to establish in this section. The relation of money to output, as distinguished from money to prices, sets Keynes's new theory apart from his *Treatise on Money*.

IV THE MONETARY THEORY OF EMPLOYMENT

We turn now to the monetary theory of employment in the *General Theory* in its finished form. Entrepreneurs maximise their profits at the point of intersection of the aggregate demand function and the aggregate supply function (*CW*, VII, p. 25). Of the two components of the volume of effective demand thus determined, the schedule of the propensity to consume is 'a fairly stable function' so that employment can increase only if investment increases (*CW*, VII, pp. 95, 96, 98, 113).

The generally pervasive influence of money on employment is focused on the two determinants of investment: the marginal efficiency of capital and the rate of interest. The marginal efficiency of capital is the ratio that equates the discounted returns (quasi-rents) from a capital asset to its present supply price. The expected returns on durable capital assets extend some time into the future and are fraught with great uncertainty. Although the ability to produce physical output at future dates is a relatively simple engineering problem, the difficult economic problem centres around the terms on which future physical output can be converted into money. The essential character of a monetary economy is the realisation in terms of money of the value of the real output produced by business firms. In a dynamic setting of changing technology, foreign competition, changes in tastes, and other uncertain factors, the initial expectations made at the time of investment may prove disappointing, that is, conversion of output into money may be on unfavourable terms and lead to money losses by the firm.

The intimate relation of durable capital assets and money in the concept 'marginal efficiency of capital' is one aspect for Keynes's definition of a monetary economy. If the link with the future is made by investing in capital assets, the result is favourable to employment; if the link is made by preferring to hold cash, the effect on employment is unfavourable; and if, after an investment is made, expectations are disappointing, employment will also suffer. In the Preface to the *General Theory*, Keynes gives one of his definitions of a monetary economy: 'A monetary economy . . . is essentially one in which changing views about the future are capable of influencing the quantity of employment and not merely its direction' (*CW*, VII, p. vii). A statement attributing similar characteristics to capital assets appears in the last paragraph of chapter 11 on the marginal efficiency of capital: 'It is by reason of the existence of durable equipment that the economic future is linked to the present. It is, therefore, consonant with, and agreeable to, our broad principles of thought, that the expectations of the future should affect the present through the demand price for durable equipment' (*CW*, VII, p. 146).

In discussing the appropriate major divisions of economic theory, Keynes writes: 'But as soon as we pass to the problem of what determines output and employment as a whole, we require the complete theory of a Monetary Economy' (*CW*, VII, p. 293). In the following paragraph in discussing the way in which changing views about the future can affect the present, he writes, in italics: '*For the importance of money essentially flows from its being a link between the present and the future*' (*CW*, VII, p. 293).

There follows a paragraph which places money and capital assets as dual and alternative links with the future. In the real world in which previous expectations are subject to subsequent disappointment 'the peculiar properties of money as a link between the present and the future must enter into our calculations . . . Money in its significant attributes is, above all, a subtle device for linking the present to the future' (*CW*, VII, p. 294). These statements are to be interpreted in relation to Keynes's discussion of long-term expectations in chapter 12, and to the essential properties of interest and money in chapter 17. Chapter 12 tells us that under *laissez-faire* capitalism, the socially necessary activity of investing in capital assets is based on very little solid knowledge and takes place within an irrational setting. Because of the fetish for individual liquidity, stock exchanges may gyrate wildly and the capital development of a country 'becomes a by-product of the activities of a casino' (*CW*, VII, p. 159). Because of this dynamic, unstable, irrational setting, capital investment is not made on the basis of general social advantage. The stock exchange facilitates the mobilisation of capital by providing liquidity to individual investors, who are able through the exchange to convert securities into cash at any time. However, this is a fragile arrangement and can lead to disaster, as it did in 1929 with a sudden collapse of long-term expectations, leading security holders to rush simultaneously to become liquid. If the matter involved only a small number of speculators, it could be dismissed as socially insignificant, but actually the collapse of confidence in the future earnings of capital assets leads also to a collapse of real capital formation and in turn to large-scale unemployment. Keynes's emphasis on links between the present and the future reflects a critical attitude toward financial institutions, which he views as a major weakness of capitalism. In ideal circumstances, the financial accounting for the production and reproduction of durable capital assets would reflect the gradual conversion of real values into money as the capital assets were used up in physical production. In the closing paragraph of the chapter on long-term expectations Keynes wrote that he expected, in view of the instability of the marginal efficiency of capital under *laissez-faire*, to see the state assume increasing responsibility for directly organising investment on the basis of general social advantage (*CW*, VII, p. 164).

Keynes's other determinant of investment, the rate of interest, is strictly a monetary phenomenon. The rate of interest equilibrates the desire to hold wealth in the form of cash with the available supply of cash (*CW*, VII, p. 167). Money's function as a store of wealth, as distinguished from its role as a medium of exchange, is the crucial function in Keynes's schema. In the certain world of classical economics, only a lunatic or a miser would hold money as a store of wealth (*CW*, XIV, p. 115). In his first major published response to reviewers of the *General Theory*, Keynes wrote:

> Our desire to hold money as a store of wealth is a barometer of the degree of our mistrust of our own calculations and conventions concerning the future. . . . The possession of actual money lulls our disquietude; and the premium which we require to make us part with money is the measure of the degree of our disquietude.
>
> (*CW*, XIV, p. 116)

The liquidity-preference schedule, which along with the quantity of money determines the rate of interest, consists of a bundle of psychological and conventional beliefs including a belief as to what is an appropriate rate of interest. Keynes believed that wise policy by central banks could establish public confidence in the appropriateness of low rates of interest. In the United Kingdom, for example, Bank Rate remained at 2 per cent between 1932 and 1939. Events such as the great price inflation of the 1970s can change conventional beliefs about normal interest rates and lead to great difficulty in lowering them to previous levels. Announcements of unexpected increases in the money supply may set off expectations of more price inflation and cause interest to rise rather than to fall along the declining liquidity-preference schedule. All these contingencies are carefully stated by Keynes (*CW*, VII, p. 173). The instability of output and prices associated with *laissez-faire* policy is probably not compatible with Keynes's belief in the feasibility of getting long-term interest rates down to low levels and keeping them there for prolonged periods.

For a monetary theory of employment, the most important chapter in the *General Theory* is 17, on 'The Essential Properties of Interest and Money'. In a pre-publication table of contents, the title of this chapter contained the additional words 'philosophical considerations' (*CW*, XIII, p. 424), which suggests a broad range of ideas not yet reduced to technical economic analysis. Keynes characterises chapter 17 as one which probes 'certain deeper perplexities' (*CW*, VII, p. 213). A year prior to publication of the *General Theory* Keynes wrote to D. H. Robertson that chapter 17 is 'posterior to' earlier chapters and is a more complex version of liquidity preference. 'I admit,' Keynes said, 'the obscurity of the chapter. A time may come when I am, so to speak, sufficiently familiar with my ideas to make it easier' (*CW*, XIV, p. 519). These several remarks suggest that in chapter 17 Keynes was pressing against new frontiers. It is, perhaps, the most esoteric chapter in the *General Theory*.

For the monetary theory of employment, a key statement in chapter 17 is the following: 'Thus in the absence of money and in the absence of . . . any other asset with the characteristics of money, the rate of interest would only reach equilibrium when there is full employment' (*CW*, VII, p. 235). Clearly money possesses some special properties that explain involuntary unemployment. The purpose of chapter 17 is to explain these essential properties of money and interest.

In attempting to maximise their respective net worths, wealth-holders as a group, by their behaviour in buying and selling, establish a market equilibrium among rates of return on different assets. Each new investment in a capital asset brings down the marginal efficiency and tends to keep it in equilibrium with rates of return on other capital assets. In equilibrium these marginal efficiencies will equal the rate of interest on money, which is an alternative way of storing wealth. If left to themselves, assets other than money would be produced until their rates of return reach equilibrium at full employment. Money, however, is different. Because of its special properties, the rate of interest on money may, and characteristically does, reach equilibrium above the rate consistent with an amount of investment in new capital assets required for full employment. The rate of interest on money sets the pace, rules the roost, and causes unemployment (*CW*, VII, pp. 235, 225).

The essential and special properties of money are zero or negligible elasticities of production and substitution and negligible carrying costs. An increase in the demand for money will raise its price (the rate of interest) but will not increase its quantity if its elasticity of production is zero. Similarly, an increase in the demand for money will not call forth substitutes if the elasticity of substitution is zero. In the case of reproducible assets, on the contrary, an increase in demand leads entrepreneurs in the private sector to employ labour and increase output of the assets for which demand has increased. Similarly, if there were some reproducible asset that could serve as a close substitute for money, a rise in the rate of interest would call forth additional employment and output of the close substitute. When an increased demand for money raises the rate of interest, which remains high, this lowers investment and increases unemployment. Within limits the central bank can hold down the rate of interest by increasing the quantity of money. It may, however, experience difficulty in lowering the rate of interest to the level required for full employment. Moreover, a low point may be reached, below which further increases in the quantity of money will not lower the interest rate: that is, the demand for money as a store of value may become perfectly elastic in the sense that wealth-owners prefer to hold money rather than part with it at the prevailing rate of interest.

According to the analysis of chapter 17, output stops short of full employment because of the desirability of holding the asset with a liquidity premium most in excess of its carrying cost. This is Keynes's way of stating the general case, but for all practical purposes in a monetary economy the asset with a liquidity premium most in excess of its carrying cost is money. Liquidity is partly a function of negligible elasticities of production and substitution. Owners of wealth would have less preference for money if its supply could be increased easily or if a rise in its price (rate of interest) would lead to the substitution of other assets for money (*CW*, VII, p. 241n). Since money also has a negligible carrying cost, its net liquidity ($l-c$) is greater than for any other asset.

The preference for holding money is enhanced because it is the unit of account and the standard of deferred payment. Money is the standard in which wages, taxes, debts, and contracts of all types are normally payable. There is an obvious advantage in holding assets in the form in which these obligations become due now and in the future. These advantages of being the standard of value interact with the other properties of money virtually to assure that it will be the asset with a liquidity premium most in excess of its carrying costs.

Abba Lerner's concept, 'the marginal efficiency of holding' money, is helpful in explaining chapter 17 (Lerner, 1952). The marginal efficiency of holding an asset is the benefit to be derived from possessing an additional unit of the asset. It differs from the rate of interest, which is the fee paid by a borrower to a lender; and from the marginal efficiency of capital, which is the benefit from increasing the output of an asset by one unit.

By recalling the barebones model of the early drafts of the *General Theory* (see above, pp. 53–4), we can get a clearer insight into the meaning of chapter 17. In this barebones model the entrepreneur holds capital assets and money with which to buy materials and to pay wages. After estimating the effective demand for his product, the entrepreneur will either make the means of employment available to the workers or withhold them and leave the workers unemployed. If the decision is to offer employment, the workers will produce real output which the entrepreneur will try to sell for more money than he had at the start of production. Alternatively, confronted with uncertain and fluctuating effective demand, the entrepreneur may decide to withhold the means of employment from the workers. In the latter case, his marginal efficiency of holding money and capital assets exceeds his marginal efficiency of investing.

The significance of chapter 17 for the monetary theory of employment is that entrepreneurs may prefer to hold idle their existing assets, which include the means of production as well as money, rather than risk a loss, or too small a gain, in the money value of their net assets. The entrepreneur's motivation, as Keynes emphasises, is to make money and not to produce real output for its own sake. The withholding of the means of employment from the workers takes place, according to Keynes, despite the fact that the value of the output per worker at the margin will exceed the marginal disutility of the extra employment.

Unfortunately the published version of the *General Theory* contains no references to co-operative or real-wage or other form of non-monetary economy in which involuntary unemployment does not occur. In the published version, chapter 17 contains the only references to a 'non-monetary economy', which Keynes defines as 'an economy in which there is no asset for which the liquidity-premium is always in excess of the carrying-cost' (*CW*, VII, p. 239). Presumably this condition would hold in a co-operative economy of the type described in the early drafts of the *General Theory*.

Keynes's non-monetary economy referred to in the *General Theory* is not a barter economy, at least not in the usual meaning of barter. When Keynes briefly uses the term 'barter' in the early draft, he immediately adds, 'Since this economy does not exclude the use of money for purposes of transitory convenience, it might be better to call it a *real-wage economy* or a *co-operative economy* as distinct from an *entrepreneur* [monetary] *economy*' (*CW*, XXIX, p. 67, Keynes's emphasis). Money would be used for transactions but not as a store of value. It would not be the basis for withholding the means of employment from workers, and create involuntary unemployment. The correct meaning of a 'non-monetary economy' is not a barter economy but a socialist economy or some other form of co-operative organisation in which the objective is not to 'make money' but to produce real output for consumption by the workers themselves (real-wage economy) or indirectly through exchange for some other real products. My interpretation of what Keynes is telling us is that involuntary unemployment, in the sense of workers being denied employment in conditions in which the value of their added output would exceed the marginal disutility of the employment to produce it, would not exist in a collective economy. Now Keynes was not a socialist, certainly not in the usual meaning of that word. But his theory does point to a flaw in the system of private ownership of the means of production that needs to be overcome through monetary policy, fiscal policy, the socialisation of investment, or whatever policy and reform would bring 'production and consumption into fruitful union' (see above, p. 52).

The conclusion that a collective (co-operative) economy would not have involuntary unemployment is interesting but not very surprising. The corollary that involuntary unemployment results from private ownership of the means of production is interesting and also significant. It is not to be found in classical or neoclassical economics, with the possible exception of Malthus.

Perhaps the most common criticism of Keynes's equilibrium at less than full employment is that it depends on the assumption of rigid wages and prices. It is argued that if wages and prices were fully flexible – whatever that means – involuntary unemployment would disappear, because real wages would be lower, profits would be higher, and entrepreneurs would have an incentive to expand output and hire more workers until everyone who wanted to work could find a job. Keynes addresses these issues in chapters 2 and 19 and, at a different level, in chapter 17. These arguments are well known and will not be repeated here. In chapter 19 Keynes concluded that a flexible wage policy might have the same effects as a flexible monetary policy although his analysis in arriving at this result is very different from the classical analysis. However, all this was mainly by way of making and answering debating points. The important point for the critics was to 'prove' that Keynes's theory rests on special assumptions of rigid wages and prices and therefore is not a general theory nor even a new theory. Hardly any economists really believed that a flexible wage policy was superior to a flexible money policy.

Those who use the flexible-wage-and-price argument as a theoretical, if not a practical, refutation of Keynes's theory of involuntary unemployment overlook the central message of chapter 17. In order to function as a standard of prices, the value of money must be relatively stable. Assume a condition of substantial unemployment. A national policy of moderate downward flexibility in money-wages rates will create the expectation of further falls in money-wages and lead to a condition of sagging investment and employment because of the adverse effects of expectations on the marginal efficiency of capital. If full, all-out flexibility of money-wages were the policy, prices might fall so rapidly, as wages fell, that money would lose its usefulness as the standard for transactions and contracts. Abba Lerner pointed out that wage and price stability is a necessary property of money. 'The usefulness of money depends intimately on a certain degree of stability in its purchasing power . . . Price rigidity is not an appendage that can be removed without harm. Wage and price rigidity is an essential property of money' (Lerner, 1952). Experience teaches that hyperinflation causes money to lose its place as a standard for transactions. We may safely assume that hyperdeflation would have a similar result. The important conclusion is that sticky wages are a corollary of the properties of money. Therefore sticky wages cannot in any meaningful sense be the cause of involuntary unemployment.

V SUMMARY AND CONCLUSION

In a monetary economy, entrepreneurs make the decisions whether to hire or not to hire workers. Wage-earners do not employ the means of production but are employed by them. Workers can do relatively little to influence decisions as to whether they are to be employed. If the marginal efficiency of holding money is in equilbrium with both the rate of interest and the marginal efficiency of capital at a level which results in a volume of investment less than necessary for full employment, then the means of production will be withheld from some workers. They are involuntarily unemployed. They would be willing to work for a value equivalent to what they would produce but are denied this opportunity because their employment would not be profitable for the entrepreneur. Workers are involuntarily unemployed because money, one of the key institutions of capitalist production, is a more preferred form of wealth than the real output that could be produced by putting money capital to use to hire workers to produce additional output. Money as capital is both the means and the end of capitalist production. Keynes variously describes money 'as purchasing power as such', 'a bottomless sink of purchasing power', 'wealth as such', 'the power of disposal over assets'.

In a capitalist economy, money is private property *par excellence*. It is the general equivalent of other forms of wealth. It is the socially recognised form of private wealth.

References

Acton, Lord (1886) *English Historical Review*. I: 40.

Dillard, Dudley (1948) *The Economics of John Maynard Keynes: The Theory of a Monetary Economy* (New York: Prentice-Hall).

——(1954) 'The Theory of a Monetary Economy', in *Post-Keynesian Economics*, ed. Kenneth K. Kurihara (New Brunswick, N. J.: Rutgers University Press) pp. 3–30.

——(1980) 'A Monetary Theory of Production: Keynes and the Institutionalists', *Journal of Economic Issues*, Vol. XIV (June) pp. 255–73.

——(1984) 'Keynes and Marx: A Centennial Appraisal, 1883–1983', *Journal of Post Keynesian Economics*. Vol. VI no. 3 (Spring).

Keynes, John Maynard (1971–86) *The Collected Writings of John Maynard Keynes* (London: Macmillan for the Royal Economic Society).

Lerner, Abba P. (1952) 'The Essential Properties of Interest and Money', *Quarterly Journal of Economics*, Vol. LCVI (May) pp. 172–93.

Patinkin, Don (1982) *Anticipations of the General Theory? and Other Essays on Keynes* (Chicago: University of Chicago Press).

Section II
Macroeconomic Equilibria

3 Non-Walrasian Equilibria and Macroeconomics

Antoine d'Autume

I INTRODUCTION

The theory of non-Walrasian equilibria provides a method for analysing the problems of allocation in an economy with imperfectly functioning markets. This method is new, and represents a direct line of development which in our view can be traced from Clower's original (1965) article to the construction of general non-Walrasian equilibrium models. It is also general, and thus capable of being applied to numerous areas in macroeconomic theory.

The novelty behind this line of thinking is that, in the absence of perfect flexibility of prices, agents' awareness of the quantitative constraints they face and the rationing that they endure causes them to modify considerably their behaviour. The theoretical expression of this intuition is recognition of a new type of information which is not strictly limited to prices, as in traditional Walrasian theory, but rather is based on quantities. This leads naturally to the definition of non-Walrasian equilibria as situations characterised by the compatibility of the quantitative signals emitted and perceived by agents who adapt very imperfectly to the general condition of disequilibrium.[1]

The importance of Clower's (1965) contribution lies in the fact that he was able to emphasise from the beginning the points at issue. The study of an economy in which prices do not play the role of co-ordinating *a priori* the decisions of agents brings to mind the Keynesian intuitions. In particular, one of the non-Walrasian equilibrium regimes, i.e. one of the obtainable sub-models, appears to be a formalisation of the Keynesian theory of unemployment. The distinction between Keynesian unemployment due to insufficient effective demand, and classical unemployment, due to insufficient profitability, represents one of the tangible contributions of the new approach. Clearly, this is not something that can be considered as really new, but its integration in a unique conceptual framework permits a more correct perspective on both types of unemployment.

These initial results, which have strongly influenced subsequent development, have been obtained within a very simplified macroeconomic model suggested in particular by the works of Barro and Grossman (1971), Benassy (1977) and Malinvaud (1977) (see also Muellbauer and Portes, 1978, and d'Autume, 1980a). It is not our intention here to discuss these first-generation models; rather our survey of the literature will be limited to the analysis of two principal themes: the role of investment and capital accumulation on the one hand, and the place of international trade on the other. In these particular areas the macroeconomic applications of non-Walrasian equilibrium theory have not been very numerous.

Before turning to discussion of these applications, it is useful to pursue our methodological reflections a little further in order to provide a general judgement of the non-Walrasian equilibrium approach to economic analysis. In the first place we must discern the position of the approach with respect to traditional Walrasian theory. Does it represent a radical break, or is its objective simply to complete the Walrasian analysis by applying it to consideration of certain 'frictions' in the adjustment process? Similarly, is it an equilibrium or a disequilibrium theory?

The answer to the second question is merely a matter of terminology, but it seems to us that it is preferable to speak of it as an equilibrium theory. Economists have traditionally used equilibrium methods to study what appear, *a priori*, to be disequilibrium situations. Thus, the temporary equilibrium conception of the Swedish economists and of Hicks is applied to conditions in which expectations are incompatible and incorrect. In addition the equilibrium method can be used to analyse short-period situations as well as the faraway stationary state. In the same way, non-Walrasian equilibria permits the study of situations involving disequilibria between supply and demand.

The answer to the question of whether the new theory simply introduces complications into the standard Walrasian analysis seems to require a twofold response. At the level of temporary equilibrium the answer is negative. The non-Walrasian equilibria have an autonomous logic. They lead to blocked situations, characterised by cumulative multiplier processes which do not respond to Walrasian mechanisms. On the other hand, considered dynamically, the answer must be more ambiguous. Price adjustments are largely stabilising and make the economy gravitate towards the Walrasian equilibrium which is still the irreplaceable point of reference in the theory.

In the second place, it does not seem to us that it is necessary to claim for this approach the statute of 'the microfoundations of macroeconomics'. Rather it is a fundamental method of macroeconomic analysis. It makes reformulation of numerous old-fashioned analyses possible by reference to their dependence on a particular disequilibrium regime. But, contrary to initial expectations, it has not been possible to develop really satisfactory microeconomic foundations for it. Imperfect flexibility of prices is taken as given, without further justification. The affirmation of the monetary character of exchange really only plays a secondary role. Even non-Walrasian equilibrium requires the supposition of the process of *tâtonnement*. The degree of co-ordination of agents' decisions is diminished with respect to Walrasian theory, but this co-ordination is not the result of a genuine dynamic process. The fruitfulness of such an approach cannot be denied, but it has succeeded in completing only a part of the programme it originally set for itself. Experience has shown that we are still far away from the formulation of a synthetic theory of individual behaviour and of the operation of the market mechanism in conditions of imperfect information with transactions costs. Investigation of the problem of the microeconomic foundations of microeconomics thus proceeds along varied and often contradictory lines.

Also in opposition to original intentions is the development of macroeconomic applications of non-Walrasian equilibrium theory which has placed its contributions as a sort of prolongation of a continuing Keynesian tradition of analysis. Does this not imply another case of neglect of the true originality of Keynes's book? Our impression is that if a selective reading of the *General Theory* is carried out this position is not illegitimate. Even the author of the *General Theory* himself occasionally gives more stress to the role of quantity adjustments than to the imperfections of the capital market or producers' short-term expectations. In the end, the core of the non-Walrasian equilibrium approach must be recognised as simply Keynes's well-known affirmation that it is the level of employment and not the rate of interest that assures the equality of savings and investment.

II THE FOUNDATIONS OF INVESTMENT BEHAVIOUR IN DISEQUILIBRIUM

At the level of general principles the analysis of investment in conditions of disequilibrium only requires a transfer to an inter-temporal framework of behaviour under constraints, which is common to the non-Walrasian equilibrium theory. In particular we can easily see the importance of market constraints. Grossman (1972) has indeed shown some time ago that the foundations for the behaviour underlying the accelerator can be provided in this way. However, the impact of these ideas has turned out to be more limited than originally expected. The analytical difficulty of the problems to be resolved and the necessarily arbitrary character of the specification of expectations, in addition to any attempt to take into account the attitude of firms to uncertainty and imperfections in capital markets, explains this state of affairs. There is no disequilibrium model of investment that has both rigorous microeconomic foundations and is analytically satisfying and rich in interpretation. Therefore we must consider the attributes of a great number of models, all of which differ in their simplifying hypotheses.

A. The Desired Stock of Capital

A common point of departure is the determination of the producer's desired level of capital within a static framework, i.e. for given levels of factor costs and given quantity constraints. With the usual notation we may represent the producer's optimisation problem as follows:

$$\left.\begin{aligned} &\max F(K, L) - \rho K - wL \\ &F(K, L) \leqslant \bar{Q} \\ &L \leqslant \bar{L} \end{aligned}\right\} \qquad (1)$$

We assume constant returns to scale and that the couple (ρ, w) of capital costs and the level of the real wage yields positive profits, i.e. it corresponds to a point within the factor price frontier. If production is with complementary factors: $L \geqslant aQ$ and $K \geqslant bQ$, the desired capital which is the solution to the problem given in (1) is

$$K^* = \min(b\bar{Q}, b\bar{L}/a) \qquad (2)$$

If production takes place with factor substitution the problem becomes more delicate. Let us introduce some new notation.[2]

$$\begin{aligned} &j = L/K && f(j) = F(1, j) \\ &r(j) = f(j) - jf'(j) && R(j) = r(j)/f'(j) \end{aligned} \qquad (3)$$

$r(j)$ is the marginal productivity of capital and $R(j)$ is the ratio of the factor marginal productivities. We define three functions:

$$\left.\begin{aligned} &\bar{j}(w) && \text{such that } f'(\bar{j}) = w \\ &\bar{\bar{j}}(\rho) && \text{such that } r(\bar{\bar{j}}) = \rho \\ &\hat{j}(\rho/w) && \text{such that } R(\hat{j}) = \rho/w \end{aligned}\right\} \qquad (4)$$

Thus there are three levels of capital intensity which respectively assure the equality of the factors' marginal productivity with its cost of production or the ratio of the marginal productivity with the ratio of factor costs. We can show that the couple (ρ, w) is located on the factor price frontier if $\bar{\bar{j}}(w) = \hat{j}(\rho/w) = \bar{j}(\rho)$, while for a couple located below the factor price frontier, i.e. assuring a positive profit we have

$$\bar{\bar{j}}(w) > \hat{j}(\rho/w) > \bar{j}(\rho) \tag{5}$$

Finally let us define the function H showing the minimum necessary level of capital for the level of production and the level of employment:

$$K = H(Q, L) \Leftarrow \Rightarrow Q = F(K, L) \tag{6}$$

We are now able to solve the optimisation problem given in (1) for the case of factor substitution as follows:

$$K^* = \left\{ \begin{array}{ll} \bar{Q}/f(\hat{j}) & \text{if } f(\hat{j})/\hat{j} > \bar{Q}/\bar{L} \\ H(\bar{Q}/\bar{L}) & \text{if } f(\bar{j})/\bar{j} > \bar{Q}/\bar{L} > f(\hat{j})/\hat{j} \\ \bar{L}/\bar{j} & \text{if } \bar{Q}/\bar{L} > f(\bar{j})/\bar{j} \end{array} \right\} \tag{7}$$

In the first case the producer is confronted with market constraints: he minimises his production costs and therefore equalises the ratios of factor marginal productivities to the ratios of their factor costs. In the third case the producer is confronted with an employment constraint and therefore equalises the marginal productivity of capital to its cost. In the intermediate case he is confronted with both constraints and he uses the minimum necessary level of capital.

It is of interest to geometrically represent the influence of the constraint of the level of sales on the one hand, and the constraint of the level of employment on the other on the desired level of capital, because they give very particular curves such as those given in Figures 3.1 and 3.2.[3]

Given $\bar{L}$, and for a low level of the $\bar{Q}$ constraint, the producer is only subject to the sales constraint: when $\bar{Q}$ rises, K^* rises proportionally. When he is confronted with the employment constraint, it is still possible for him to substitute labour for capital: K^* rises more than proportionally to the level of sales. When capital's marginal productivity reaches the level of capital costs it no longer pays to increase production and K^* becomes constant.

Given $\bar{Q}$, K^* increases proportionaly to the constraint on the demand for labour as long as the market constraints are not reached. When the producer is confronted with this constraint it is in his interest to substitute capital for labour: the desired capital thus decreases in step

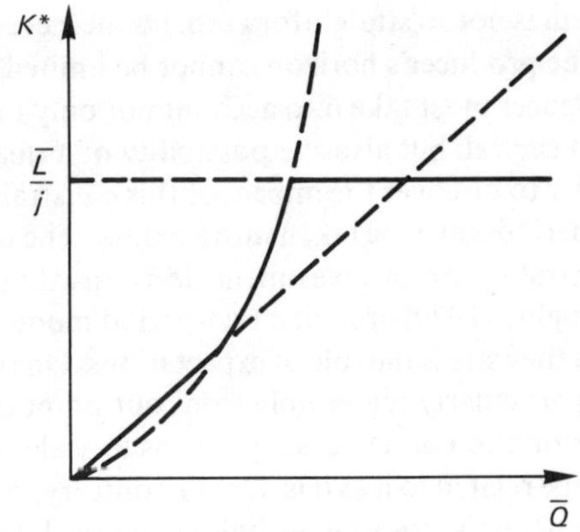

Figure 3.1

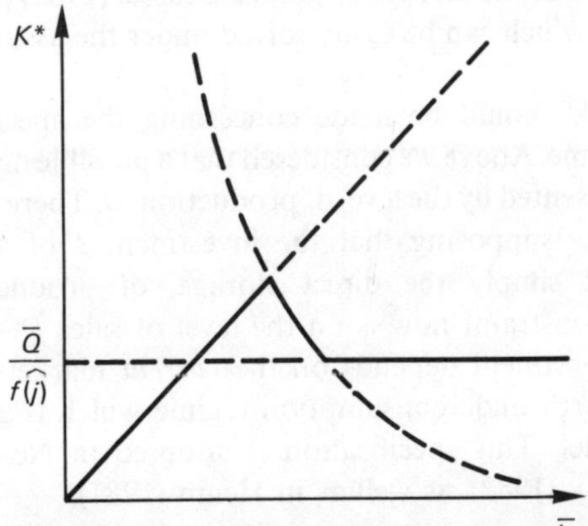

Figure 3.2

with the relaxation of the employment constraint until the minimum of production costs is reached.

After having established the determination of desired capital stock, it is necessary to look at the determination of the level of investment. The transition is immediate if we assume that all capital is circulating capital: the producer's horizon is limited to the following period; desired investment is then simply equal to $K^*_{t+1} - K_t$, where K^*_{t+1} depends on the expected constraints and actual capital is given by K_t. If this is not the case, the problem is not so straightforward, because even if second-hand markets exist the producer's horizon cannot be limited to only the next period: the producer must take into account not only the expected price of second-hand capital, but also the possibility of a quantity constraint on sales. In order to discover the impact of this constraint his behaviour in subsequent periods must be taken into account. The usual property of temporal decentralisation of investment decisions thus disappears.

Neary and Stiglitz (1979) present a two-period model with circulating capital in which they stress the role of expectations. One of the properties of this model, particularly regrettable from our point of view, is that it relies on the assumption of decreasing returns to scale so that the above analysis cannot be related to it as it is. On the contrary, demand functions are studied with an interesting technique derived from Neary and Roberts (1980) based on the concept of shadow prices. Benassy (1982) presents a model with two periods in which investment takes the simplified form of the storage of goods. Laussel (1982) presents a multi-period model which can be easily solved under the assumption of static expectations.

One remark should be made concerning the specification of the rationing scheme. Above we considered that a possible market constraint could be represented by the level of production, Q. There is an alternative which involves supposing that the investment I of a firm is not a purchase, but simply the direct storage, of produced goods: the quantitative constraint now is on the level of sales $Q-I$. Under such conditions investment depends on the *current* market constraint and suggests a fourth underconsumption regime which is absent from the standard model. This specification is adopted in Neary and Stiglitz (1979), Benassy (1982), as well as in Henin (1981).

B. Adjustment Costs and Tobin's 'q'

An ancient tradition includes adjustment costs in the determination of the optimal level of investment which can thus no longer be reduced to simply the amount of investment necessary to close the gap between the current and the desired stock of capital. From this point of view one is led to the comparison of the marginal cost of investment and its 'profitability', i.e. the increment of profit that can be obtained by means of an additional unit of capital.

A very static method of evaluating this profitability is to take the optimisation problem (1) under the assumption that the capital stock is fixed, i.e. by adding the constraint: $K = \bar{K}$. Profitability can then be defined as the dual variable π associated with this constraint. Thus, when the production function is considered under the assumption of complementarity of factors and *when neither the $\bar{Q}$ or the $\bar{L}$ constraints are binding*, we have:

$$\pi = 1/b(1 - wa - \rho b) \tag{8}$$

When the production function is considered under the assumption of factor substitutability in the face of both the $\bar{Q}$ and $\bar{L}$ constraints the following results may be obtained for the optimal level of employment L and profitability, π:

$$\left.\begin{array}{ll}
\text{(i)} & L = \bar{K}\bar{\bar{j}} \text{ and } \pi = F'_K - \rho \\
& \text{if } \bar{L} \geqslant \bar{K}\bar{\bar{j}} \text{ and } \bar{Q} \geqslant \bar{K} f(\bar{\bar{j}}) \\
\text{(ii)} & L \text{ such that } \bar{Q} = F(\bar{K}, L) \text{ and } \pi = w\, F'_K / F'_L - \rho \\
& \text{if } \bar{Q} \leqslant \bar{K} f(\bar{\bar{j}}) \text{ and } \bar{Q} < F(\bar{K}, \bar{L}) \\
\text{(iii)} & L = \bar{L} \text{ and } \pi = F'_K - \rho \\
& \text{if } \bar{L} \leqslant \bar{K} f(\bar{\bar{j}}) \text{ and } \bar{Q} \geqslant F(\bar{K}, \bar{L}) \\
\text{(iv)} & L = \bar{L} \text{ and any } \pi \text{ such that } w\, F'_K / F'_L - \rho \leqslant \pi \leqslant F'_K - \rho \\
& \text{if } Q = F(\bar{K}, \bar{L}) \text{ and } \bar{L} < \bar{K}\bar{\bar{j}}
\end{array}\right\} \tag{9}$$

The first three regimes correspond respectively to a case where there is no binding quantity constraint, to a case where the $\bar{Q}$ constraint is binding and to a case where the $\bar{L}$ constraint is binding. The fourth regime is a limit case where both quantity constraints are binding and where profitability is therefore indeterminate; at the macroeconomic level it may be considered as a fourth regime of underconsumption. It is therefore logical to suppose that investment is exclusively a function of the current level of profitability, or alternatively of a variable q such that $q - 1 = \pi/\rho$. The q variable may be interpreted as the marginal valuation of the stock of capital. We thus are led, within the framework of disequilibrium theory, to the theory of investment developed by Tobin (1979). The novelty lies in the fact that here the expression for q differs according to the regime.

This is the path that we have followed in earlier work (d'Autume, 1982), presenting q more as a market price than a shadow price, but this does not affect the results of the analysis. One drawback of this approach is that it represents investment behaviour as being very myopic. The producer not only formulates static expectations about the environment, the price and quantity constraints, he does not take into account the fact that his future profits will differ from his current profits because of the very investment that he plans to carry out.

A more satisfactory approach would thus consist of explicitly posing the producer's intertemporal optimisation problem which would permit the determination of profitability as a dual variable of a dynamic model. For example:

$$\left.\begin{array}{l} \max \displaystyle\int_0^{+\infty} e^{-\int_0^t r(s)ds}(F(K(t), L(t)) - w(t)L(t) - g(I(t))dt \\ \dot{K}(t) = I(t) - \mu K(t) \\ F(K(t), L(t)) \leqslant \overline{Q}(t) \\ L(t) \leqslant \overline{L}(t), \quad K(t) \geqslant 0, \quad K(0) = K_0 \end{array}\right\} \quad (10)$$

where μ is the rate of depreciation and $g(I)$ is a convex function of adjustment costs such that $g(0) = 0$ and $g'(0) = 1$.

If we introduce a dual variable $q(t)$ associated to the adjustment equation for K, the application of the Pontryagin maximum principle leads to a level of investment such that: $g'(I) = q$. Investment is then zero if $q = 1$ and is an increasing function of the difference between q and unity. We thus reproduce Tobin's initial intuition: q is the sole factor determining investment. The problem is that the current value of q cannot be easily determined. Formally, the Pontryagin principle gives the adjustment equation of q that must be integrated between 0 and positive infinity to define the value of $q(0)$. This reflects the fact that this marginal evaluation of the capital stock is influenced by all expectations concerning the future.

Below we will return to the analysis of this type of investment theory which was initiated by Lucas (1967) and was developed within the framework of Walrasian equilibrium by Hayashi (1982) and Abel and Blanchard (1983). Blanchard and Sachs (1982) present an application within the framework of non-Walrasian equilibrium. d'Autume an Michel (1983) furnish some additional analytical elements, while the papers by Michel (1982) and Henin and Michel (1982b) apply a similar approach. This intertemporal disequilibrium approach exemplified in the article of Blanchard and Sachs is extremely seductive because it offers a clear and rigorous treatment of expectations. Its sole drawback is that numerical simulation is required to provide a solution of a model which is analytically intractable.

C. The Presence of Uncertainty

A different type of investment function has been introduced by Malinvaud (1978, 1980) and has been used in particular by Picard (1981, 1982). This function supposes the complementarity of productive factors. Profitability and the level of capacity utilisation are its two arguments. The first is expressed here as expression (8) above. The second is presented by the difference between desired capital, defined as in (2) above, and existing capital, or alternatively, by the difference between corresponding levels of production. In this latter case it is represented by the difference, V, between the level of possible and desired production y^*, defined by the perceived quantity constraints, and productive capacity, $\bar{y}$.

$$V = y^* - \bar{y} = K^*/b - K/b \tag{11}$$

If the investment function is linear we have:

$$I = \alpha\left(\frac{1 - wa - \rho b}{b}\right) + \beta(y^* - \bar{y}) = \alpha\pi + \beta V \tag{12}$$

where α and β are two positive parameters.

In addition to its simplicity this function is of interest because of its resemblance to similar specifications used in some recent macro-econometric models (e.g. the DMS model, INSEE, 1980). However, the eclecticism of such a formulation deserves some explanation. First of all it would seem in fact that the notion of profitability adopted is only applicable when productive capacity is fully used. Why should one invest when there is still available capacity? New elements must be introduced into the model to answer these apparent objections. Without doubt the first candidate is the presence of uncertainty, and in particular the uncertainty attached to the behaviour of demand. Malinvaud (1980, pp. 31–3) presents a simple formalisation of this idea to which we now turn.

The producer determines his desired productive capacity, $\bar{y}^d$ by maximising the mathematical expectation of expected returns R^e on his investment. This expected return is uncertain because the level of expected possible production, y^{*e}, determined by expected quantity constraints, is uncertain. More precisely, it is supposed that y^{*e} is the sum of a certain normal level, y_0^* of a variable, and of a random factor ε with a zero expcted value and with a distribution function F independent of y_0^*

The producer thus determines the level $\bar{y}$ by maximising $E(R^e)$ with:

$$R^e = (1-wa)\min(y^{*e}, \bar{y}) - \rho b\, y, \text{ and } y^{*e} = y_0^{*e} + \varepsilon.$$

It is easily seen that the solution of this problem leads to the choice of a level of productive capacity such that:

$$(1-wa)\,P(y^{*e} > \bar{y}^d) = \rho b, \text{ or better}$$
$$(1-wa)\,[1 - F(\bar{y}^d - y_0^*)] = \rho b \tag{13}$$

It is thus suitable to equate the marginal gain, weighted by the probability of the productive capacity being actually used, with the cost of financing the investment. Equation (13) implicitly defines a desired, average level of excess capacity which is a decreasing function of factor costs which may be either positive or negative, i.e.

$$\bar{y}^d - y_0^* = \phi\left(\frac{1-wa}{\rho b}\right) \lesseqgtr 0$$

The investment function is derived by supposing that investment is a function of the difference between desired productive capacity and current capacity and by determining the normal, expected level of y_0^*. The simplest way is to define it as equal to the current level: $y_0^* = y^*$. Defining the adjustment parameter as γ, we thus obtain:

$$I = \gamma\,(\bar{y}^d - y) = \gamma[(\bar{y}^d - y_0^*) + (y_0^* - \bar{y})]$$

$$I = \gamma\left[\phi\left(\frac{1-wa}{\rho b}\right) + (y^* - \bar{y})\right]$$

Aside from linearity, the function that is thus obtained approximates (11): the producer is forced to balance the influence of profitability and the influence of the degree of capacity utilisation. We can also give a geometric representation of this idea by noting that we necessarily have $E\min(y^{*e}, \bar{y}) < \min(E(y^{*e}), \bar{y})$. The curve representing the first term of this inequality as a function of $\bar{y}$ has the general form given in Figure 3.3. The consideration of expectations makes the 'kink', which is implied *a priori* by the presence of the MIN operator, disappear. The maximisation of expected returns thus leads the producer to choose a level of capacity $\bar{y}$ which may be above or below the expected value of the future constraint $E(y^{*e})$.

Finally we note that the simultaneity of the influence of profitability and of the level of capacity utilisation on investment can be justified in

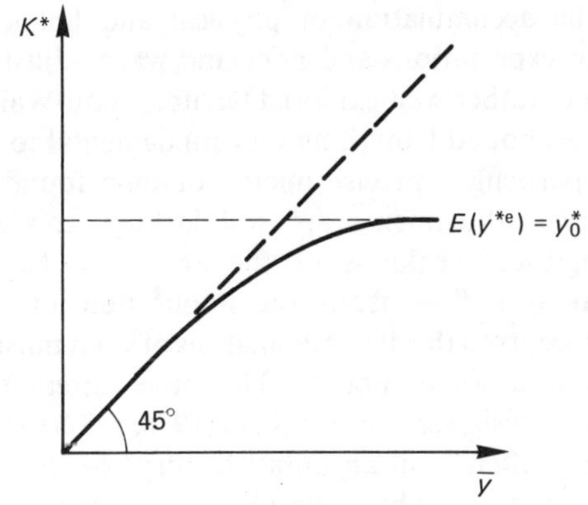

Figure 3.3

an entirely different manner. It is sufficient to consider a simple (Marshallian?) idea which suggests that productive capacity increases as long as *effective* profitability, i.e. taking account of the degree of capacity utilisation, is positive. We would then have:

$$I = \alpha\left(\frac{1-wa}{\rho}\frac{y}{K}-1\right) \tag{14}$$

where current production is $y = \min(y^*, bK)$. The difference from equation (11) is that the possible production y^* only applies when it is inferior to productive capacity. The reader is referred to Picard (1982, annex) for an application in this sense. To complete our analysis of investment in conditions of disequilibrium we note the empirical study of Artus and Muet (1983) which is based on a model of several regimes. In the same general sense is the article of Artus, Laroque and Michel (1982) which presents a simplified macroeconomic model of non-Walrasian equilibrium using French data.

III DYNAMIC ANALYSIS

Macroeconomics cannot be reduced to the analysis of instantaneous equilibria. It is more natural to study dynamics considered as a succession of non-Walrasian equilibria. The driving forces in such analysis are the accumulation of physical and financial assets, the modification of expectations and price and wage adjustments. In fact, here we return to rather well-explored territory: non-Walrasian equilibrium theory does not add anything very fundamental to the analysis of dynamics. In particular, precise microeconomic foundations for the analysis of price adjustments are still lacking; this represents the principal recognised weakness of the approach. Nevertheless, undeniable advantages flow from the application of non-Walrasian equilibrium concepts to the dynamic analysis of what must be recognised as completely traditional models. The other attempts at dynamic disequilibrium analysis, e.g. those of Stein (1976, 1982) to refer to some of the better ones, suffer from an unsatisfactory specification of instantaneous equilibrium. What happens when the limits of full employment of labour and machines are reached? Traditional models are neither explicit nor convincing on these points. The clear definition of different regimes is an incontestable advance in this respect.

A. Some Characteristic Themes

Before going on to the characterisation of stationary equilibrium, we shall first take up some of the more significant themes dealt with in the study of dynamics.

The first theme concerns the respective roles of profitability and sales. *A priori*, each of these variables belongs to a specific regime: Keynesian unemployment is caused by insufficient sales, while classical unemployment has its origin in insufficient profitability and is thus a supply problem. One of the attractive aspects of Malinvaud's investment function (11) is that it softens this strict separation. Profitability influences investment and therefore the level of demand and production in Keynesian conditions. Conversely, one can conceive of a sudden collapse of demand leading to a similar fall in investment so that Keynesian unemployment is transformed into classical unemployment, productive capacity becoming scarce. The role of profitability, and therefore the question of the elasticity of the level of employment with respect to real wages, clearly will then be more complex. They can only be adequately studied within a dynamic framework. This theme is developed in particular by Malinvaud (1982) and in several of his other works.

The possibilities for substitution between capital and labour also intervene to modify the influence of wages on employment, but here also an analysis in dynamic terms is required. Can investment, a part of effective demand, stimulate employment in the short term, yet be a substitute for labour in the long term? This is precisely the type of result found in d'Autume (1982). An interesting possibility would be the introduction of elements of disequilibrium into a model of vintage capital goods. This has not yet been done, but Malinvaud (1981, vol. 1, ch. 6; and 1982) presents a model which attempts to capture the spirit of a putty-clay model.

Expectations of quantity constraints also play a crucial role, as has been emphasised already by Hildenbrand and Hildenbrand (1978). There are several possibilities with respect to the specification of the formation of expectations. The simplest approach is to specify exogenously the levels of the constraints expected (cf. Benassy, 1982a; Neary and Stiglitz, 1979). Further, the way in which current non-Walrasian equilibria and the type of regime prevailing are influenced by expectations may be studied. Neary and Stiglitz believe that they have shown a tendency for anticipations to be self-fulfilling, in the sense that, for example, an expectation of Keynesian unemployment tomorrow leads to the risk of the immediate appearance of such unemployment today. It is also possible to study the multipliers: does the recognition of the role of expectations increase them or decrease them? It is easy to see the importance of this question for the stability of the economic system and the efficacy of economic policy. Unfortunately, it is difficult to get general results which would, in any event, require the endogenisation of expectations. At this point, the choice is between an adaptive-expectations and a rational-expectations formulation. The first possibility has been little studied, possibly because of the analytical difficulties associated with such a model. On the contrary, the formation of rational expectations about the expected constraints has been the object of a number of papers: Neary and Stiglitz (1979) use a two-period model whose application in this context is dubious, an analysis in terms of overlapping generations being much more appropriate (cf. also Blanchard and Sachs, 1982; and Michel, 1982). This type of model is often criticised *a priori* because it combines the hypothesis of rationality in the formation of expectation and the absence of rationality in the formation of prices. This criticism does not seem very convincing. The rigidity of prices need not be considered as the expression of irrational behaviour, but rather of the non-co-operative character of the relations existing between agents. Moreover, the hypothesis of rational expectations must be understood as a means of introducing forward-looking attitudes into the behaviour of agents. This is the only way to study the actual effects of expected future shocks.

B. The Analysis of Stationary States

A number of dynamic models, with or without the accumulation of capital, have already been presented: Dehez and Gabszewicz (1977), Bohm (1978), Honkapohja (1979), Malinvaud (1980), Picard (1981, 1982), d'Autume (1980b). The structure that is common to all these models may be presented *grosso modo* as follows:

$$\left.\begin{aligned} \dot{s}/s &= \lambda_1 Z_L + \delta_1 (\dot{p}/p)^e \\ \dot{p}/p &= \lambda_2 Z_Q + \delta_2 (\dot{s}/s)^e \\ \dot{k}/k &= I/K - n = \frac{\alpha\pi + \beta V}{K} + \delta_3 n - n \\ \dot{m}/m &= \theta - \dot{p}/p - n \end{aligned}\right\} \quad (15)$$

The equations for the movement of nominal wages, *s*, and the level of prices, *p*, translates the influence of relative excess demands for labour and of goods Z_L and Z_Q, as well as the influence of expected increases in prices and wages. To describe the evolution of capital per man we again adopt Malinvaud's investment function (11), taking into account the exogenous rate of growth, *n*, of the supply of labour, L_0. Finally, *m* is the amount of real balances per head and θ the rate of growth of the money stock.

To complete the specification of this representative model it is necessary to define the disequilibrium indicators, Z_L and Z_Q. Such a definition is by nature partially arbitrary because it must reflect the necessarily subjective character of agents' perceptions of the constraints on those markets where they are not rationed (cf., for example, d'Autume, 1980b, ch. 2). The models thus differ from each other and some of them may be criticised for failing to provide continuity of these indicators between one regime and another. This continuity poses a particular problem with reference to the frontier between the regime of Keynesian unemployment and the regime of repressed inflation. It is an open question whether it is best to consider all the points on this frontier as situations of supply and demand equality in all markets (as Benassy, 1977, and Picard, 1982 assume), or whether it is possible to permit discontinuity, relying, perhaps, on a suitably adapted notion of stability (as in Honkapohja and Ito, 1983).

In any event, the disequilibrium variables, Z_L and Z_Q, as well as π and V, are a function, depending on the regime, of the variables $w = s/p$, k, m

and eventually the rate of growth θ of the money stock which is considered exogenous. It is thus possible to determine the stationary points of the system without any precise formulation of the process by which expectations are formed since it is sufficient to consider them as being verified by the conditions of the stationary state.

It is, however, necessary to define a stationary Walrasian equilibrium, that is, a state that might be attained when prices are perfectly flexible. We define it as a triplet (w^*, k^*, m^*), such that all markets are in equilibrium and profit is zero: thus $Z_L = Z_Q = \pi = 0$. In addition some technical conditions must be fulfilled to assure satisfactory specification of stationary equilibrium. First, the definition of excess demand of good Z_Q and of the degree of capacity utilisation, V, have to be such that a zero value for one implies the same value for the other. Further, the importance of the term δ_3 in the investment function should be noticed. The presence of this term, which we have not yet discussed, represents an autonomous trend growth of capital to which one must add the influence of the disequilibrium represented by π and V. It is assumed that this trend is equal to the natural rate n. Further, coefficient δ_3 should be equal to unity in order for a stationary value of capital per man to be compatible with elimination of disequilibrium represented by the zero values of π and V. If, on the contrary, this coefficient is eliminated, as is done, for example, by Picard (1982), the stationarity of k requires the maintenance of positive profitability, which seems dubious. We shall thus suppose that $\delta_3 = 1$.

In such conditions when indexation is complete ($\delta_1 = \delta_2 = 1$) the stationary Walrasian equilibrium is a stationary point in system (15): the influence of rigidities disappear in the long run. When indexation is imperfect ($\delta_1 < 1$, $\delta_2 < 1$) we come back to the viewpoint of the well-known long-term Phillips curves. In the long run a trade-off persists between inflation and the disequilibrium tensions in the labour and the goods markets. According to the exogenous value of θ and thus of inflation we will have in the long run either a situation of excess supply on the two markets (Keynesian unemployment) with deflation, or a situation of excess demand on the two markets (repressed inflation). In any event, conditions of classical unemployment can be no more than transitory.

In such an analysis the choice of instruments for economic policy plays an equally important role, and it will be necessary to insure that the budgetary constraint of the government is satisfied. Most models suppose that the government directly controls the real rate of interest. The only possibility of integrating real and monetary phenomena is thus the real balance effect. A less extreme perspective which gives a greater role to the rate of interest would be very desirable. It would thus be possible to rediscover, at least for the regime of Keynesian unemployment, a short-term equilibrium of the *IS–LM* type (in this respect cf. d'Autume, 1980b, 1982; Danthine and Peytrignet, 1981; Benassy, 1982; and Henin and Michel, 1983).

The preceding argument was based on the hypothesis that the rate of growth of the money stock was exogenous. Several authors (Dehez and Gabszewicz, 1977; Malinvaud, 1980) on the other hand assume that this rate of growth is endogenous, the result of economic policy decisions. This approach does not call into question the association of a positive or negative rate of inflation with stationary equilibria regimes of repressed inflation or Keynesian unemployment, but it raises the possibility of existence of both types of stationary equilibria. Indeed, within this context and assuming the absence of open market operations, the creation of money appears as the surplus of the private sector or identical to the public sector deficit. In general, this deficit appears as a decreasing function of the level of income, for example because public expenditure is largely independent of the level of income while tax receipts are dependent on the level of income. But the exact influence exercised by the level of real balances on the level of income depends on the particular regime. More precisely, provisionally neglecting growth and price adjustments, we may suppose that the behaviour of real cash balances is determined by the equation: $\dot{m} = G - T(y(m))$, where G represents exogenous public expenditure. Tax receipts are a function $T(y)$ of income. Income is a continuous function $y(m)$ of real balances. In conditions of Keynesian unemployment this function is increasing (stimulation of aggregate demand), but decreasing in conditions of repressed inflation (exacerbated rationing). The result is that for a range of values of G there exist two stationary values of m, one for Keynesian unemployment and the other applying to repressed inflation. Since $\partial\dot{m}/\partial m$ is negative in the first case and positive in the second, Keynesian equilibrium is stable and the inflationary equilibrium unstable. We thus have a presumption that should be verified in conditions of price adjustment which we have provisionally neglected. The application of this result is clear since it suggests that there will be a general long-term tendency to Keynesian depression. Nevertheless we must be aware of the fact that it strongly depends on the hypotheses concerning the choice of instruments of economic policy.

Finally, it should be pointed out that one of the points of interest in Picard's (1982) approach is the introduction of aspects of inflation caused by a lack of consensus into the adjustment process of prices and wages: nominal wages are determined not only by the state of disequilibrium in the labour market, but equally by the difference between workers' desired real wages and the actual level. The stationary states then depend on the level of the desired real wage, and in particular on its relation to the level of wages compatible with Walrasian equilibrium.

IV INTERNATIONAL EXCHANGE IN DISEQUILIBRIUM CONDITIONS

A. The Elasticity of Employment with Respect to Real Wages

The macroeconomic applications of non-Walrasian equilibrium theory are not limited to the closed economy. Indeed, it is necessary to expand the analysis to determine the influence of international exchange on the economic policy prescriptions that have been obtained in their absence. The first lesson that may be discovered from the recognition of international exchange is a bias in favour of classical prescriptions, which limits the scope of economic policies to eliminate unemployment[4].

If we make the assumption of a 'small country' which can buy and sell without limit in international markets at world prices, there can never be, by definition, a sales constraint. Thus, in Dixit's (1978) model with a single good, unemployment can only be classical: a reduction in wages will always stimulate exports and production. Yet the recognition that there will be 'protected' sectors whose products are not traded internationally restores the possibility of Keynesian phenomena. As shown in Neary (1980; see also Steigum, 1980) an increase in wages has a positive effect on employment when the Keynesian effects of the expansion of demand in the non-traded goods sector more than offset the classical effects of contraction of demand in the open sector. It is not then possible to give an *a priori* judgement of the effects of an increase in wages. The necessity of making precise evaluation of the often contradictory effects of economic policy measures on the open and non-traded goods sectors is certainly not new to French economists, for this was one of the basic themes underlying some initial work on economic planning (cf. Courbis, 1975).

It is thus extremely difficult to give an unequivocal answer to the problem of the elasticity of employment with respect to real wages. In an analysis which is both theoretical and empirical, Dreze and Modigliani

(1981) report negative elasticities for the case of Belgium, with the long-term impacts much stronger than the short term.

B. The Effects of Devaluation

But the assumption of a 'small country' is much too extreme. There is a long tradition of analysing open economies in which a country faces an infinitely elastic supply curve of imports at an internationally fixed price and a well-defined demand curve for its own exports as a function of price. If this price does not adjust instantaneously, exporters may experience sales constraints. We now turn to such a model in which the small-country assumption only applies to imports.

We shall concentrate on the effects of devaluation in a general model drawn from the work of Picard (1982b), showing that they differ according to the regime. Cuddington (1980) has studied a similar model, and Younes (1978) and Owen (1981) obtain similar results in models of several countries.

The model under consideration has the traditional structure of Keynesian models of an open economy, but does not take financial markets into account. The first good is imported without limit at a fixed price, p_2. One of the innovations of Picard's model is the assumption that the imported good may be both consumed and used as an input (oil). The second good is consumed domestically or exported. A quantity, y, of this good is produced in the country with the aid of labour, L, and imported raw materials, z. The production function with complementarity of factors and decreasing returns to scale may then be written:

$$y = min\,[F(L), G(z)] \qquad (16)$$

The two functions F and G are increasing and concave. The price of the produced good, p_1, and the nominal wage, w, are rigid. The exchange rate is given by e, the real wage by $w = s/p_1$, and competitivity by $x = ep_2/p_1$. We will not repeat Picard's analysis of agents' behaviour and the operation of markets, but rather proceed directly to the demonstration that the traditional absorption approach, with some modifications, may serve to summarise this analysis.

The volume of imports is an increasing function $J(y, x)$ of the level of output and of income, y, and decreasing when competitivity, x, increases. The volume of demand for exports is an increasing function of competitivity $D(x)$. Absorption is defined as the aggregate domestic demand for goods 1 and 2, valued in terms of good 1. It is an increasing function $A(y, x)$ of money income, y. The influence of the degree of competition on absorption is complex and ambiguous: it leads to a modification of the structure of domestic demand, modifies the valuation of its two components and further diminishes the size of national income because it increases the costs of imported intermediate consumption. Therefore we shall not make a particular assumption concerning the impact of this influence.

Finally, we suppose that the Marshall–Lerner conditions are satisfied. Other things remaining the same, a devaluation increases the trade balance, volume effects dominating the terms of trade effects:

$$\varepsilon = \frac{\partial}{\partial x}[D(x) - xJ(y, x)] > 0.$$

We call γ and η the propensities to save and import, and δ the sensitivity of absorption to competitivity:

$$\gamma = 1 - (\partial A/\partial y) > 0, \quad \eta = x\,(\partial J/\partial y) > 0, \quad \delta = \partial A/\partial x?$$

In conditions of Keynesian unemployment the level of domestic production is determined by demand. It is the solution to the equation:

$$y - A(y, x) = D(x) - x\,J(y, x) \tag{17}$$

Calling B the equilibrium trade balance, that is, the common value of the two terms of equation (17), we may write:

$$dy/dx = \frac{\varepsilon + \delta}{\gamma + \eta} \quad dB/dx = \frac{\gamma\varepsilon - \eta\delta}{\gamma + \eta} \tag{18}$$

If we assume that the sensitivity of absorption is low [5], and that the δ term is dominated, these two multipliers are positive: a devaluation instantly improves both employment and the trade balance.

Thus within the context of the first regime the model retains the results of the traditional Keynesian approach, but we shall now see that this is not the case for the other regimes. In conditions of classical unemployment the level of production is equal to the notional supply of goods, which is a decreasing function of factor costs w and x:

$$y = y^s\,(w, x) \tag{19}$$

It is easy to see that if the cost of a factor increases, the quantities employed of both factors decreases: by hypothesis there is no factor substitution but the fact of decreasing returns diminishes the optimum scale of output.

Conditions of excess demand imply rationing of domestic demand or of exports. If we assume that domestic demand is given priority, then exports, E, are given as a residual by the following equation:

$$y - A(y, x) = E - x\,J(x, y) \tag{20}$$

Thus the characteristic equality of the absorption approach is still valid: now it acts to determine the (constrained) level of exports, income being determined elsewhere. From (19) and (20) we may write:

$$\frac{\partial y}{\partial x} < \int O \frac{dB}{\partial x} = \gamma \frac{\partial y}{\partial x} - \delta < 0,$$

again assuming that δ is dominated. By increasing the price of imported inputs devaluation diminishes profitable productive capacity and thus employment. Devaluation similarly diminishes the exportable surplus and thus the trade balance.

In conditions of repressed inflation the analysis is identical to that for classical unemployment, except the level of production is now determined by the notional supply of labour. Relation (19) is replaced by:

$$y = F(l^s(w, x)) \tag{21}$$

and the volume of exports is again determined by (20).

The elasticity of the supply of labour with respect to the rate of unemployment is without doubt weakly negative. It is thus difficult to assume that the term δ is dominated in this case. The effect of devaluation on the trade balance is uncertain, but in any event will be weak. In summary, we can see the interest of the disequilibrium approach in demonstrating the profound differences in the effects of devaluation from one regime to another.

C. The Impact of the Oil Crisis

The analysis of the preceding section conceals a paradox which we have chosen to ignore up to this point. If p_2 is interpreted as the price of oil, it implies that an increase in the price of oil has the same effect as a devaluation: that is, it implies an improvement of employment and the trade balance in conditions of Keynesian unemployment. The oil crisis should have had favourable effects! This paradox is due in part to the excessive degree of aggregation of the model. The sole imported good serves as both a consumption good and as an imported raw material input, and these two roles may at times be incompatible. It is possible to show that if the imported good is only considered as an imported input some of the paradoxical conclusions of the analysis given above may be corrected, allowing a more satisfactory analysis of the impact of the oil crisis on a developed country that does not produce oil domestically. It still remains true, however, that the level of aggregation of the model forbids a distinction between the effects of an oil shock and those of a devaluation, or, shall we say, a 'dollar shock'. Further refinement of the model to take into account two imported goods would be highly desirable.

Suppose that imports are composed only of oil used as an input in the production of the domestic good. Let us further simplify by assuming that the quantity imported is proportional to domestic production. Formally the function G that acts in (16) is linear and defined $G(z) = z/\alpha$. The function J is then reduced to $J(y) = \alpha y$. For a level of production, y, domestic value added, the sum of wages and profits, is given by $y - x\alpha y = (1 - x\alpha)y$. The two components of absorption are the value of imports $x\alpha y$ and the domestic demand for good 1 which is assumed to depend exclusively on an increasing function of the level of domestic value added. Absorption thus becomes: $A(y, x) = a[(1 - x\alpha)y] + x\alpha y$. Domestic demand for good 1 is thus a decreasing function of 'competitivity', x, because of the income effect linked to the payment of the petroleum account[6]. The demand for exports is still an increasing function, $D(x)$ of competitivity, but rather than a substitution effect it is more reasonable to interpret this as an income effect linked to the payment of the oil 'rent'. Adopting the same notation used in the preceding section we may then write:

$$\varepsilon = D' - \alpha y$$
$$\gamma = (1 - x\alpha)(1 - a') > 0$$
$$\eta = x\alpha > 0$$
$$\delta = \alpha y(1 - a') > 0, \quad \text{as well as,}$$
$$\varepsilon + \delta = D' - \alpha y a'$$
$$\gamma\varepsilon - \eta\delta = (1 - a')(\varepsilon - x\alpha D')$$

It seems reasonable to suppose that $D' - \alpha y a' < 0$, which is equivalent to supposing that the propensity to consume in developed countries is higher than the propensity in oil producing countries. A transfer of income from the former to the latter would then lead to a decrease in demand for good 1. We thus would have $\varepsilon + \delta < 0$, so that $\varepsilon < 0$. The Marshall–Lerner conditions are then not satisified because the negative effect of the terms of trade dominate. We thus also have $\gamma\varepsilon - \eta\delta < 0$. In such conditions the formulae of the preceding section show that the oil crisis (or a devaluation) has an unfavourable impact on employment and the trade balance in all regimes.

In this version of the model we lose what we considered as the most interesting characteristic of the preceding model – the demonstration of the different effects in the different regimes. But the very fact that the effects are all of the same sign leads to a new question. Starting from conditions of Walrasian equilibrium would an oil crisis plunge the economy into conditions of Keynesian unemployment or classical unemployment when wages and prices are rigid? The answer is not straightforward because both the notional supply of goods (19), and the Keynesian equilibrium effective demand solution to (17) are reduced. If the impact on supply is stronger than the impact on demand the economy will be subject to classical unemployment, while Keynesian unemployment occurs in the opposite case.[7]

The double impact of oil prices on profitability and on world demand has been known for some times (cf. notably, Malinvaud, 1980, p. 85). It is also the basis of the work of Bruno and Sachs (1981, 1982) which relies on a more eclectic framework. Even if the analysis that we have reported above has not been able to eliminate the ambiguity in the effect of oil prices, at least it has allowed us to identify the important factors for the analysis. Nevertheless the drawbacks of the static framework in which it was carried out must be recognised. The propensity to consume of a country is not an exogenous given: it is deeply influenced by agents' expectations. Therefore, the important question concerns the evolution of this propensity over time: will the oil account be paid directly or will the payment be spread out, possibly over a period which is too long? A satisfactory analysis of the effects of the oil crisis would thus require an inter-temporal approach reflecting agents' attempts to adapt their consumption and investment plans in an optimal way to the sudden shock, also taking into account their expectations about prices and quantity constraints. The reader is referred to Henin (1982) for a simple model of this type, and to Giavazzi, Odekon and Wyplosz (1982) for a more ambitious study in the framework of a simulation model similar to that used by Bruno and Sachs.[8]

V CONCLUSIONS

The non-Walrasian equilibrium approach above all represents an important contribution to macroeconomic analyses of the short term. We have seen how it might be integrated into dynamic analyses, but that such an integration is too frequently based on an excessively schematic description (in particular too myopic) of agent behaviour. The adoption of a more rigorous inter-temporal approach is certainly required for further theoretical progress. This would allow a more precise description of stocks and flows, of the role of the accumulation of these stocks, as well as of expectations. There can be no doubt that this would also lead to an improved description of monetary and financial phenomena which are often only given passing consideration in existing models. Indeed, this proposal is similar to a recent widespread tendency in developments in macroeconomics in the analysis of investment and foreign trade outside the field of disequilibrium analysis. It seems realistic to expect important progress in fields of research inspired both by non-Walrasian equilibria and other approaches to dynamic macroeconomics.

Notes

1. General analysis of non-Walrasian equilibrium models may be found, for example, in Benassy (1976) and Drazen (1980).
2. See d'Autume (1980b, 1982) and Laussel (1980, 1982).
3. The form of the first diagram is taken from Laussel (1982, fig. 3).
4. These results correspond closely to positions currently taken in economic policy debates by countries such as France. 'Classical' economists, whether consciously or unconsciously, always invoke the existence of the external constraint to justify their choice of economic policy options.
5. Picard (1982b) can only demonstrate this property because he eliminates the income effect by supposing that profits are not immediately distributed to households. The impact of increasing prices of imported raw materials inputs is offset, given real wages, by these profits without this implying a reduction in domestic demand. We return to this point in the next section.
6. Picard (1982b) explicitly assumes, on the contrary, that domestic demand is an increasing function of competitivity because of the substitution effect.
7. Formally, the frontier of the Keynesian and classical regimes is given by the equation $y^s = y^k$, given respectively by equations (19) and (17). The point at issue is how it will move as the result of an oil crisis.
8. Our survey of the non-Walrasian equilibrium analysis of international trade is purposely not exhaustive. Because they treat related themes, the work of Azam (1982) on the role of imported intermediate goods, and Berthelemy (1981, 1982) on the problem of transfers, should also be mentioned.

References

Abel A. B. and Blanchard O. J. (1983) 'An Intertemporal Model of Saving and Investment', *Econometrica*, vol. 51, no. 3.

Artus P. and Muet P. A. (1983) 'Investissement, contrainte de débouchés, d'emploi, contraintes financières: estimation d'un modèle à plusieurs régimes', Observatoire Français des Conjonctures Economiques, Paris.

Artus P., Laroque G. and Michel G. (1982) 'Estimation of a quaterly macroeconomic model with quantity rationing', Document de travail, ENSAE, no. 8209.

d'Autume A. (1980a) 'L'influence des effets de répartition sur l'unicité et la stabilité de configurations macroéconomiques de déséquilibre', in Henin (1980).

d'Autume A. (1980b) 'Equilibres non-walrasiens et macroeconomie', Ph.D. Thesis, Université Paris II.

d'Autume A. (1982) 'Un modèle de croissance en déséquilibre', in Henin and Michel (1982a).

d'Autume A. and Michel P. (1983) 'Epargne, investissement et monnaie dans une perspective intertemporelle' *Revue Economique*, vol. 36, no. 2, March 1985.

Azam J. P. (1982) 'L'impact macroéconomique de la politique commerciale en déséquilibre', *Revue Economique*, vol. 33, no. 6.

Barro R. J. and Grossman H. I. (1971) 'A General Disequilibrium Model of Income and Employment', *American Economic Review*, vol. 61, no. 1.

Benassy J. P. (1976) 'Théorie du déséquilibre et fondements microéconomiques de la macroéconomie', vol. 27, no. 5.

Benassy J. P. (1977) 'A Neokeynesian Model of Price and Quantity Determination in Disequilibrium', in *Equilibrium and Disequilibrium in Economic Theory*, ed. G. Schwodiauer (Boston: D. Reidel Publishing Company).

Benassy J. P. (1982a) 'Developments in Non-Walrasian Economics and the Microeconomic Foundations of Macroeconomics', in *Advances in Quantitative Economics*, ed. W. Hildenbrand (Cambridge University Press).

Benassy J. P. (1982b) 'The Three Regimes of the IS-LM Model: a Non-Walrasian Analysis', CEPREMAP.

Berthelemy J. C. (1981) 'La théorie des transferts: une approche en termes de déséquilibres', *Revue Economique*, vol. 32, no. 1.

Berthelemy J. C. (1982) 'Les prélèvements pétroliers et les déséquilibres macroéconomiques mondiaux: une analyse en termes de transferts', *Revue Economique*, vol. 33, no. 4.

Blanchard O. J. and Sachs J. (1982) 'Anticipations, récessions et politique économique: un modèle de déséquilibre intertemporel', *Annales de l'INSEE*, no. 47–48.

Böhm V. (1978) 'Disequilibrium Dynamics in a Simple Macroeconomic Model', *Journal of Economic Theory*, vol. 17.

Boissieu C. de, Parguez A. and Zagame P. (1977) '*Economie du Déséquilibre*' (Economica).

Bramoullé G. and Giran J. P. (eds) (1981) '*Analyse du déséquilibre*' (Economica).

Bruno M. and Sachs J. (1981) 'Supply Versus Demand Approaches to the Problem of Stagflation', in *Macroeconomic Policies for Growth and Price Stability*, ed. E. Giersch (Tübingen: J. C. B. Mohr).

Bruno M. and Sachs J. (1982) 'Input Price Shocks and the Slow-down in Economic Growth: the Case of UK Manufacturing', *Review of Economic Studies*, vol. XLIX, no. 5.

Clower R. W. (1965) 'The Keynesian Counter-Revolution: a Theoretical Appraisal', in *Monetary Theory*, ed. R. W. Clower (Penguin).

Courbis R. (1975) *Compétitivité et Croissance en Economie Concurrencée* (Dunod).
Cuddington J. T. (1980) 'Fiscal and Exchange Rate Policies in a Fix-Price Trade Model with Export Rationing', *Journal of International Economics*, vol. 10 (April).
Danthine J. P. and Peytrignet M. (1981) 'Intégration de l'analyse graphique IS-LM avec la théorie des équilibres à prix fixes', in Bramoulle and Giran (1981).
Dehez P. and Gabszewicz J. J. (1977) 'Saving Behavior and Disequilibrium Analysis', in *Systèmes Dynamiques et Modèles Économiques* (Editions du CNRS).
Drazen A. (1980) 'Recent Developments in Macroeconomic Disequilibrium Theory', *Econometrica*, vol. 48, no. 2.
Dreze J. H. and Modigliani F. (1981) 'The Trade-Off Between Real Wages and Employment in an Open Economy (Belgium)', *European Economic Review*, vol. 15, no. 1.
Dixit A. (1978) 'The Balance of Trade in a Model of Temporary Equilibrium with Rationing', *Review of Economic Studies*, vol. 45.
Fourgeaud C., Lenclud B. and Michel P. (1981) 'Two-Sector Model with Quantity Rationing', *Journal of Economic Theory*.
Giavazzi F., Odekon M. and Wyplosz C. (1982) 'Simulating an Oil Shock with Sticky Prices', *European Economic Review*.
Grossman H. I. (1972) 'A Choice-Theoretic Model of an Income Investment Accelerator', *American Economic Review*, vol. 62 (Sept).
Hayashi F. (1982) 'Tobin's q, Rational Expectations and Optimal Investment Rule', *Econometrica*, vol. 50, no. 2.
Hénin P. Y. (ed.) (1980) *Etudes sur l'économie en déséquilibre* (Economica).
Hénin P. Y. (1981) 'Equilibre avec Rationnement dans un modéle macro-économique avec décision d'investissement endogène', *Economie Appliquée*, no. 4.
Hénin P. Y. (1982) 'L'impact macroéconomique d'un choc pétrolier', Doc. no. 57, Conjoncture et Analyse des Déséquilibres, Université Paris I.
Hénin P. Y. and Michel P. (eds) (1982a) *Croissance et accumulation en déséquilibre* (Economica).
Hénin P. Y. and Michel P. (1982b) 'Théorie de la croissance avec rigidités salariales et contrainte de demande effective: une reformulation', in Henin and Michel (1982a).
Hénin P. Y. and Michel P. (1983) 'Une représentation IS-LM des équilibres macroéconomiques avec rationnement', Doc. no. 62, Conjoncture et Analyse des Déséquilibres, Université Paris I.
Hildenbrand K. and Hildenbrand W. (1978) 'On Keynesian Equilibria with Unemployment and Quantity Rationing', *Journal of Economic Theory*, vol. 18.
Honkapohja S. (1979) 'On the Dynamics of Disequilibria in a Macro Model with Flexible Wages and Prices', in *New Trends in Dynamic System Theory and Economics*, ed. M. Aoki and A. Marzollo (Academic Press).
Honkapohja S. and Ito T. (1983) 'Stability with Regime Switching', *Journal of Economic Theory*.
INSEE, Service des Programmes (1980) 'Une représentation de l'économie

française: le modèle DMS', *Revue Economique*, vol. 31, no. 5.
Laussel D. (1980) 'Sentiers de croissance, cyclès et dépression', *Revue d'Economie Politique*, vol. 90.
Laussel D. (1982) 'Sentiers de croissance en déséquilibre', in Henin and Michel (1982a).
Lucas R. (1967) 'Adjustment Costs and the Theory of Supply', *Journal of Political Economy*, vol. 75.
Malinvaud E. (1977) *The Theory of Unemployment Reconsidered* (Basil Blackwell). French translation: *Réexamen de la Théorie du Chômage* (Calmann-Levy, 1980).
Malinvaud E. (1978) 'Nouveaux développements de la théorie macro-économique du chômage', *Revue Economique*, vol. 29, no. 1.
Malinvaud E. (1980) *Profitability and Unemployment* (Cambridge University Press and Maison des Sciences de l'Homme).
Malinvaud E. (1981) *Théorie Macroéconomique*, 2 vols. (Dunod).
Malinvaud E. (1982) 'Salaiers et chômage', in Henin and Michel (1982a); also in *Economic Journal*, March 1982.
Michel P. (1982) 'Trois facteurs de la crise dans un modèle de croissance contrainte', *Revue Economique*, vol. 33, no. 5.
Muellbauer J. and Portes R. (1978) 'Macroeconomic Model with Quantity Rationing', *Economic Journal*, vol. 88 (Déc).
Neary J. P. (1980) 'Nontraded Goods and the Balance of Trade in a Néo-Keynesian Temporary Equilibrium', *Quarterly Journal of Economics*, no. 3.
Neary J. P. and Roberts K. W. S. (1980) 'The Theory of Household Behaviour Under Rationing', *European Economic Review*.
Neary J. P. and Stiglitz J. E. (1979) 'Towards a Reconstruction of Keynesian Economics: Expectations and Constrained Equilibria' *Quarterly Journal of Economics*.
Owen R. F. (1981) 'A Two Country Disequilibrium Model of International Finance', Centre d'Etudes et de Recherche en Sciences Sociales Economiques et Commerciales, Cergy-Pontoise.
Picard P. (1981) 'Croissance et Inflation dans un Modéle de Déséquilibre', *Revue Economique*, vol. 32, no. 6.
Picard P. (1982a) 'Inflation, croissance et déséquilibre', in Henin and Michel (1982a).
Picard P. (1982b) 'Théorie du déséquilibre et politique économique', Ph.D. Thesis, Université Paris I.
Steigum. E. (1980) 'Keynesian and Classical Unemployment in an Open Economy', *Scandinavian Journal of Economics*, vol. 82.
Stein J. (1976) 'Inside the Monetary Black Box', *Monetarism*, ed. Stein (North Holland).
Stein J. (1982) *Monetarists, Keynesians and the New Classical Economics* (Basil Blackwell).
Tobin J. (1979) 'A General Equilibrium Approach to Monetary Theory', *Journal of Money Credit and Banking*, vol. 1, no. 1.
Younes Y. (1978) 'Dévaluation et équilibre avec rationnement', *Economie Appliquée*, vol. XXXI, no. 1–2.

4 An *IS–LM* Representation of Macroeconomic Equilibria with Rationing

Pierre-Yves Hénin and Philippe Michel

The historical and pedagogical importance of the *IS–LM* scheme for the development of moderm macroeconomics suggests that we should consider it as a reference model which may be used to assess new instruments of macroeconomic analysis. A. D'Autume (1980) has shown rigorously that the *IS–LM* approach remains valid when applied to the analysis of Keynesian unemployment under conditions of equilibrium with rationing. J. P. Danthine and M. Peytrignet (1981) proposed an extension of the *IS–LM* framework to different disequilibrium configurations, but in fact their work is exclusively concerned with a reformulation of the general model of supply and demand. J. P. Benassy (1982) demonstrates the importance of certain flexibility hypotheses for a study of this kind, but his work does not explicitly consider different regimes for the formulation of *IS* and *LM* curves. H. Snessens (1981) appeals to an *IS–LM* representation, but considers *IS* as an inequality rather than an equilibrium condition. It seems possible to proceed along the path suggested by these investigators to show how an appropriate generalisation of the *IS* and *LM* curves produces a real reformulation of the concept of macroeconomic equilibrium with rationing.

In order to retain the essential link with Hicks's original (1937) contribution, we shall use a two-sector model in which the market for investment goods clears in each period.[1] Further, wages are presumed to be upwardly flexible. This eliminates all strictly positive excess demand for labour and avoids having to support the rationing scheme with arbitrary assumptions. Finally, we will start by making explicit the foundation of the analysis by providing a derivation of agents' behavioural functions before proceeding to the construction of the *IS* and *LM* curves and the study of general equilibrium.

I THE BEHAVIOUR OF REPRESENTATIVE AGENTS

The representation which we propose is grounded in the method of temporary equilibrium as elaborated by Hicks (1939) and developed by J. M. Grandmont (1976). This implies that the behavioural functions ruling in any period are consistent with inter-temporal rationality on the part of agents. In the temporary equilibrium perspective, variables inherited from the past, such as the capital stock or wealth, or determined by the future, such as expectations[2] or equilibrium prices of assets, are simply considered to be data for analysis of the current period.

A. The Framework of Analysis

We thus assume that the stock of capital is given, and that part of it is specialised to the production of investment goods, part to the production of consumption goods. This hypothesis allows us to consider the following production functions, $Q = f(N_q)$ and $C = \phi(N_c)$ are given and independent. We will also assume that they are strictly concave.[3]

The price of consumption goods, which is fixed within the period, serves as the numeraire for the system. The price of investment goods, p_Q, is flexible and clears the corresponding market. Nominal wages, or, identically, real wages in terms of consumption goods, are downwardly rigid at wage level $\bar{w}$, but upwardly flexible above this wage, thereby assuring any possible excess demand for labour.

The supply of labour to the productive sectors is a constant given by L. The consumers only hold money balances equal to M_0 at the beginning of the period and M at the end of the period.[4] During the period they acquire shares whose price is a function of the rate of interest, i.e. $a = 1/(1+r)$. As a result of the operation of arbitrage, which is implicitly assumed, the shares must earn a return that is equivalent to investment in manufacturing firms. The convention of temporary equilibrium implies that anticipated inflation in the price of consumption goods is given. To simplify notation we shall assume that it is equal to zero. The rate of interest is assumed to be flexible, adjusting the money market and thus implicitly the market for shares, given the appropriate definition of the corresponding demand function. With these hypotheses in mind we can proceed to describe the agents behavioural functions in detail.

B. Households' Behaviour

The resources of the households are composed of their initial cash balances, M_0, their current incomes which in aggregate are identical to total national income, and their expected income, y^e, from the present value, ay^e, of assets. This gives an initial wealth of $W = M_0 + y + ay^e$. Households face a double arbitrage decision, one concerning the division between savings and current consumption, and the other concerning the demand for money balances, M^d. Their demand for shares and the anticipated value, C^e, of their future consumption are then completely determined.

Consumers' preferences are assumed to be regular and may be represented by the log-linear utility function of the form:

$$U = \alpha \log C + \beta \log C^e + \gamma \log M \tag{1}$$

with $\alpha + \beta + \gamma = 1$ which implies no additional restriction. Households' optimal behaviour is composed of a choice of the values (C, C^e, M) which maximises U subject to the budget constraint:

$$aC^e \leqslant a(y^e + M) + y - C - M + M_0 \tag{2}$$

In addition, the market for consumption goods may be in disequilibrium, in which case actual current consumption, C, is determined by the minimum of supply C^s, and demand. This implies a supplementary constraint:

$$C \leqslant C^s \tag{3}$$

The solution to this optimisation problem for consumers who are not rationed (constraint 3 does not hold) gives:

$$\begin{aligned} C^* &= \alpha(y + ay^e + M_0) = \alpha W \\ C^{e*} &= \beta W/a \\ M^* &= \gamma W/ra \end{aligned} \tag{4}$$

while the solution for consumers constrained by the supply of consumption goods would be:

$$\begin{aligned} C &= C^s \\ \tilde{C}^e &= \frac{\beta}{a(\beta+\gamma)}[W - C^s] \\ \tilde{M} &= \frac{\gamma}{ra(\gamma+\beta)}[W - C^s] \end{aligned} \tag{5}$$

The rationing which affects current consumption is at the origin of forced saving and the positive relation to the demand for money.[5] By equating the 'notional demand' M^* with the effective demand $\tilde{M}$ we obtain:

$$\tilde{M} = M^* + \frac{\gamma}{ra(\beta+\gamma)}[C^* - C^s] = M^* + k(r)[C^* - C^s] \tag{6}$$

We note that the ratio coefficient k is bigger than the notional demand coefficient for money balances, γ/ra, by a factor equal to $1/(\beta+\gamma) = W/(W-C^*)$. As M^* is always positive, this relation will also be positive because C^* is necessarily less than W. On the other hand, part of the forced saving is destined for demand for shares which increases, since with $U^1_{\tilde{M}} < U^1_{M*}$, the arbitrage between shares and money balances reduces the subjective evaluation (in terms of utility) of the required yield on shares. The value of the coefficient of the ratio will then be within γ/ra and unity.

C. The Behaviour of Firms

In the framework of the hypotheses defined above, firms have to decide the level of employment, the supply of output and the level of investment. Recognition of the impact of future profits rests on the state of expectations which are taken as given in temporary equilibrium. The realised value of these profits is expressed for each sector respectively by a function of current investment and the interest rate $V^q(Q_q, r)$ and $V^c(Q_c, r)$ which is strictly increasing and concave in Q, and decreasing in r.[6]

The optimal problem for firms producing investment goods, Q, is therefore to maximise $pF(N_q) - wN_q + V^q(Q_q, r) - pQ_q$, relative to N_q and Q. A unique solution is given by the first order conditions, from which we derive the supply and demand functions for goods and the demand for labour:

$$N_q^* = F_N'^{-1}(w/p) \qquad = N_q^*(\underset{(-)}{w}, \underset{(+)}{p}) \tag{7}$$

$$Q^s = F(N_q^*) \qquad = Q^s(\underset{(-)}{w}, \underset{(+)}{p}) \tag{8}$$

$$Q_q^* = V_q^1(\cdot, r)^{-1}(p) \qquad = Q_q^*(\underset{(-)}{p}, \underset{(-)}{r}) \tag{9}$$

The reasoning behind the investment function (9) is to equate the price of the marginal demand for investment goods V_Q' to the market price of investment goods. The optimisation problem facing firms producing consumption goods is similarly constrained, but we must take into consideration in addition the possibility of rationing due the market constraint C^d with fixed prices. Introducing a multiplier m associated with this constraint we obtain:

Maximise $\phi(N_c) - wN_c + V^c(Q_c, r) - pQ_c + m\{C^d - \phi(N_c)\}$

which in the absence of market constraints yields:

$$N_c^* = \phi_N'^{-1}(w) \quad = N_c^*(\underset{(-)}{w}) \tag{10}$$

$$C^s = \phi(N_c^*) \quad = C^s(\underset{(-)}{w})$$

$$Q_c^* = V_q'(\cdot, r)^{-1}(p) = Q_c^*(\underset{(-)}{p}, \underset{(-)}{r})$$

while the case of constrained markets yields:

$$\tilde{N}_c = \phi^{-1}(C^d) = \tilde{N}_c(C^d) \tag{11}$$

and implies that the demand for investment in unaffected given the assumption of inelastic expectations of future profits.[7]

D. The Economy's Investment Function

A demand function for investment goods has been constructed for each sector. In the Keynesian tradition, represented in particular by Witte (1963), equilibrium in the market for capital goods is expressed in the macroeconomic investment function. Within the framework of the present model, where the equality of supply and demand is expressed as follows:

$$Q_q^*(\underset{(-)}{p}, \underset{(-)}{r}) + Q_c^*(\underset{(-)}{p}, \underset{(-)}{r}) = Q^s(\underset{(-)}{w}, \underset{(+)}{p}) \tag{12}$$

this point of view implies solutions for the equations determining the price and volume of capital goods of the form:

$$Q = Q(\underset{(-)}{r}, \underset{(-)}{w}), \quad p = p(\underset{(-)}{r}, \underset{(+)}{w}) \tag{13}$$

Investment 'in value terms', that is, in terms of consumption goods $I \equiv pQ$ is produced by these functions. If the elasticity of the volume of investment with respect to the wage rate which is normally negative is greater than unity in absolute value, then the value of investment will be decreasing in *w*:

$$I = I(\underset{(-)}{r}, \underset{(-)}{w}) \tag{14}$$

The derivative I'_w that is produced from the two terms of opposite sign can generally be considered to be small. The expression for the investment function (14) completes the set of behavioural functions which it is necessary to take into consideration in the study of macroeconomic equilibrium with rationing and its representation by means of *IS–LM*.

II THE MACROECONOMIC CONFIGURATIONS

Before we explain the derivation of the *IS* and *LM* curves, it will aid exposition if we first describe the various macroeconomic configurations which might result in the labour market and the market for consumption goods. The hypothesis that wages are rigid at the predetermined level, $\bar{w}$, applies only in the presence of unemployment. Conversely, wages are permitted to adjust upwards so as to eliminate the possibility of excess demand for labour. In conditions of full employment the wage must thus be considered as endogenous, as well as notional supplies, Q^s and C^s which depend on wages. There are then two cases to be distinguished, according to the conditions prevailing in the consumption goods market which determine the level of employment in this sector.

A. Full Employment and Excess Demand for Consumption Goods

When the sales constraint is not binding in the consumption goods sector, the economy in general experiences an excess demand for consumption goods and generalised inflationary pressure. The condition for full employment, which implicitly defines the equilibrium wage rate, $\hat{w}$, may be written as:

$$N_q^*(\underset{(-)}{\hat{w}}, \underset{(-)}{r}) + N_c^*(\underset{(-)}{\hat{w}}) = L \tag{15}$$

which also provides the function $\hat{w}(r)$ whose derivative $\hat{w}'_r$ is obtained by differentiation of (15):

$$\frac{d\hat{w}}{dr} = \frac{-\partial Q_q}{F'_N \partial r} \Bigg/ \left(\frac{\partial N_q^*}{\partial w} + \frac{\partial N_c^*}{\partial w} \right) \tag{16}$$

of the form $-[(-)/(-)] = (-)$. The function $\hat{w}(r)$, decreasing in r, is therefore equivalent to (15) as an expression of the full employment condition in an inflationary situation.

B. Full Employment and the Sales Constraint: Underconsumption

It is equally possible, *a priori*, that full employment coincides with a sales constraint which corresponds to the conditions of underconsumption specified in the traditional equilibrium model with rationing (Muellbauer and Portes, 1978). The demand for labour by firms producing consumption goods is then a constrained demand $\tilde{N}_c(C^d)$ where $N(y, r)$, which gives the following equation as the condition for full employment:

$$N_q^*(\underset{(-)}{w}, \underset{(-)}{r}) + \tilde{N}_c(\underset{(+)}{y}, \underset{(-)}{r}) = L \tag{17}$$

defining the equilibrium wage $\tilde{w}(y, r)$ whose derivatives may be derived by differentiation of (17) as:

$$\frac{d\tilde{w}}{dr} = -\left[\frac{1}{F'_N}\frac{\partial Q_q}{\partial r} + \frac{1}{\phi'_N}\frac{\partial C^d}{\partial r}\right] \Big/ \frac{\partial N_q^*}{\partial w} \tag{18}$$

$$\text{of the form } -\frac{(-)}{(-)} = (-)$$

$$\text{and } \frac{d\tilde{w}}{dy} = -\frac{1}{\phi'_N} C'_y \Big/ \frac{\partial N_q^*}{\partial w}$$

$$\text{of the form } -\frac{(+)}{(-)} = (+)$$

The function $\hat{w}(\underset{(+)}{y}, \underset{(-)}{r})$ is an equivalent expression to the labour market equilibrium given in equation (17).

C. The Classification of Macroeconomic Configurations

By consideration of the various combinations of conditions prevailing in the labour market and the consumption good market, it becomes possible at this stage to identify four types of macroeconomic configuration (see Table 4.1), each characterised by an expression for consumption and the wage.

It is important to notice that at present this classification only deals with potential situations whose realisation as equilibrium with rationing has yet to be established. This appears clearly when one proceeds to the graphical presentation of this classification by subdivision of the (y, r) space.

1. *The Equilibrium Frontier in the Consumption Goods Market* (CC')

In conditions of unemployment this condition may be written

$$C^s(\overline{w}) = C^d(y, r) \tag{19}$$

Table 4.1 *The four macroeconomic configurations*

Goods market \ Labour market	Unemployment	Full employment
Excess supply	Keynesian unemployment $\begin{cases} C = C^d(y, r) \\ w = \bar{w} \end{cases}$	Underconsumption $\begin{cases} C = C^d(y, r) \\ w = \tilde{w}(y, r) \end{cases}$
Excess demand	Classical unemployment $\begin{cases} C = C^s(w) \\ w = \bar{w} \end{cases}$	Inflation $\begin{cases} C = C^s(w) \\ w = \hat{w}(r) \end{cases}$

which may be represented by a curve CC' of positive slope

$$\frac{dy}{dr} = -\frac{C'_r}{C'_y} \text{ of the form } -[(-)/(+)].$$

In conditions of full employment this becomes

$$C^s(\hat{w}) = C^d(y, r) \tag{20}$$

which is also equal to $C^s(\tilde{w})$ and equivalent to

$$\tilde{w}(\underset{(+)}{y}, \underset{(-)}{r}) = \hat{w}(\underset{(-)}{r})$$

whose differential makes possible the calculation, with the use of the obvious notation for partial derivatives, of

$$\frac{dy}{dr} = \frac{C'_w \hat{w}'_r - C'_r}{C'_y}$$

a positive expression with slope greater than $-C'_r/C'_y$.

2. *The Full Employment Frontier* (LL')

The full employment frontier derived here corresponds to the given value of the wage, $\bar{w}$. When the sales constraint is binding the frontier emerges simply from the equation

$$\bar{w} = \hat{w}(r) \tag{21}$$

satisfied for the unique value $\hat{r} = \hat{w}^{-1}(\bar{w})$. On the contrary, in conditions of excess supply of consumption goods the full employment frontier with $\bar{w}$ fixed becomes:

$$\bar{w} = \tilde{w}(y, r) \tag{22}$$

with slope

$$\frac{dy}{dr} = -\frac{\tilde{w}'_r}{\tilde{w}'_y} \text{ of the form } -[(-)/(+)].$$

Note that, using the same notation, the equilibrium frontier in the consumption goods market (20) becomes

$$\frac{dy}{dr} = \frac{\hat{w}'_r - \tilde{w}'_r}{\tilde{w}'_y} < -\frac{\tilde{w}'_r}{\tilde{w}'_y}$$

because $\hat{w}'_r$ is negative. This determines without ambiguity the respective positions of the frontiers just identified and assures the existence of four distinct regions as represented in Figure 4.1. It should be recalled that the division of Figure 4.1 is based on variables which are endogenous to macroeconomic equilibrium, so they must be considered again as representing potential situations and not the equilibria with rationing previously defined, as in the traditional approach to equilibrium with rationing. It is thus necessary to proceed to the definition of the possible positions of equilibrium.

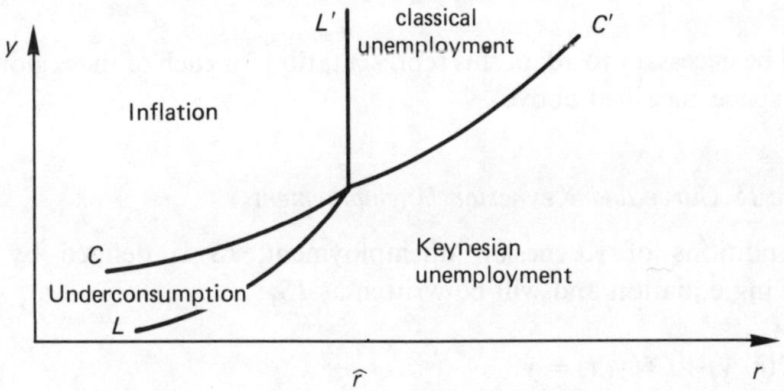

Figure 4.1 *Classification of macroeconomic configurations*

III *IS–LM* CURVES AND EQUILIBRIUM WITH RATIONING

Before showing how the *IS* and *LM* curves can help to define equilibria with rationing for the model under consideration, it should be recalled that there are two possible alternative formulations that may be used to generalise the *IS–LM* scheme to conditions of disequilibrium. The first approach retains the basic features of the traditional framework by constructing an 'aggregate quasi-demand' curve from an *IS–LM* model, and extends it to conditions of inequality between the value of aggregate demand and the value of income created. This perspective leads to the derivation of an 'aggregate effective quasi-demand' curve (Henin, 1982).

The alternative formulation retains a much stronger equilibrium condition expressed by the *IS* curve and attempts the formulation of equilibrium with rationing in terms of the intersection of equilibrium with rationing in terms of the intersection of the *IS* and *LM* curves. In this perspective the *IS* relation expresses the mechanism which equilibrates effective savings and investment. This generalises the usual definition to the extent that these values can be affected by rationing experienced by agents. The analysis which follows adopts this second orientation.

A. Derivation of the *IS* Curve

The equation for the *IS* curve, expressing the equalisation of realised investment and effective saving, can be written in the general form:

$$I(r, w) + \mathrm{Min}[C^s(w), C^d(y, r)] = y \tag{23}$$

It will be necessary to adapt this representation for each of the regions of (y, r) space classified above.

1. *The IS Curve and Keynesian Unemployment*

In conditions of Keynesian unemployment, *IS* is defined by the following equation and will be written as IS_1:

$$I(r, \bar{w}) + C^d(y, r) = y \tag{24}$$

whose differential allows us to determine the slope as:

$$\frac{dy}{dr} = \frac{(I'_r + C'_r)}{(1 - C'_y)}$$

where the obvious notation is adopted for the partial derivatives. The IS_1 curve corresponds to the traditional *IS* curve.

2. *The IS Curve in Conditions of Classical Unemployment*

In conditions of Classical unemployment, the IS_2 curve is defined by the equation

$$I(r, \bar{w}) + C^s(w) = y \tag{25}$$

which implies a slope of

$$\frac{\mathrm{d}y}{\mathrm{d}r} = I_r'$$

IS_2 is thus of lesser slope that IS_1, due to the absence of the multiplier effect and variation in consumption.

3. *IS and Underconsumption*

When there is a underconsumption with full employment and the sales constraint is binding, the curve IS_3 is defined by the equation

$$I(r, \tilde{w}) + C^d(y, r) = y \tag{26}$$

with $\tilde{w} = \tilde{w}(y, r)$, which allows derivation of the following expression for the slope of IS_3:

$$\frac{dy}{dr} = \frac{I_r' + C_r' + I_w' \tilde{w}_r'}{1 - C_y' - I_w' \tilde{w}_y'} \tag{27}$$

With respect to the slope of IS_1, that is the case of Keynesian unemployment, it may be remarked that the numerator and the denominator are diminished by a term including I_w', representing the impact of the wage rate on the value of investment. I_w' is negative if the absolute value of the elasticity of the volume of investment with respect to the wage is large (greater than one). In this case the slope of IS_3 is reduced relative to the slope of IS_1, but remains positive as long as the direct effects dominate, which may be considered as the general case.

4. *IS in Inflationary Conditions*

The equation for the *IS* curve under inflation, identified as IS_4, may be written

$$I(r, \hat{w}) + C^s(\hat{w}) = y \tag{28}$$

with $\hat{w} = \hat{w}(r)$ and slope

$$\frac{dy}{dr} = \{I_r' + (I_w' + C_w')\,\hat{w}_r'\}$$

For negative I'_w, or positive, but not dominating C'_w, and since $\hat{w}'_r$ is itself negative, the slope of IS_4 is much greater in absolute value than the slope of IS_2 (Classical unemployment). Yet, in general, the coefficient of dy is relatively greater than in conditions of underconsumption (disappearance of the multiplier), while the coefficient of dr is generally lower because the amplifying effect C'_r disappears, and the effect of $C'_w\,\hat{w}'_r$ is of opposite sign. In the diagram we thus adopt the case in which the slope of IS_4 lies between that of IS_2 and that of IS_3.

5. *The Economy's IS Curve*

The continuity of the function (23) and the definition of the wage at the frontiers of the different classifications gives the *IS* curve of the economy as the branches IS_1 to IS_4, or at least a part of them.

When the price of the consumption good is fixed, and despite the flexibility of wages at full employment, there is nothing to guarantee that the point *W*, representing the intersection of *LL'* in full employment with fixed wages and *CC'*, the goods market equilibrium, may be attained, or that it satisfies the *IS* condition. Thus, if we write $E(y, r)$ for the function of excess saving $E = y - C - I$, there are three cases that can be distinguished according to the value of this function at point *W*.

(a) The Case of the System with Appropriate Prices If the *E* function disappears at *W*, then *IS* passes through this point, which may be represented as in Figure 4.2. In these conditions neither an underconsumption equilibrium nor a classical unemployment is possible.

(b) The Case of Non-zero Excess Savings at W If excess saving, E_w, is positive at the point of full equilibrium, *W*, the *IS* curve for the economy will necessarily cut *CC*' southwest of *W*, as in Figure 4.3(a). On the other hand, negative excess saving E_w implies the case represented in Figure 4.3(b). Note that the *IS* curve may never be represented simultaneously by branches of the type IS_2 (classical unemployment) and IS_3 (underconsumption).

B. Derivation of the *LM* Curve

The definition of the *LM* curve as a series of equilibrium points for the supply and demand for money, does not present the same difficulty of interpretation that we experienced in the case of the *IS* curve. Under the hypotheses of our model the *LM* equation expresses the equality

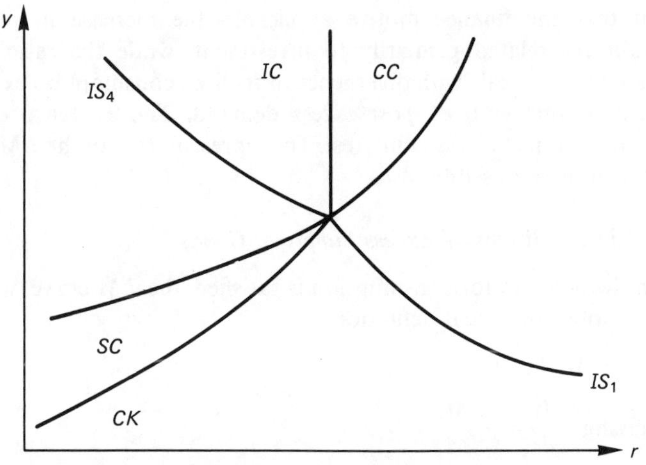

Figure 4.2 The IS curve with the appropriate price system

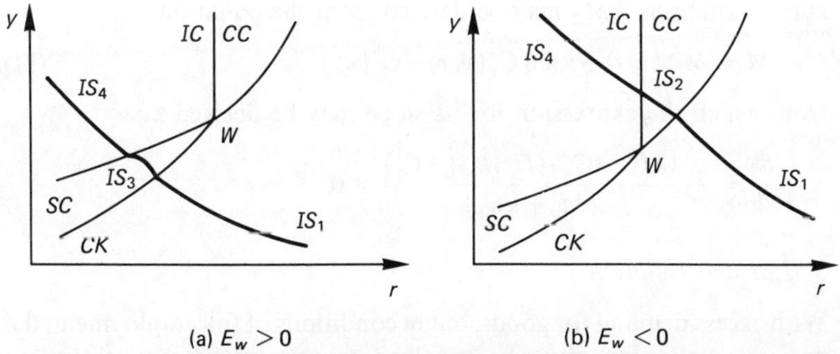

Figure 4.3 The IS curve for the economy

between the effective supply and effective demand for money, or

$$\bar{M} = \tilde{M}^d = M^*(y, r) + k(r)\,\mathrm{Min}\{C^d(y, r) - C^s(w), 0\} \qquad (29)$$

where $k(r) = \gamma/\{ra(\beta+\gamma)\}$ is the ratio coefficient which results from the maximisation problem faced by the household. The extension of the traditional *LM* curve is achieved by the introduction of a ratio term for the disequilibrium observed in the goods market, which is not too dissimilar to the Keynesian discussions of the 'finance motive' (Tsiang, 1966; Bramoulle, 1981). This similarity remains limited, however, to the extent that the finance motive applies to the increase in planned expenditures related primarily to investment, while the ratio effect indicated above deals with divergence of realised consumption expenditures, and thus with *ex post* excess demand. The existence of this similarity is none the less of interest. The representation of the *LM* curve comprises three possible cases.

1. *LM in Conditions of Excess Supply of Goods*

When the demand for consumption is satisfied, the *LM* curve, written, LM_1, implies the usual definition:

$$\bar{M} = M^*(y, r) \tag{30}$$

giving $\dfrac{dy}{dr} = -\dfrac{M'_r}{M'_y} > 0$

2. *LM and Classical Unemployment*

In conditions of excess demand for goods and unemployment, the *LM* curve written as LM_2 may be derived from the equation:

$$\bar{M} = M^*(y, r) + k(r)[C^d(y, r) - C^s(w)] \tag{31}$$

from which the expression for its slope may be derived as:

$$\frac{dy}{dr} = -\frac{\{M'_r + (C^d - C^s)k'_r + kC'_r\}}{\{M'_y + kC'_y\}} > 0.$$

3. *LM and Inflation*

With excess demand for goods, but in conditions of full employment, the previous definition must be modified to take into account the endogeneity of the wage rate and the endogeneity of the supply of consumption goods which this implies. The LM_3 curve then has the slope

$$\frac{dy}{dr} = -\frac{\{M'_r + (C^d - C^s)k'_r + k(C'_r - C'_w w'_r)\}}{(M'_y + kC'_y)}$$

Note that the additional term, the product of two negative derivatives and preceded by a minus sign, reinforces the negative terms of the numerator and increases the absolute value of the slope of LM_3 with respect to the slope of LM_2. We can thus give the following representation of *LM*, taking an excess supply of money at *W* as an example (Figure 4.4).

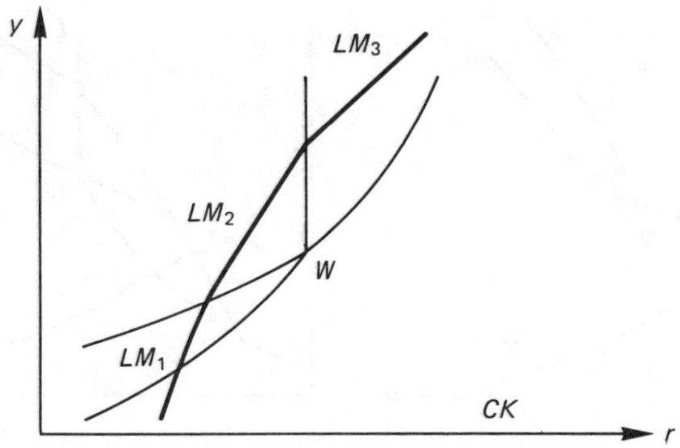

Figure 4.4 The LM curve with excess supply of money at W

C. Equilibria with Rationing

Having discussed the generalisation of the *IS* and *LM* curves required by the possibility of rationing of economic agents, we can now proceed, as in the traditional model, to consideration of the points of intersection of the *IS* and *LM* curves as representations of possible situations under given conditions, here understood as equilibrium with rationing.

1. *The IS–LM Representation of the Different Configurations*

By way of example, it is possible to describe the four different equilibrium classifications given above in terms of *IS–LM* equilibria.

The graphical representations given in Figure 4.5 easily suggest comparative static exercises which might be carried out on the basis of the present model. The realised equilibrium can in fact be made to coincide with the equilibrium at *W* by the appropriate shifts in the *IS* and *LM* curves, and thus of their constituent branches. In such an exercise we should keep in mind that the equilibrium positions of *LL'* and *CC'* in the *y*, *r* space are not invariant to the different economic policy instruments which may be applied. It is, however, important to note that manipulation of the current supply of money, $\bar{M}$, is one of the measures which may be applied with impact on the reference lines *LL'*–*CC'*.

2. *The IS–LM Model and the Definition of Equilibrium with Rationing*

The proposed model is not only meant to demonstrate how an *IS–LM* representation of equilibria with rationing can be achieved. It develops an original definition of equilibrium with rationing within an *IS–LM*

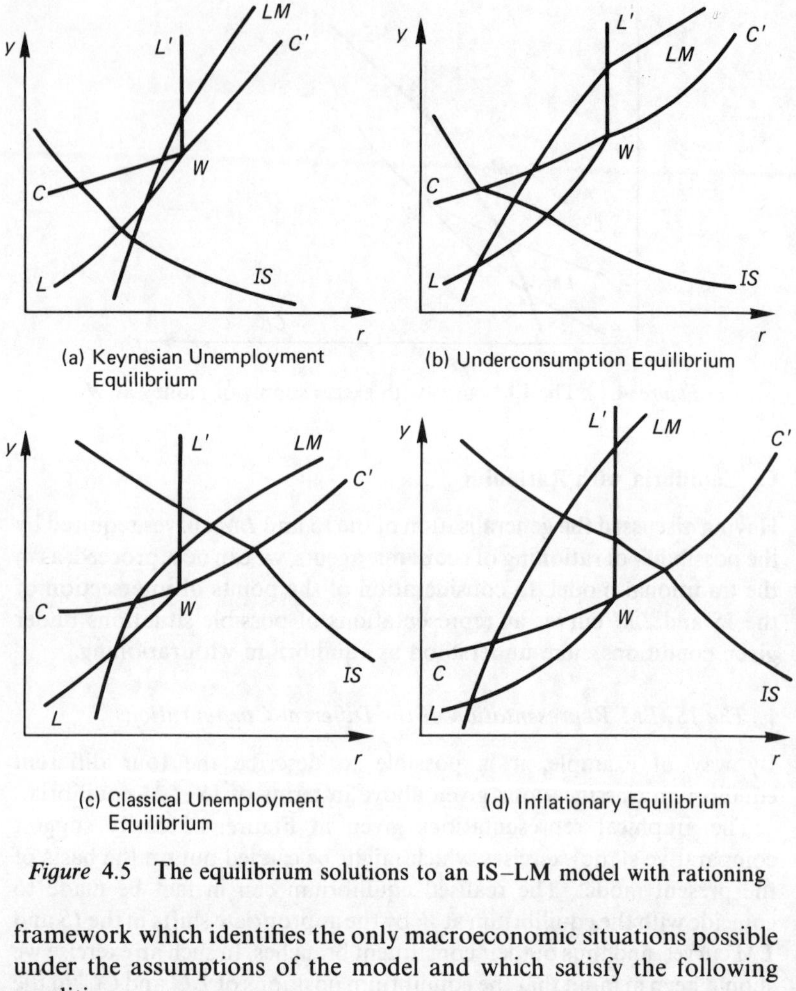

Figure 4.5 The equilibrium solutions to an IS–LM model with rationing

framework which identifies the only macroeconomic situations possible under the assumptions of the model and which satisfy the following conditions:

(1) Firms maximise profits in the short and the long run, taking into account given expectations and rationed sales in the consumption goods market.
(2) Consumers take their current decisions in order to maximise their inter-temporal utility, taking account of possible rationing of consumption goods.
(3) Effective investment equals *ex post* saving.
(4) Effective demand for money equals supply.

IV FINAL REMARKS

The reconstruction of the *IS–LM* model to take into account the different possible forms of rationing with which agents may be confronted in disequilibrium, leads us to a redefinition of macro-economic equilibria with rationing. Under the hypotheses of the model, it appears that a unique equilibrium will be normally attained and that it will be represented by one of the four possible classifications, or at their frontier. Without doubt, the results that we have obtained depend on the particular hypotheses that we have chosen, but we expect that the main results should be robust with respect to these hypotheses. In particular the hypothesis of upwardly flexible wages at full employment is not essential and could be replaced by an appropriate rationing scheme. The same applies to the investment goods sector which could be modified without damaging the basic correspondence between the *IS–LM* solution and equilibrium with rationing. Finally, it is a surprising illustration of the fruitfulness of the *IS–LM* framework that it lends itself so easily to generalisation, the change of hypothesis showing the relativity, not only of the framework itself, but of the very figure in which it has been confined for the last forty-six years.

Notes

1. The similarity between the present model and that set out in Henin and Michel (1982) is represented by its bi-sectoral fix-price flex-price structure.
2. Under the hypothesis of perfect foresight. With adaptive expectations, expectations themselves become variables determined by the past.
3. In addition, assume ϕ'_N, $F'_N \rightarrow \infty$ if $N \rightarrow 0$.
4. The end of period balances necessarily correspond to the exogenous supply of money.
5. J. Gabillon (1982) calls this 'forced hoarding'.
6. In addition we shall assume that $V'_q \rightarrow \infty$ for $Q \rightarrow 0$.
7. See Henin (1981, p. 721) for the hypothesis that current market conditions influence expected profit.

References

d'Autume A. (1980) 'Equilibres Non Walrasiens et Macroéconomie', Ph.D. Thesis, University of Paris II.

Benassy J. P. (1982) '*The Three Regimes of the IS–LM Model: A Non Walrasian Analysis* (Cepremap) April.

Bramoulle G. (1981) 'Demande de monnaie et déséquilibres de marché', in *Analyse du Déséquilibre* (Economica) pp. 173–204.

Danthine J. P. and Peytrignet M. (1981) 'Integration de l'analyse graphique IS–LM avec la théorie des equilibres à prix fixes: Une note pédagogique', in *Analyse du Déséquilibre* (Economica) pp. 115–31.

Gabillon J. (1982) *Un modèle de désequilibre avec fonction d'investissement et marché des titres* (Faculte des Sciences Economiques, Toulouse) Cahier no. 114.

Grandmont J. M. (1976) 'Théorie de l'équilibre temporaire général', *Revue Economique*, Décember, pp. 822–32.

Henin P. Y. (1981) 'Equilibres avec rationnement dans un modèle macro-économique avec décision d'investissement endogène', *Economie Appliquée*, no. 4, pp. 697–728.

Henin P. Y. (1982) *Sur quelques definitions de l'équilibre global: Un modèle pour deux paradigmes*, Document C.A.D. no. 60 (University of Paris I).

Henin P. Y. and Michel P. (1982) 'Equilibre avec rationnement dans une economie à deux secteurs prix fixes, prix flexibles', in *Croissance et accumulation en désequilibre* (Economica) pp. 45–80.

Hicks J. R. (1937) 'Mr Keynes and the "Classics"', *Econometrica*, April, in Critical Essays in Monetary Theory (Clarendon Press, 1967) pp. 126–42.

Hicks J. R. (1939) *Valeur et Capital*, trans. (Dunod, 1956).

Muellbauer J. and R. Portes (1978) 'Macroeconomic Models with Quantity Rationing', *Economic Journal*, December.

Snessens H. (1981) *Rationing Macroeconomics: A Graphical Exposition*, C.O.R.E. Discussion Paper 8129.

Tsiang S. C. (1966) 'Walras' Law, Say's Law and Liquidity Preference in General Equilibrium Analysis', *International Economic Review*, September.

Witte J. G. (1963) 'On Microfoundations of Social Investment Function', *Journal of Political Economy*, October.

Section III
The Foundations of the *General Theory*

5 Equilibrium and Probability: A Reinterpretation of the Methodological Foundations of the *General Theory*

Fausto Vicarelli

I INTRODUCTION[1]

Most of Keynes's interpreters have considered the analysis proposed in the *General Theory* as having no relation to the vision of capitalism which emerges from his earlier, fundamental works. This has created considerable and, in some instances, insuperable difficulties, both in understanding Keynes's message (his theory) and in the analysis of the functioning of the economic system (his method).

It is above all on this second aspect of the controversy that I would like to concentrate in this chapter.[2] The basic problem to which I would like to call attention is the use of the neoclassical concept of equilibrium in the interpretation of the *General Theory* and in the various attempts to formalise its main propositions. Given that even in the broadest sense, as used by F. Hahn,[3] this concept is rooted in the tradition of general equilibrium theory and thus in the deductive methodological framework of this approach, it is inevitable that those interpretations centred around this concept lead to a *rapprochement* between Keynes and Walras. In view of Keynes's background in Marshall this might seem to be something of a paradox, and in many senses it is. The fact remains that Keynes's challenge to the traditional theory on the highly delicate ground of its generality was bound to lead to comparisons with Walras's paradigm, which J. R. Hicks's works had introduced into the Cambridge citadel.[4]

But the most original feature of Keynes's vision of capitalism, that of a world in which expectations lie at the base of real and financial economic decisions, has proved difficult to interpret within the framework of neo-classical equilibrium. This is very apparent to J. R. Hicks and J. Tobin, the two economists who have paid most attention to the theoretical implications of Keynes's message. These difficulties have been recently explained and emphasised by Hicks,[5] while Tobin has had to accept the existence of different prices for the same capital goods.[6]

The *General Theory* is, however, independent of the concept of equilibrium, in the sense that it is founded methodologically on an analytical philosophy – the same as that which Keynes had already expounded in his *Treatise on Probability* – which is completely alien to the neo-classical notion of equilibrium. This philosophy enables Keynes, on the basis of his observations of aspects of capitalism he believes to be significant, to inductively derive conclusions logically connected to this reality. The degree of rational belief that we can grant to these kinds of conclusions, that is to say, their probability, has nothing to do with actual economic events. In its relation to the plan underlying the *General Theory*, the comparison between *ex ante* and *ex post* values, which it is impossible to avoid within an equilibrium approach, lies at a completely different level of analysis.

The powerful analytical ability which the *General Theory* derives from this method is that of explaining, at the highest possible level of abstraction, the forces which determine levels of income and employment at a given moment in time, without having to refer to time periods. Emphasising, as it does, the coexistence, at any given time, of decisions based on short- and on long-term expectations, this interpretation shows the incompatibility between Walrasian equilibrium, and so full factor employment, and Keynes's vision of capitalism.

II PROBABILITY, UNCERTAINTY AND EXPECTATIONS

'Between two sets of propositions, therefore, there exists a relation, in virtue of which, if we know the first, we can attach to the latter some degree of rational belief. This relation is the subject matter of the logic of probability.'[7]

The argument which I want to put forward, in a way that I hope to prove is not at all paradoxical, is that if, starting the *General Theory*, Keynes had recalled this point from his *Treatise on Probability*, interpretation of his principal work would have proceeded along very different lines from those assumed by the so-called neo-classical synthesis. In my opinion, the Keynesian definition of probability, applied to the *General Theory*, suggests significant points both of content and of method. The questions of content are centred around expectations and the way in which these make the *General Theory* into a theoretical expression of Keynes's vision of capitalism; the methodological points regard certain important aspects of the logical process whereby underemployment equilibrium is determined.

In both of these cases it is important to bear in mind the sense in which Keynes considers Probability as belonging to Logic. In the *Treatise on Probability* the terms 'certain' and 'probable' indicate the differing degrees of rational belief which differing levels of knowledge allow us to attribute to given propositions. Probability may thus appear to be something subjective. Keynes, however, is eager to point out that from a logical point of view this is not so: 'It [probability] is not, that is to say, subject to human caprice.'[8] Once the facts on which our knowledge is founded are given, the probability of a proposition is completely objective: 'the theory of probability is logical, therefore, because it is concerned with the degree of belief which it is rational to entertain in given conditions, and not merely with the actual beliefs of particular individuals which may or may not be rational'.[9]

The basis of probability, in other words, and the reason for its belonging to Logic rather than to Mathematics, lies in the fact that it establishes what rational beliefs may be derived from a set of facts with which one is directly aquainted.[10] As a consequence, the object of the theory of probability is the knowledge which can be obtained by argument from direct acquaintance with facts. The choice of the facts or propositions used to aquire knowledge by argument is naturally subjective, but 'the relations, in which other propositions stand to these, and which entitle us to probable beliefs, are objective and logical'.[11]

Ten years after the publication of the *Treatise on Probability*, in a review of a collection of studies by F. Ramsey, published posthumously,[12] Keynes reviewed his position in the light of criticism from the young philosopher who had so prematurely departed. Ramsey had criticised the approach taken in the *Treatise* on the basis of a line of thought which led him to make a distinction between 'human' and 'formal' logic. According to this argument, formal logic has as its object the rules of coherent reasoning. 'Human logic', on the other hand, consists of the analysis of certain 'useful mental habits' by means of which the human mind uses the information supplied by perception, memory and other channels to achieve knowledge. Although he believed Ramsey had not succeeded in distinguishing rational degrees of belief from belief in general, Keynes accepted that the concept could enrich probability theory:

> The application of these ideas to the logic of probability is very fruitful. Ramsey argues, as against the view which I had put forward, that probability is concerned not with objective relations or propositions but (in some sense) with degrees of belief, and he succeeds in showing that the calculus of probabilities simply amounts to a set of rules for ensuring that the system of degrees of belief which we hold shall be a consistent system. Thus the calculus of probabilities belongs to formal logic. But the basis of our degrees of belief – or the *a priori* probabilities, as they used to be called – is part of our human outfit, perhaps given us merely by natural selection, analogous to our perceptions and our memories rather than to formal logic. So far I yield to Ramsey – I think he is right.[13]

There is a significant echo of this admission in chapter 12 of the *General Theory*, dedicated to long-term expectations, where Keynes states that the state of long-term expectations depends not only on the most likely predictions but also on the 'confidence' attached to these. Economic decisions have to be taken, not in a context of risk, as in the case of repeated trials where probabilities can be calculted on the basis of frequencies, but rather in a context of uncertainty, characterised by a scarcity of information. 'Human logic' can thus help us in understanding the mechanisms which together go to determine the state of 'confidence', that is to say the complex of conditions to which economic actors attach fundamental importance in their decisions.

Recognition of the validity of Ramsey's criticism thus allows Keynes to enrich the essence of the approach of the *Treatise on Probability* when he comes to apply it. A note to chapter 12 of the *General Theory*[14] in which he states that 'very uncertain' should not be taken to mean 'very improbable' refers directly back to chapter 6 of the *Treatise*, which discusses the 'weight' of arguments whose probability is to be ascertained. Here the term 'weight' is used as a synonym for 'relevant knowledge' and is clearly distinct from the concept of probability:

> As the relevant evidence at our disposal increases, the magnitude of the probability of the argument may either decrease or increase according as the new knowledge strengthens the unfavourable or the favourable evidence: but something seems to have increased in either case – we have a more substantial basis upon which to rest our

conclusion. I express this by saying that an accession of new evidence increases the weight of an argument. New evidence will sometimes decrease the probability of an argument, but it will always increase its weight.[15]

As a result, the uncertainty which dominates expectations throughout the *General Theory* is expressed, in the language of the *Treatise*, in terms of scarcity of information, that is to say of the slim basis on which conclusions have to be based. Probability, on the other hand, lies at a different, independent level of analysis and remains solidly anchored to the concept of a logical relationship between premises and conclusions. The uncertainty of the elements which go to form expectations reduce 'confidence', but exert a neutral effect on probability and thus on the degree of rational belief which it is possible to assign to future events on the basis of their relationship with events which have actually been observed. The probabilistic approach to expectations, in the sense of the *Treatise*, is thus left unaffected by the importance the *General Theory* attaches to uncertainty.

This conclusion is a very important one, in that it allows us to take a new view of the significance of Keynesian theory with respect to the crucial role of expectations in explaining the marginal efficiency of capital and liquidity preference, two key pillars in Keynes's theoretical construction. On publication of the *General Theory* a review by J. R. Hicks[16] immediately grasped the strategic importance which Keynes attributed to expectations. What he emphasised, however, were the limitations and dangers of this approach. In his view, these limitations were implicit in the hypothesis of the invariancy of expectations with respect to events occurring, to use his own terminology, within the 'period' considered in the analysis. The dangers lay in the risk that in long-run applications the analytical effectiveness of the expectations method might 'peter out'.[17]

The neo-classical synthesis of Keynesian thought has not paid much attention to expectations, relegating these among the exogenous elements capable merely of shifting functional relationships which in all other respects are considered to be stable. The development of macro-economic theory along so-called neo-classical lines, has led, on the other hand, via the rational expectations paradigm, to the incorporation of this aspect of the Keynesian anomaly within the orthodoxy of Walrasian equilibrium. A line of interpretation of the *General Theory* which refers back to the Cambridge tradition accepts the significance of expectations but none the less considers these the least essential element in Keynes's construction, incapable of preventing traditional theory from reducing the most innovative features of his thought to the prevailing orthodoxy.[18]

The weakness of a theory based on expectations is alleged to consist of the lack of a link with objective elements and the consequently arbitrary nature of its assumptions and conclusions. Any attempt to explain the workings of the capitalist system without first identifying precise laws showing the tendencies of its forces towards objective conditions is, according to this view, wasted effort, or at any rate devoid of theoretical validity. In this sense, then, apart from questions of method, the resort to expectations is alleged to undermine the heuristic content of the *General Theory*.

If, however, we interpret expectations in the light of a Keynesian concept of probability, we discover that this criticism is unfounded. Let us consider, for example, the formation of the long-term expectations used in the calculation of the marginal efficiency of capital. Keynes begins – or rather he assumes that entrepreneurs begin – with the observation of a series of data which the market supplies on a regular basis. From these he derives a series of elements which can be used in evaluating the prospective return on an investment. Here we have exactly the same approach as that used in the *Treatise*: the knowledge of certain propositions supplied by the evidence is used to derive knowledge by argument of non-observable propositions on the basis of the logical relationship existing between the former and the latter.

The strength of this conception of expectations thus lies in the way the argument is based on the most objective possible datum, namely observed reality. The subjective factor exists: it lies, however, in the choice of the aspects of reality taken as a starting-point. This has nothing to do with the supposedly arbitrary nature of the conclusions; rather it consitutes the key point in the whole theory.

III VIRTUAL EQUILIBRIUM AT A POINT IN TIME

In his review of the *General Theory*, Hicks views Keynes's analysis in terms of expectations as a contribution to economic method: 'From the standpoint of pure theory, the use of the method of expectations is perhaps the most revolutionary thing about this book'.[19] At the same time, however, he sees limitations and dangers in the way Keynes argues from expectations. If we put these limitations and dangers at a purely methodological level, the problem we have to face up to is the meaning of Keynesian equilibrium, undoubtedly one of the most intricate questions in the confused mass of interpretative literature surrounding the *General Theory*.

Here again the leading role belongs to Hicks, the author of the *IS–LM* model, the paradigm which has polarised the interpretative debate, as well as the most recent and profound discussion of the subject.[20] Hicks, as we see in his writings in recent years,[21] has reconsidered the interpretative ability of his original model. In his recent 'explanation' of *IS–LM*, he devotes considerable space to the interpretative difficulties which arise when one reasons in terms of a time-period. It is on this point that I would like to concentrate my attention.

The idea of summarising the analytical content of the *General Theory* in *LS–LM* curves derives from an application of Walras's analysis of exchange to the Keynesian markets for goods, labour, money and bonds.[22] Hicks proves that the model can still be coherently applied when wages are given and when labour demand and supply are not in equilibrium and there is no difficulty in considering the price of goods as fixed. The complications arrive when it is necessary to identify the curves used to determine effective demand and employment, the basis for the *IS* curve. One of these curves showing the dependency of effective demand on employment can be identified immediately: in the *General Theory*, for any given level of investment, effective demand grows with the growth of employment as a result of increased consumption. The converse relationship, on the other hand, whereby employment depends on effective demand, is, in Hicks's view, difficult to identify, once one takes into account the time factor.

The fact that the realisation of production plans requires time, implies that within the period chosen as an objective of analysis (Hicks's 'week'), current employment is determined with respect to expectations of future demand. It cannot thus be considered a function exclusively of current demand unless it is supposed that the gap between production and current demand is the only factor involved in orientating the current input of labour. This hypothesis, Hicks observes, is an arbitrary one and cannot be assumed as a rule of conduct for entrepreneurs. It is unlikely that the latter's behaviour should be uninfluenced by what they expect to happen in future periods. In Hicks's view, however, taking account of successive periods makes it necessary to abandon an analysis based on single periods and to move towards Lindhal-style, sequential models of analysis, alien to the *IS–LM* approach.

There is one way to avoid these difficulties, namely to suppose that production plans are actually fulfilled, that is to say that current production is equal to effective demand. In conditions of equilibrium, when demand and production coincide, it is in fact reasonable to consider current demand as a reference point for labour input. The period within which equilibrium is achieved must not, however, be too short: it has to allow a minimum of time for the adjustment of plans to demand (not a 'week' but a 'year'). There is, in any case, a further problem concerning the equilibrium between the supply and demand for money as stock which underlies the *LM* curve. Here it is sufficient to bear in mind that the stock equilibrium has to be guaranteed for the whole period and that this implies the realisation of expectations within the period considered.[23] If, however, expectations are systematically achieved there is no longer any uncertainty, the principle underlying liquidity preference.

There is no way of escaping from this impasse without resorting to *ad hoc* hypotheses which are equally unsatisfactory.[24] It is thus natural to ask whether there might not be some other way, outside the equilibrium paradigm, of supplying a logical interpretation of the analytical message of the *General Theory*. As in the case of expectations, here too a solution can be found in an interpretation based on Keynes's concept of probability.

Let us concentrate our attention on the fundamental proposition contained in chapter 3 which sums up all the others proposed by the *General Theory*, namely that unemployment is a consequence of insufficient aggregate demand. In the light of the *Treatise*, unemployment should be seen as an observed reality, of which we have direct knowledge (a 'secondary' proposition in the language suggested to Keynes by W. E. Johnson). That aggregate demand is insufficient is a proposition known by argument (the 'primary proposition'). The explanation of the economic forces at work, given in the same chapter, is the logical relationship between the observation and the conclusion. In other words, an increase in investment leads to a (more than proportional) increase in income.

Here it is the increase in investment which constitutes the evidence on which to base our argument, while the increase in income is a conclusion drawn with a probability determined by the degree of rational belief which can be attributed to the conclusion. This probability, however, has nothing to do with the result effectively obtained in terms of income level. The conclusion indicated above could be derived with the highest possible degree of probability (that is to say, with certainty) and still fail to correspond to factual reality, which is influenced by a vast range of circumstances. The comparison between logical conclusions and factual reality is illegitimate and cannot constitute a decisive element in the evaluation of a theory. An illogical argument could lead to conclusions coherent with reality; this would not be enough, however, for us to grant it scientific respectability.

If we interpret the *General Theory* as an analysis of what happens within a given period of time, the comparison between *ex ante* values (conclusions by argument) and *ex post* values (factual reality) becomes inevitable, and the notion of equilibrium appears as the only way of making the comparison innocuous.[25] Although, on this ground, the *General Theory* authorises many ambiguities of interpretation, Keynes's authentic version, printed just one year after its publication, is very clear:

> The expected results are not on a par with the realised results in a theory of employment. The realised results are only relevant in so far as they influence the ensuing expectations in the next production period . . . Income on the other hand is realised result . . . Time relationship between effective demand and income incapable of being made precise . . . No definite relationship between aggregate effective demand at one time and aggregate income at some later time. This does not matter.[26]

Keynes's emphasis on the validity of his theory even in conditions of equilibrium is the most convincing argument that equilibrium is not required, that the theory is constructed outside an equilibrium framework of analysis. If we read chapter 3 of the *General Theory* without regard for the Marshall-style language in which it is written, we see clearly that what Keynes is aiming to do is to identify the forces on which income and production depend at a given point in time. Given that entrepreneurs decide production levels on the basis of their demand and price expectations,[27] it is the forces of demand, summed up in the propensity to consume and the marginal efficiency of capital, which influence the level of production. This proposition is independent of equilibrium. If, at a given point in time, aggregate demand should be in excess of production, this is nothing more, *ceteris paribus*, than one more element to bear in mind in the formulation of expectations and thus in production plans. Keynes warns us that to achieve an understanding of capitalism, we have to be willing to accept a high degree of abstraction in its analysis.

The logical model with which he represents us is based on the method of induction, as defined in the *Treatise on Probability*. It makes it possible to identify those forces which, at a given point in time – that is to say, independently of the passage of time – determine income and employment. The operation of these forces may be formalised in a mathematical model the determinacy of which confirms the logical nature of the process of induction. The solution to this model can be called 'equilibrium'. It is clear, however, that what we are dealing with here is a 'virtual equilibrium' in which all the magnitudes appear as *ex ante* values and in which expectations are an exogenous variable.[28] The comparison with the effective values of the magnitudes in question and verification of whether or not expectations are fulfilled implies a different level of analysis to which Keynes has no intention of devoting himself.

IV INCOMPATIBILITY BETWEEN EFFECTIVE DEMAND AND FULL FACTOR EMPLOYMENT

The interpretation of the *General Theory* as an analysis of the forces which at a given point in time determine income and employment, enables us to clarify an important point in Keynes's logical model, namely the meaning and consequences of the coexistence of short- and long-term expectations. Entrepreneurs' production decisions depend on short-term expectations concerning the return on sales on completion of the production process. Decisions to increase productive capacity depend on long-term expectations concerning the net return on investment. The functioning of the capitalist system is characterised by the fact that at any given time there are forces at work deriving from both kinds of decision.

The reference to the short and the long term in Keynesian expectations has nothing to do with Marshall's short and long period. Keynes's distinction refers to the time-horizon referred to in decision-making and not, as with Marshall, to phenomena occurring within periods of differing length. This approach places the analysis at a high level of abstraction and the maximum possible level of generality: all the real phenomena considered to be of significance can be taken into account at the same time. In this way we can talk in terms of an analysis in real time, not in the sense that the analysis claims to determine what happens with the passage of time, but in the sense that no phenomenon of relevance to action at a given point of time is ignored.

It is thus incorrect to attribute to the *General Theory* a method based on a short-term analysis in which rates of profit differ, as opposed to a long-term method in which the latter are uniform.[29] The question of whether or not current rates of profit are levelled belongs to that part of analysis in which *ex ante* and *ex post* values are compared, a problem into which Keynes does not intend to enter. From the logic underlying his analysis we may conclude, however, that the possibility of competitive forces achieving convergency towards a uniform rate of profit does not depend on the passage of time. There are basically two reasons for this, and these are not completely independent of each other. The circumstances, the systematic and the non-systematic forces, which oppose the working of competition are always in action, at any given point in time, theoretically with the same intensity. However much entrepreneurs may learn from experience, expectations concerning the future return on investment can never be reduced to observed reality. On this last point Keynes is very explicit:

> Express reference to current long-term expectations can seldom be avoided. But it will often be safe to avoid reference to short-term expectation, in view of the fact that in practice the process of revision of short-term expectation is a gradual and continuous one carried on largely in the light of realised results . . . Nevertheless, we must not forget that, in the case of durable goods, the producer's short-term expectations are based on the current long-term expectations of the investor; and it is in the nature of long-term expectations that they cannot be checked at short intervals in the light of realised results . . . Thus the factor of current long-term expectations cannot be even approximately eliminated or replaced by realised results.[30]

This passage clearly shows that Keynes is willing to concede that short-term expectations are essentially determined by realised results and may thus be definitively identified with these, but that he completely rules out the possibility of this also being so for long-term expectations.[31]

But then, if we take long-term expectations as exogenously given and assume that short-term expectations are realised (so that money interest rates are equal to the 'own rates'), the coexistence of both kinds of expectations makes a Walrasian formulation of the Keynesian system over-determined. Full employment is therefore logically impossible: it could be obtained only by chance.

Now, in the neo-classical synthesis of Keynes, models are actually determined. But we have to realise that the determinacy of the models sacrifices precisely that aspect of capitalist reality on which Keynes bases his interpretation of the forces in action at a given point in time. As we have seen, this consists of the coexistence of three distinct decision-making processes. Two of these are short-term decisions: decisions by owners of wealth about assets to hold; decisions by entrepreneurs who plan their combination of factors in the short-term horizon. The third one is a long-term decision: decisions by entrepreneurs to create demand for new capital goods[32] on the basis of their long-term expectations.

The exogenous nature of investment – that is to say, the way in which it depends on exogenous long-term expectations – constitutes, together with liquidity preference, the most important fruit of the heresy of the *General Theory* with respect to the dominant neo-classical theory. It is a fruit of Keynes's programme of research – the study of a monetary economy necessarily in conditions of uncertainty – and of his approach – to achieve his conclusions inductively, from the observed facts. Investment decisions may prove to be right or wrong: the *General Theory* tells us nothing about this. If they are wrong, the mistake will influence the formation of expectations at some future point in time. Even if they are correct, however, this does not mean that decisions will be repeated (for example, that the volume of investment or the rate of increase in capital stock will remain the same). There exists no 'normal' level of investment or 'normal' rate of accumulation or plant utilisation to which long-term expectations tend to comply.

It is here that we discover the analytical power of Keynes's inductive method as compared with the deductive method used in neo-classical equilibrium. To argue that in the course of time the rate of profit and investment will tend to certain 'normal' values thanks to the fact that the forces which hinder this trend will tend, in time, to be neutralised, implies the definition of postulates from which one deduces which forces are to be considered temporary and which permanent. In classical economic thought this distinction might have been justified. Here the theoretical and institutional environment, characterised by the identification of centres of savings with centres of investment, was completely different. Today, however, the distinction is purely arbitrary, facilitating the attempts of the neo-classical interpretation of the *General Theory* to transform long-term expectations into an endogenous variable.[33]

Should we conclude that Keynes was not interested in the long-run future of the economic system? 'In the long run we are all dead. Economists set themselves too easy, too useless a task if in tempestuous seasons they can only tell us that when the storm is long past the ocean is flat.'[34] This well-known sentence cannot be interpreted, as has been done so often, as a reply in the negative. If anything, it expresses a severe condemnation of tautological statements, devoid of an analysis of the causal links underlying current events.

Actually Keynes relegates the long-term prospects for capitalism to the last chapter of the *General Theory*, dedicated to the 'social philosophy' underlying the work. This is not a change in the method used – from an analysis of a point in time to one in the course of time. Rather it consists of an enunciation of normative propositions derived from the positive economic reasoning of the rest of the book. At the basis of this 'philosophy' of Keynes lies a deep dissatisfaction with an economic society incapable of providing full employment and in which the distribution of wealth and income is 'arbitrary and unjust'.

Even in the long run, Keynes sees the instability of the marginal efficiency of capital as the worst danger to full employment. He believes that a policy of low interest rates is a necessary but not a sufficient condition to achieve the desired volume of investment. It is from this view that he derives his policy of 'socialising' investment, an idea which comes to the surface in other parts of the *General Theory* and which he believes to be fully compatible with his free-enterprise vision of the economy:

> it seems unlikely that the influence of banking policy on the rate of interest will be sufficient by itself to determine an optimum rate of investment. I conceive, therefore, that a somewhat comprehensive socialisation of investment will prove the only means of securing an approximation to full employment; though this need not exclude all manner of compromises and of devices by which public authority will co-operate with private initiative . . .
>
> Whilst, therefore, the enlargement of the functions of government involved in the task of adjusting to one another the propensity to consume and the inducement to invest, would seem to a nineteenth-century publicist or to a contemporary American financier to be a terrific encroachment on individualism, I defend it, on the contrary, both as the only practicable means of avoiding the destruction of existing economic forms in their entirety and as the condition of the successful functioning of individual intiative.[35]

Keynes expresses just one doubt, confirming that he entrusts the long term to his normative hopes rather than to tendencies already at work: 'Is the fulfilment of these ideas a visionary hope? Have they insufficient roots in the motives which govern the evolution of political society? Are the interests which they will thwart stronger and more obvious than those which they will serve?'[36]

Notes

1. A previous draft of this paper benefited from useful critism from Profs. M. Amendola, M. Draghi, C. Gnesutta, J. Kregel, G. Martinengo, G. Nardozzi, A. Roncaglia, S. Parrinello, P. Sylos-Labini. Responsibility for any weaknesses or mistakes present in the text are mine alone.
2. As far as the content of Keynes's message is concerned, see my own *Keynes: the Instability of Capitalism*, Pennsylvania University Press, and Macmillan, 1984.
3. 'An economy is in equilibrium when it generates messages which do not cause agents to change the theories which they hold or the policies they pursue' – F. Hahn, *On the Notion of Equilibrium in Economics, An Inaugural Lecture* (Cambridge University Press, 1973) p. 25.
4. It is sufficient to observe that Hicks's review of the *General Theory* is already centred around the legitimacy or otherwise of the use of the adjective 'general'.
5. See, in particular, J. R. Hicks, '*IS–LM*. An Explanation', in J. R. Hicks, 'Money, Interest and Wages', *Collected Essays in Economic Theory*, vol. II (Oxford: Blackwell, 1982).
6. J. Tobin, 'A General Equilibrium Approach to Monetary Theory', *Journal of Money, Credit and Banking*, February 1969.
7. J. M. Keynes, *Treatise on Probability*, 1921, in *Collected Writings of J. M. Keynes CW*, VIII: pp. 6–7.
8. *CW*, VIII: p. 4.
9. Ibid. p. 11.
10. Keynes's conception of probability is thus a much broader one than that based on the statistical frequency of a phenomenon. Keynes, recalling the evolution of philosophical and mathematical thought on probability, emphasises how the dominance of frequency-based theory has restricted the application of probabilistic theory to repeatable events, identifying probability with its quantitative measure. There can be no doubt that economists are familiar precisely with this frequency-based approach, and that they nearly always reason in terms of probability distributions attaching economic significance to means, variance etc. The *Treatise on Probability* calls for a broadening of conceptual horizons, inviting economists to reason in terms of the logical relationship between direct and indirect knowledge.
11. *CW*, VIII.
12. J. M. Keynes, *Essays on Biography*, *CW*, X.
13. *CW*, VIII: pp. 332–9.
14. J. M. Keynes, *The General Theory of Employment, Interest and Money*, *CW*, VII: p. 148.
15. J. M. Keynes, *Treatise on Probability*, p. 77. On this line, see E. R. Weintraub, 'The 4,827th Reexamination of Keynes' System', chap. 3, in E. R. Weintraub, *Microfoundations* (Cambridge University Press, 1979).
16. J. R. Hicks, "Mr Keynes's Theory of Employment", *Economic Journal*, June 1936; 3, also in 'Collected Essays', in *Economic Theory*, vol. II, Blackwell, Oxford, 1982.
17. In order to understand the effective importance of these comments on expectations, it should be borne in mind that Hicks was interpreting the

General Theory in the light of G. Myrdal's approach. The latter's method, based on the distinction between *ex ante* and *ex post*, has been reviewed by Hicks ('A Review of Myrdal', in *Collected Essays*). See, on this point, J. A. Kregel, 'Microfoundations and Hicksian Monetary Theory', in *De Economist*, vol: 130, no. 4 (1982).

18. See, in particular, P. Garegnani, 'On a Change in the Notion of Equilibrium in Recent Work on Value. A Comment on Samuelson', in M. Brown, K. Sato and P. Zarembka (eds) *Essays in Modern Capital Theory* (Amsterdam, North-Holland, 1976).
19. J. R. Hicks, 'Mr. Keynes' Theory of Employment', p. 86.
20. J. R. Hicks, 'Mr Keynes and the "Classics": A Suggested Interpretation', in *Econometrica*, January 1937; and J. R. Hicks, '*IS–LM*, an Explanation'.
21. See in particular, J. R. Hicks, *The Crisis in Keynesian Economics* (Oxford: Blackwell, 1974), and J. R. Hicks, *Causality in Economics* (Oxford: Blackwell, 1979).
22. See J. R. Hicks, '*IS–LM*. An Explanation', pp. 320–1.
23. See J. R. Hicks, *Capital and Growth* (Oxford University Press, 1965).
24. See J. R. Hicks, '*IS–LM*. An Explanation', pp. 329–30.
25. That Keynes's method of expectations has nothing to do with the analysis of the Swedish school has been argued very lucidly by J. A. Kregel, in 'Economic Methodology in the Face of Uncertainty: the Modelling Methods of Keynes and the Post-Keynesians', *Economic Journal*, June 1976.
26. J. M. Keynes, *CW*, XIV: pp. 179–80. The passage is contained in a series of notes with the significant title 'ex-post and ex-ante', prepared by Keynes for his lectures in 1937.
27. If we assume perfect competition, individual firms' expectations can only be based on the expected market price. See, on this point: S. Parrinello, 'The Price Level Implicit in Keynes' Effective Demand', *Journal of Post-Keynesian Economics*, Autumn 1980; and C. Casarosa, 'The Microfoundations of Keynes's Aggregate Supply and Expected Demand Analysis', *Economic Journal*, March 1981.
28. F. Hahn's 'conjectural' equilibrium seems the closest concept to what is meant here by 'virtual' equilibrium. See F. Hahn, 'On Non-Walrasian Equilibria', *Review of Economic Studies*, February 1978. It seems to me that the logical approach is fully coherent with the concept of 'contemporary causality', recently proposed by Hicks (see J. R. Hicks, *Causality in Economics*) and used to conduct his 'explanation' of the *IS–LM* model. But the avoidance of any form of period analysis makes it possible to keep here faith with Keynes's principle of given expectations.
29. There is an interesting discussion of this point in A. Vercelli, 'Equilibrio e disequilibrio nella Teoria Generale di Keynes: il Ruolo dei salari monetari e le difficoltà di un metodo di puro equilibrio', in A. Graziani, C. Imbriani and B. Jossa (eds), *Studi di Economia Keynesiana* (Liguori, Naples, 1981).
30. J.M. Keynes, *General Theory*, pp. 50–51.
31. There is a clear contrast here with the theory of rational expectations, developed over the last ten years on the basis of contributions by R. E. Lucas. In its most general formulation this theory is based on the hypothesis that decision-makers' subjective probability distribution with respect to the

future values of variables coincides with the objective distribution, based on the information supplied by the model. As a result, any systematic gap between forecasts and reality has to be identified and explained. For Keynes, on the other hand, while decision-makers' forecasts are assumed to be logical, the probability of the conclusions (long-term expectations) has nothing to do with whether the events actually happen (as pointed out in note 10 above, Keynes's concept of probability is not measured in terms of the frequency of events). In this view it is the lack of systematic errors which deserves an explanation.

32. The price of existing capital goods is assumed to be the same as that of newly produced capital goods. It might be objected that this is not completely correct, in that existing goods are used in the current phase of production whereas newly produced goods are employed only in a subsequent phase. If this were thought necessary, it would be possible to take account of this distinction introducing a separate price for newly produced goods, thereby following Keynes. Given, however, that there is a necessary relationship between these two prices (in equilibrium the difference might be equivalent to the price of services for a single productive phase), this would not change the substance of the argument. If, on the other hand, one accepts the hypothesis of J. Tobin's general equilibrium model (J. Tobin, 'A General Equilibrium Approach'), namely that the two prices are completely independent, one arrives at different conclusions. For a critique of this approach, see C. Gnesutta, 'Equilibrio del conto capitale e meccanismo di trasmissione degli impulsi monetari', in F. Vicarelli (ed.), *La Controversia Keynesiana* (Il Mulino, Bologna, 1974).
33. The impossibility of reducing long-term expectations to past and present events is upheld with force by J. Tobin in his critique of the theory of rational expectations. See J. Tobin, *Asset Accumulation and Economic Activity* (Blackwell, Oxford, 1980).
34. J. M. Keynes, *A Tract on Monetary Reform*, *CW*, IV: p. 65.
35. J. M. Keynes, *General Theory*, pp. 378–80.
36. *General Theory*, p. 383.

6 Keynes's *General Theory*: Foundations for a Heterodox Political Economy?

Jean Cartelier

The passage of time has led to the realisation that the veritable novelty of Keynes's ideas may not necessarily lie in those aspects of his work where it appears most obvious: that is, in the diagnosis of the causes, and the proposed remedies for the elimination, of persistent unemployment. Support for this statement may be found in the fact that the standard representations of these aspects of Keynes's work have all adopted the framework of traditional theory (Hicks, Patinkin and the modern theories of non-Walrasian equilibrium).

The greatest interest in Keynes's ideas, some fifty years after the publication of the *General Theory*, would seem to lie elsewhere, in the possibility that they offer as a basis for innovations in economic analysis *outside* the principal themes of the dominant theory. The *General Theory*, in fact, implied a sharp break from orthodox theory in three specific areas: the *units* of measure appropriate to political economy, the theory of *effective demand*, and of the *absence of adjustment*.

This triple rupture forms the basis of an economic heterodoxy in the sense that it justifies the elaboration of an alternative representation of the essential elements of economic activity. The first part of this chapter seeks to provide a simple framework which highlights the 'new horizons' offered by the *General Theory*.

While heterodoxy must, by definition, lie outside of the dominant theory, it need not necessarily be opposed to it. This is for two reasons. The first is that the investigation of non-*tâtonnement* analysis by general equilibrium theorists may lead to interesting results which may be compatible with the heterodox point of view. The second is the recognition that the problems which cannot be resolved within the heterodox framework are sufficiently serious to prohibit ostracism. After all, in scientific endeavour, heterodoxy is not a virtue in itself. The second part of the chapter discusses one of these problem areas: the determination of the rate of interest.

* * *

(1) By choosing 'to make use of only two fundamental units of quantity, namely, quantities of money-value and quantities of employment',[1] Keynes rejects in one simple sentence a fundamental postulate of orthodox theory: the existence of a 'nomenclature of goods', generally identifiable by means of their physical characteristics which are considered to be independent of any particular social framework. At the same time, Keynes eliminates the problems of the determination of the prices of these 'goods' (on the basis of another postulate, the law of one price) and the variation of real wealth over time (surplus and accumulation).

Such a radical departure was difficult for economists to accept. A general idea of the difficulty may be gained by reference to the work of B. Schmitt, a follower of Keynes who has done as much as anyone to emphasise this point, which none the less has still not eliminated the idea of real wealth. Yet it should be easy to see that none of the arguments put forward by Keynes in the *General Theory*, save, perhaps chapter 17, requires a specification of the physical characteristics of goods.

This point would have been sooner, and more widely, recognised had Keynes taken the trouble explicitly to call attention to the fact that money is the exclusive object of economic activity. The greater part of the task thus still remains to be accomplished.

(2) Giving pride of place to money, rather than to the nomenclature of goods, is not independent of the rules of the game formulated by Keynes under the name of the theory of *effective demand*. It is a question of the determination of the *initial magnitudes* with which economic activity will be concerned. In the *General Theory* these magnitudes are quantities of employment but, for a given W, they can also be expressed in terms of money.

The only economic agents involved in the determination of these initial magnitudes are the *entrepreneurs*. For Keynes this was such an obvious expression of the world in which he lived as to preclude further explanation. *The initial magnitudes are set by the entrepreneurs as they think best*. This seems to be the most precise statement of the principle of effective demand. Besides being precise, it has the advantage of highlighting the absence of any co-ordination or interaction, among entrepreneurs or between them and other agents. The question of whether it is possible to give a rational explanation for entrepreneurs' decisions, or whether it is sufficient simply to note their volatility, is of secondary importance with respect to their essential characteristic: *the absence of any objective interaction prior to the taking of decisions.*

However, since Keynes was addressing himself to professional economists he developed his argument in terms of economic calculation. Three elements of rational calculation are suggested in the *General Theory*: effective demand, formally speaking (chapter 3); the equalisation of the marginal efficiency of capital and the rate of interest (chapter 11); and the equalisation of own rates of interest (chapter 17). It is possible to give a unique and explicit expression to these three elements which will help us to clarify the problems that have to be resolved.

At this stage it may be useful to reintroduce the existence of goods in order to demonstrate more clearly the reasons why their particular physical characteristics may be neglected.

A ONE-GOOD ECONOMY

Consider an economy with one single good (wheat) in which entrepreneurs determine the quantity of wheat that they will advance in support of current production. The following two factors are presumed given and known:

(1) The entrepreneur's *state of expectation*, which may be represented by the relation between the *expected receipts* (written as d) and the quantity of wheat advanced. These two magnitudes are expressed as quantities of wheat. This relation can then be written as $d = d(q)$. It applies to the jth entrepreneur considered, and only exists 'in his mind'. Following Keynes, we presume that $d' > 0$ and $d'' < 0$ (see Figure 6.1). The state of expectation extends over a unique period which is defined as separating the moment of decision, (t_0), and the moment when the results are expected, (t_1).

(2) *The cost function* linking the necessary costs of production to the quantities advanced. This is evidently a relation of the form $q = q$ (represented by the 45 degree line in Figure 6.1) since cost and the quantity advanced are one and the same thing.

It is thus possible to define a relation between the expected *net yield* ($y = d - q$) and cost: $y = y(q)$, where $y(q) = d(q) - q$, with $y' > 0$ and $y'' < 0$.

On the basis of these elements, it is easy to construct the relation between the *marginal efficiency of capital* (written e) and the initial quantity advanced. Recall that the marginal efficiency of capital is 'that rate of discount which would make the present value of the series of annuities given by the returns expected from the capital asset during its life just equal to its supply price' (*General Theory*, *CW*, VII, 1973, p. 135). The value of e must be such that $(d(q)-q)/(e)=q$, where $e(q)=(d(q)/q)-1=tg\alpha$ (see Figure 6.1).

As a result of the hypothesis concerning the state of expectations ($d'>0$ and $d''<0$), the marginal efficiency of capital is a decreasing function of the initial quantity of wheat advanced. This does not, however, permit the determination of the latter quantity, which would, in a certain sense, be equivalent to determining the amount of capital invested. As Keynes notes:

> I would, however, ask the reader to note at once that neither the knowledge of an asset's prospective yield nor the knowledge of the marginal efficiency of the asset enables us to deduce either the rate of interest or the present value of the asset. We must ascertain the rate of interest from other source, and only then can we value the asset by 'capitalising' its prospective yield. (p. 137)
>
> *General Theory*, *CW*, Vol. VII,

In other words, the givens (1) and (2) are not sufficient to give a rational explanation to the entrepreneurs' decisions lying behind the principle of effective demand. It is necessary to add:

(3) *The rate of interest*: without further explanation it will be supposed that the jth entrepreneur has an idea of the rate of interest: $i=i^*j$.

In such conditions the amount of wheat advanced by entrepreneurs will be that which satisfies:

$$y/q^*=(d(q^*)/(q^*))-1=i^*j.$$

This result, which emerges from the equalisation of the marginal efficiency of capital and the rate of interest, is the same as would be obtained by applying the principle of effective demand *stricto sensu* (chapter 3), if we make the correction of *discounting the expected receipts*. From the equalisation between the (discounted) expected receipts and the supply function we can, in fact, obtain:

$$(d(q))/(1+i^*j)=q=(d(q)/q)-1=i^*j.$$

Similarly, we note that the jth entrepreneur is indifferent between the possession of a quantity of wheat, q^*, now (in t_0) or a quantity $d^* = d(q^*)$, later (in t_1). The own rate of interest for wheat for the jth entrepreneur is thus $r_j = (d(q^*)/q^*) - 1$, which is also equal to i_j^*. Now, if i_j^* is interpreted as the own rate of interest of 'something' which is called money, then we immediately see that q^* is also determined by the principle of the equalisation of the own rates of interest formulated by Keynes in chapter 17 of the *General Theory*. *The three principles of determination for the initial magnitudes are thus formally equivalent: they constitute three expressions of a unique principle: effective demand.*

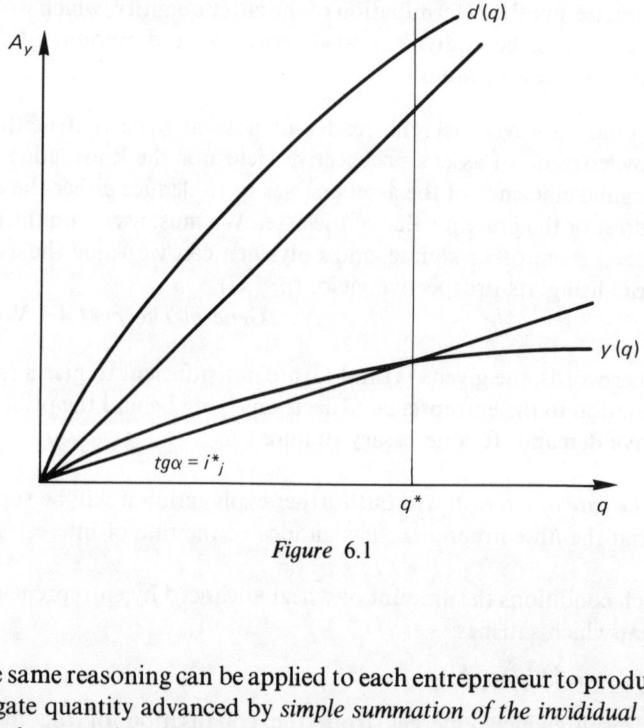

Figure 6.1

The same reasoning can be applied to each entrepreneur to produce an aggregate quantity advanced by *simple summation of the invididual* q_j^**'s.* While the quantities, q_j^*, may be summed, the relations expressing the state of expectations may not; the former are the objective expression of entrepreneurs' decisions, but the latter are purely subjective relations which can only be surmised. In fact, there is no *objective interaction* between the plans of the various entrepreneurs at this stage, since everything takes place 'in their minds'. It is impossible to discover any social co-ordination process, such as the *market*, at work at this level.

THE λ GOODS ECONOMY

The introduction of a second good (iron) or, more generally, of λ goods, will complicate the analysis slightly without affecting its basic conclusions. The complications arise from the multiplicity of possible production projects offered to the *j*th entrepreneur: one for each good in the case of simple production, an infinity in the case of joint production. However, this complexity is of little importance if the question to be resolved by the *j*th entrepreneur remains that of the initial magnitudes (employment or money), and if one leaves aside the problems of the choice of techniques and associated considerations. *It is possible to abstract completely from the diversity of use values, retaining only the entrepreneur's state of aggregate expectations and the form of the expected cost function.* This can be seen by a very rapid reference to a very simple example, that of two goods: wheat and iron.

Given the *j*th entrepreneur's expectations, which include the expected exchange ratio between wheat and iron, it is possible to represent, in the same diagram, the wheat-state of expectations and the iron-state of expectations, as well as the corresponding cost curves, on the condition that the unit of account in which the expected exchange ratios are expressed is the same (wheat, for example). Figure 6.2 shows the resulting curves of expected net receipts. The curve that is of interest from the point of view of the principle of effective demand is an envelope composed of 'the best' portions of each particular curve. In the limit it may be composed of an infinite number of curves corresponding to the multiplicity of possible production projects (it is given by the heavy line

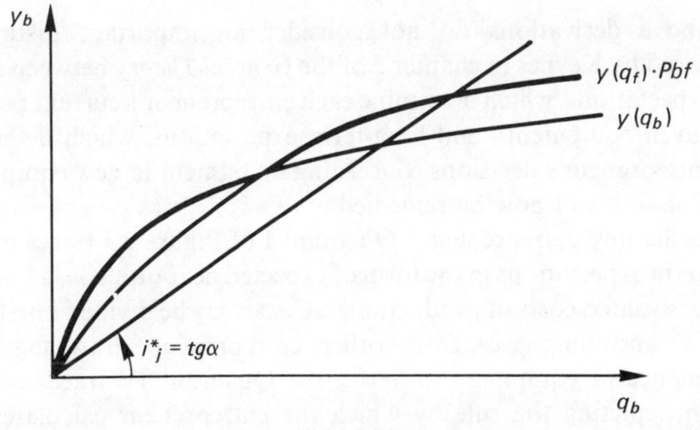

Figure 6.2

in Figure 6.2). Depending on the level of the rate of interest i_j^*, the jth entrepreneur will decide on the magnitude of his expenditure which will take the form, in terms of use value, of the production of wheat or iron.

While it is possible to abstract from use values, it is also possible to take them into account in order to apply the relation set out by Keynes in chapter 17, linking the own rates of return of the two goods and the expected variation in their exchange ratio. Let us suppose, for a given state of expectations, that the jth entrepreneur is indifferent between producing wheat and iron, irrespective of the rate of interest. This amounts to saying that the expected net revenue and the expected cost relations form an identity (all being expressed in terms of wheat). Given i_j^*, the jth entrepreneur will undertake productive expenditures amounting to q.

Now let us suppose that, everything else remaining the same, the jth entrepreneur expects an increase in the price of iron equal to $\dot{p}$ (in percentage change). In this case the curve $y_f = y_f\ (q)$ for iron is higher since costs (at current prices) have not changed, while expected receipts, expressed in wheat, are higher. To be precise,

$$y_f = (1+\dot{p})\, d\ (q) - q = rf = (1+p)\, d\ (q)/q - 1.$$

Since y_b is unchanged $r_b = (d(q)/q) - 1$ and thus $(1+r_b)\,(1+\dot{p}) = (1+rf)$, which is the relation set out by Keynes in chapter 17 of the *General Theory* (p. 223).

GENERALISATION OF THE PRINCIPLE OF EFFECTIVE DEMAND

The above derivations do not consider an important distinction introduced by Keynes in chapter 5 of the *General Theory* between short-term expectations, which determine each entrepreneur's current production (given equipment), and long-term expectations, which determine each entrepreneur's decisions concerning investment in new equipment. This omission will now be remedied.

Consider any entrepreneur j. Quadrant I of Figure 6.3 traces out his short-term expectations in the form of expected net output, m, a function of the associated costs of production, c. Costs may be divided into factor costs, z, and purchases from other entrepreneurs (raw materials, maintenance of equipment) a: $c = a + z$. Quadrant IV traces out the relation depicting the rule by which the entrepreneur calculates this division of his costs.

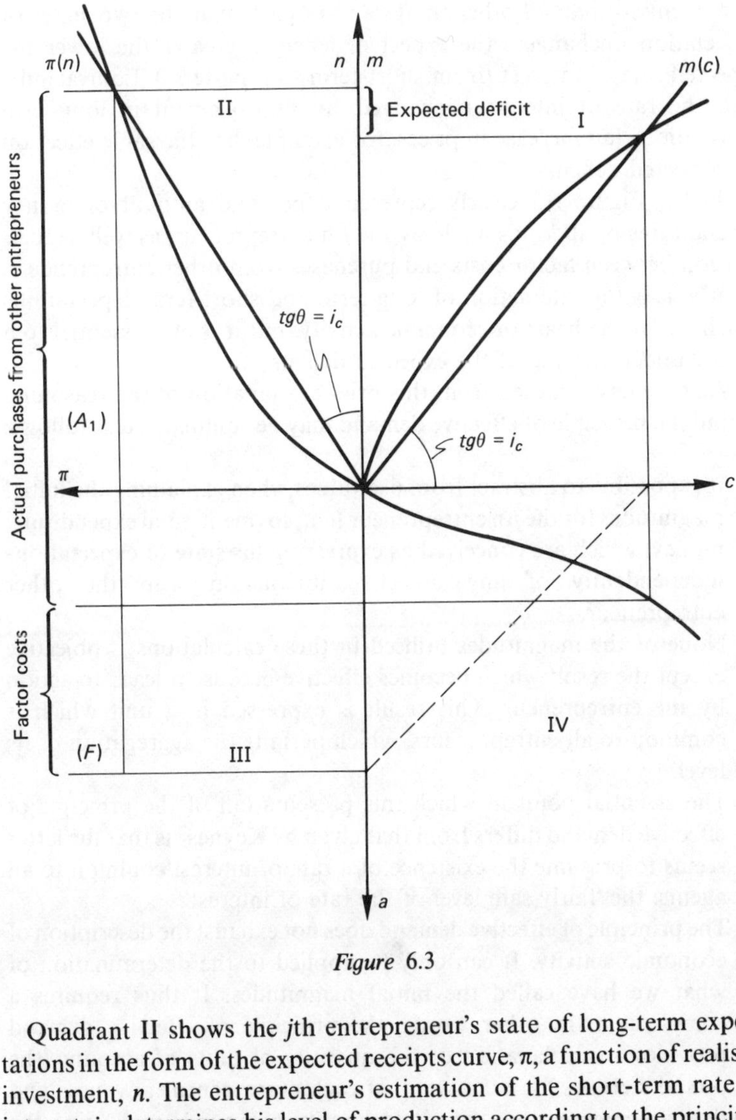

Figure 6.3

Quadrant II shows the *j*th entrepreneur's state of long-term expectations in the form of the expected receipts curve, π, a function of realised investment, *n*. The entrepreneur's estimation of the short-term rate of interest, i_c, determines his level of production according to the principle $m/i_c = c$. The estimate of the long-term rate of interest, i_λ, determines the level of investment, i.e., his purchase of new equipment consistent with $\pi/i_\lambda = n$.

The two decisions taken together lead to the determination of an expected short-term – i.e. in the current period – surplus or deficit. It can be recognised that, all other things and in particular the two states of expectation unchanged, the expected deficit is greater the lower the expected rate of interest (from short-term to long-term). Equivalently, with the rate of interest unchanged, an improvement in long-term expectations (an increase in prices, for example) has the same effect on the expected deficit.

Finally, Figure 6.3 clearly represents the total amount of money expenditures of all kinds made by the *j*th entrepreneur, as well as their division between factor costs and purchases from other entrepreneurs. Clearly, it is the interaction of long-term and short-term expectations which lies at the heart of economic activity, but it is also essential to a proper understanding of the expected deficits.

What we have learned from this brief examination of the reasoning behind the principle of effective demand may be summarised as follows:

(1) It is possible to abstract from use values when explaining the initial magnitudes for the *j*th entrepreneur (employment, total expenditure, money) which are conceived as expressing his state of expectations independently of any objective interaction with the other entrepreneurs.
(2) None of the magnitudes utilised in these calculations is objective except the result which becomes effective because it leads to action by the entrepreneur. This result is expressed in a unit which is common to all entrepreneurs, which permits the aggregation of its level.
(3) The essential point in which this presentation of the principle of effective demand differs from that given by Keynes[2] is that the latter seems to presume the existence of a rate of interest common to all agents: the 'fairly safe level of the rate of interest'.
(4) The principle of effective demand does not exhaust the description of economic activity. It can only be applied to the determination of what we have called the initial magnitudes. It thus requires a complement. In other words, the principle of effective demand provides an explanation of the quantity of units of account (the pound sterling, for example) that each entrepreneur advances and thus, by aggregation, the total quantity of pounds measuring the magnitude of the circular flow of income. Nothing has yet been said about the consequences of these economic actions, notably the eventual existence and functioning of some process of adjustment, or interaction between entrepreneurs. It is now necessary to examine these factors.

THE CIRCUIT WITHOUT ADJUSTMENT

The point of departure, the initial magnitudes, of the Keynesian circular flow process is thus given by effective demand. If there are λ entrepreneurs, effective demand may be represented in the form of a vector $h = z + a + n$, or $h + z + \bar{n}$, where $\bar{n} = a + n$.

It is possible, following Keynes, to *aggregate* these magnitudes since they are homogeneous, being expressed in the same units, and effective, being expressed in the market. It is useful, however, to recognise the new magnitude which appears in the form of the *total purchases from entrepreneurs* (A). This magnitude can be calculated by adding user costs (here equal to A_1) to expenditures by factors, by definition equal to expenditures on *consumption*. This magnitude can only be discovered by consideration of *ex post* effective demand as it is actually realised – that is to say, by the confrontation of expectations and results.

By construction, on the aggregate level, the relations between entrepreneurs are necessarily confirmed. It is not necessarily the same for factors. This is the aspect which Keynes was to call, in chapter 8, the fundamental psychological law ($C < F$).

By defining *aggregate income* as the sum of expenditures, it is obvious:

(1) that it is a category that only has meaning at the level of realised magnitudes;
(2) that it is inferior to the aggregate of actual expenditures which leads to a deficit equal to $F - C$ for entrepreneurs.

By definition, income is also the sum of investment A, and consumption. If saving is defined as the excess of *aggregate income* over consumption, it can be seen that *saving* is simply another name for investment: $A - C \equiv A_1$, because $C \equiv A - A_1$. However, if we consider saving as being only the excess of factors' incomes (F) over consumption (they are the only possible consumers), it can be seen that *saving is just another name for the entrepreneurs' deficit*, that is, the difference between their expenditures (investment) and their income, defined by Keynes as being equal to $A - F$:

$$A_1 - (A - F) \equiv F - C \equiv F - (A - A_1).$$

The determination of income is not, then, the result of a convergent process. It is brought about by means of the existence of a *difference which is not eliminated* and is the entrepreneurs' deficit, or, what comes to the same thing, the savings of factors. All of this evidently invalidates the usual interpretations of Keynes, both the traditional type based on the idea of the multiplier, and the newer variants set out in terms of temporary equilibrium.

The absence of any reference to what in fact constitutes an essential pillar of *orthodox economics, is not without a number of delicate problems.* Among the numerous questions which come to mind in light of the preceding discussion, there are two points which cannot be ignored: What are the consequences, or the effects, of non-adjustment? How is the rate of interest determined?

A. The Effects of the Deficit

The circular flow cannot be fulfilled, for on one side entrepreneurs incur deficits, while factors possess a surplus of an identical amount. The former are thus incapable of satisfying the condition, not explicitly mentioned by Keynes but none the less imperative, of making cash payment. It is thus possible that they may be unable to pay their debts.

On this basis is it necessary to consider that the economy might collapse in generalised bankruptcy in the absence of adjustment, or better, to admit that by construction the surplus of one side is available, under certain conditions, to settle the deficit of the other?

This aspect of the question is not discussed by Keynes. It does, however, suggest the possibility of introducing an element of realism into the analysis of the circular flow. With reference to Marx, we might call it the *formation of finance capital.* Keynes only identifies the point at which such additional research would be necessary. B. Schmitt has already provided a part of the necessary analysis elsewhere.

In this respect the essential problem to be resolved would seem to be how financial operations might be integrated into the analysis: are they a part of the circular flow as here defined? In this case the framework set out above is incomplete: it would be necessary to take into account, at the same time and at the same level, the realisation of financial operations. It might be supposed, for example, that entrepreneurs attempt to finance their *expected deficits* by selling financial assets at predetermined conditions, thus making it possible for factors and the financial system to cover a part of these deficits according to an extended version of the 'fundamental psychological law'. The difference is then taken up *ipso facto* by financial intermediation (B. Schmitt's composite element which closes the circuit).

Are they a distinct element? The doubt on this point is generated by the fundamental uncertainty concerning the status of *F*, which is clarified only by its realisation as *C*. In this case, the elimination would be analysed as the emergence of the magnitude *F–C* as finance capital, and the operations required to close the circular flow would be conceptually distinct (independently of the prior analysis of agents' behaviour, etc.).[3] The problems surrounding the determination of the rate of interest also lie at the heart of this question.

B. The Question of the Rate of Interest

As we have seen, Keynes established the principle of effective demand on the assumption that the rate of interest was already given and known. But if we go on to consider a multiplicity of possible expectations, the point raises analytical problems. We note that this is the only variable which remains to be determined, and that it is basically a question, as in the above discussion, of closing the system.

THE PROBLEMS OF THE KEYNESIAN THEORY OF THE RATE OF INTEREST

Keynes's conception (or conceptions) of the rate of interest is to be found in chapters 13 and 17 of the *General Theory*. The traditional exposition is well known: on the money market a demand for money, determined by liquidity preference, cuts the exogenous supply curve, determining the equilibrium level of the rate of interest. The analysis set out in chapter 17 has produced little comment, for it appears to be in contradiction to this presentation.

It will therefore be necessary to reconsider these questions briefly, keeping in mind the spirit of the framework set out in the first part of the present chapter.

A. The Approach of Chapter 17

The three elements which constitute the own rate of interest – net yield, carrying cost and the liquidity premium – are values expected by agents, in particular by entrepreneurs, at the moment of demand effective. In fact, this has been more or less implicitly taken into account in the above exposition since the equality of the own rates of interest expected by each entrepreneur for each good determined the amount of effective expenditures. In this framework, Keynes's basic proposition is clear: if there exists a good whose expected rate declines less (or not at all) when its expected quantity increases, this good will limit the quantity employment of all the others.

This proposition is general; it is necessarily contained in the theory of effective demand and, as such, does not produce spectacular results. What does give it strategic importance are *two complementary characteristics*:

(1) The good in question will in fact be the good whose *own rate of interest will represent the rate of interest*, thereby resolving the problem of the determination of i^*.
(2) The good in question will be endowed with particular properties which require that it be *a non-produced good which cannot be used in production.*

In this way the Keynesian system is closed. Two examples are given by Keynes: *land and money*. If we ignore the former we can see the route that Keynes followed to arrive at what he was to call *the monetary theory of interest*.

Keynes deduces the characteristic form of the curve of net revenues expected from the holding of money on the basis of the essential properties of money.

(a) We know that expected variations in the exchange ratios of goods affect the form of the $y_i(q_i)$ curves and thus, *ceteris paribus*, the entrepreneur's production decision. However, if the good in question is that *in which the exchange ratios are expressed*, its curve has no reason to be affected. Keynes does not make this argument; instead he refers to the essential property of a *zero elasticity of substitution*. The context clarifies the point: it is a question of an argument in which 'its utility [of money] is solely derived from its exchange-value, so that the two rise and fall *pari passu*, with the result that as the exchange value of money rises, there is no motive or tendency, as in the case of rent-factors, to substitute some other factor for it' (*CW*, VII: p. 231). It certainly would have been clearer to say that since money has a monopoly in effecting transactions and in representing the value of goods, there will never be a possibility of substitution.

(b) There is no question that this monopoly position is due to money's high *liquidity premium*, even if Keynes suggests that monopoly is not a sufficient condition (*CW*, VII: p. 236).

Another essential property, in Keynes's view, was *its zero carrying cost*. For all other goods the liquidity premium is diminished because greater holding of the good in question leads to proportionate increases in storage costs or losses due to physical deterioration. For money, there is no change with respect to quantity held for, 'beyond a certain point money's yield from liquidity does not fall in response to its quantity' (*CW*, VII: p. 233).

If we only consider these latter two elements as constituting the own rate of interest, holding increasing quantities of the good would not necessarily be accompanied by a decrease in the expected yields or, more exactly, *the expected net yield divided by the quantity is a constant*. The curve corresponding to such a good is then a straight line passing through the origin of slope *im* (see Figure 6.4). If money was a good 'like any other', except for these two above mentioned properties, effective demand would be indeterminate, for any point beyond q^* would be satisfactory, good *m* being the only one employed.

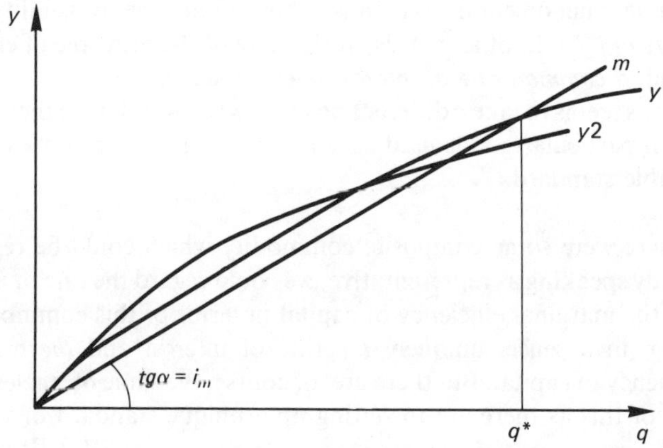

Figure 6.4

But this happy result is eliminated by the fact that money possesses a third property, that of being a *non-produced good* or, rather, according to Keynes, having *a zero elasticity of production*: 'elasticity of production meaning, in this context, the response of the quantity of labour applied to producing it to a rise in the quantity of labour which a unit of it will command' (*CW*, VII: p. 230).

The fact that it is not possible to produce money, or to use it in the production of other goods, thus constitutes an absolute obstacle:

> Unemployment develops, that is to say, because people want the moon; . . . men cannot be employed when the object of desire (i.e.

> money) is something which cannot be produced and the demand for which cannot be readily choked off. There is no remedy but to persuade the public that green cheese is practically the same thing and to have a green cheese factory (i.e. a central bank) under public control. (*CW*, VII: p. 235).

Taking the arguments marshalled in support of the essential properties of money into account, it appears that *the linear character of the curve of expected yields applies generally because it is derived from observed social, not individual, conditions.* Certainly, Keynes is silent on this point; a silence which surrounds the conditions concerning the explanation of the existence of money. But for all this, it is not necessarily the case that the straight lines are the same for all entrepreneurs, since the liquidity premium is by nature an essentially subjective phenomenon. We must thus admit the possibility of a *plurality of* i^*j's. In other words, at the level of the principle of effective demand, *a common rate of interest does not exist.*

Keynes seems to take a different position when he refers to the relation between particular goods used as standards of measure and Ricardo's invariable standard:

> If there were some composite commodity which could be regarded strictly speaking as representative, we could regard the rate of interest and the marginal efficiency of capital in terms of this commodity as being, in a sence, uniquely *the* rate of interest and *the* marginal efficiency of capital. But there are, of course, the same obstacles in the way of this as there are to setting up a unique standard of value. (*CW*, VII: p. 225).

Sraffa has subsequently resolved the obstacle to which Keynes refers. But this does not resolve the problem. Being a non-produced good, it is not easy to see how Keynes's money might be related to the standard commodity of the classical system. The existence of money cannot be the result of the system of production, which seems to be completely indeterminate, given the procedure that Keynes adopts. Its existence can only be postulated, *a priori*, for it must be available for entrepreneurs to employ as an instrument of calculation, and above all, as the only vehicle capable of carrying out the decisions based on their expectations.

In summary, then, *at the moment of the determination of the level of effective demand there is no money rate of interest.* There do exist, on the other hand, as many expected rates, i^*_j, as there are enterepreneurs, with

i_j^* interpreted, following Keynes, as the liquidity preference of the *j*th entrepreneur.

Let us now turn to Keynes's analysis in chapter 13 to see if it might provide the determination of the rate of interest.

B. The Approach of Chapters 13 and 15

In order to assess Keynes's position we shall start with a rapid summary. Keynes distinguishes the marginal efficiency of capital from the rate of interest: 'The schedule of the marginal efficiency of capital may be said to govern the terms on which loanable funds are demanded for the purpose of new investment, whilst the rate of interest governs the term on which funds are being currently supplied' (*CW*, VII: p. 165).

The ambiguity of this position should be noted. At the level of effective demand it would certainly be possible, given our previous discussion, to state that the rate of interest i_j^*, could be described, for all *j*, as the liquidity premium on money or what the entrepreneur is ready to pay in order to meet the expected cost of his production plan, that is, in order to obtain the money necessary to initiate this plan. Under such conditions the entrepreneur can undertake his plan Oq^*, taking account of the expected yield, i.e. the marginal efficiency of capital.

In no case does the comparison in question take place in *a market*, and there is no way to make sense of Keynes's references to the market determining the rate of interest, *except by giving up the principle of effective demand.*

It is on a different level of abstraction that Keynes carries on this argument, on the level of *realisation.* Once the consumption decision has been taken, and this can only logically be done by the factors, *F*, *the form in which the surplus, F-C, will be held* has to be decided. 'But this decision having been made, there is a further decision which awaits him, namely, in *what form* he will hold the command over future consumption which he has reserved, whether out of his current income or from previous savings' (*CW*, VII: p. 166). We are thus here solely concerned with the *choices of non-entrepreneurs.* This implies that the application of the principle of liquidity preference concerns agents that are distinct from those for whom we have identified the i_j^*'s. *The rate of interest is here considered a remuneration for the renunciation of liquidity.*

This approach seems to indicate:

(1) that the amount that is to be divided is fixed and known (here, beginning *ab ovo*, it refers to *F-C*);

(2) that it is always possible to give it a more liquid form; *Keynes here seems to combine money (circulation) and the liquid form of capital*;
(3) that it is equally possible to give it a different use, *consumption and investment being excluded by construction*. Since this decision also excludes the operation of the market (Patinkin, from his own perspective, is right in suggesting that the idea of a market cannot be restricted to one point in the system and that it should normally be extended, if it exists, to produce general interdependence of markets), it may be helpful to give a different interpretation to the celebrated proposition that 'It [the rate of interest] is the "price" which equilibrates the desire to hold wealth in the form of cash with the available quantity of cash (*CW*, VII: p. 167).

The link which Keynes establishes between the rate of interest and liquidity preference is *the uncertainty of the future*. 'This necessary condition is the existence of *uncertainty* as to the future of the rate of interest, i.e. as to the complex of rates of interest for varying maturities which will rule at future dates' (*CW*, VII: p. 168). The fact that Keynes only considers perpetual bonds explains the apparent uniqueness of *i*.

More precisely, it is a question of the expectation of variations of the value of wealth held in perpetual bonds, relative to the expected movements in the rate of interest. This consideration leads Keynes to state that 'the schedule of liquidity preference relating the quantity of money to the rate of interest is given by a smooth curve which shows the rate of interest falling as the quantity of money is increased (*CW*, VII: p. 171). The reasoning behind this position is given in chapter 15, in particular in terms of what may be called *speculation*, because this is what is responsible for this relation (*CW*, VII: p. 197): 'what matters is not the *absolute* level of *r* but the degree of its divergence from what is considered a fairly *safe* level of *r*, having regard to those calculations of probability which are being relied on' (*CW*, VII: p. 201).

Here it is clear that the operation of 'expectation', rather than the 'aggregate reaction of the market', two factors which Keynes constantly mingles together, is implied. A reduction in *r*, given the state of expectations of those who have to determine the form in which to hold their wealth, will produce an increase in the share held in liquid form. With the 'fairly safe level' of the rate of interest unchanged, a reduction in *r* would increase the risk of illiquidity (the probability of a future increase in *r*) and diminish the current yield which compensates for illiquidity.

The lower the rate of interest, the more a very slight increase in expectations is sufficient to compensate for this gain and produce an increased demand for liquidity. For a current rate, r_0, and a future rate, $r_1 = (1+\gamma)r_0$ we have for an asset earning 1 pound in perpetuity the possible gain:

$$\frac{1}{r_0(1+\gamma)} - \frac{1}{r_0} = \frac{-\gamma}{r_0(1+\gamma)}$$

from which the condition

$$\frac{\gamma}{r_0(1+\gamma)} = 1 \Rightarrow \gamma = \frac{r_0}{1-r_0}$$

For $r_0 = 0.10$, an increase in r of around 10 per cent is necessary (that is 0.111 for r_1). For $r_0 = 0.02$, around 2 per cent is required (i.e. 0.0204!).

If, in addition, it is recognised that for r^* constant, the lower r, the greater the possibility of a rise, it is possible to see why the demand for liquidity might be infinite below a certain rate of interest.

Should this relation then be interpreted as a 'demand function for money', whose intersection with the supply function determines the level of the rate of interest? This is what traditional interpretations have supposed Keynes to have intended, but the point requires closer examination.

If we consider the *identity* between the surplus, *F-C*, and the entrepreneurs' *deficit* within the framework which we have set out here, and which Keynes used, it is necessary to exclude the market in the usual sense. The choice of holding the surplus in a more or less liquid form is a choice that should be considered as similar to the choice between consumption and saving, that is, on the level of realisation. This can be vaguely recognised in some of Keynes's remarks on the possibility of the monetary authority basing its policy on this relation.

The problem is then to provide an explanation of the *aggregate* form of this relation on the basis of a purely *individual* analysis involving the state of expectations. This explanation should convince us that *the theory of liquidity preference does not possess the significance that Keynes attributed to it since it does not determine the level of the rate of interest.*

For each individual component of *F* (or of *F-C*) there will exist an associated 'fairly safe level of r, r_i^*'. For a determinate rate r (it should be asked, determined by whom?), the position of each individual as given by his share of the surplus, will depend on r_i^*. Depending on whether $r_i^* < r(1+\gamma)$, where $\gamma = \frac{r}{1-r} \Rightarrow r_i < \frac{r}{1-r'}$, the ith agent will prefer to hold a bond or liquidity. (See Figure 6.5.)

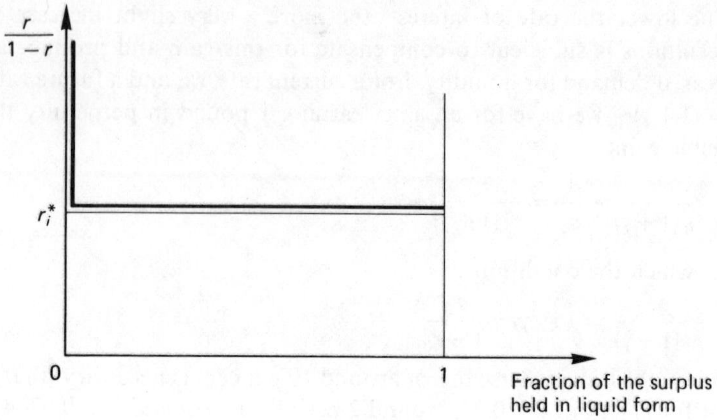

Figure 6.5

For each individual, representing a proportion μ_i of the surplus $\Sigma\mu_i = 1$, it follows that ordering the *i* according to the decreasing r_i^*, we obtain an aggregate curve (see Figure 6.6)

Figure 6.6

that can be approximated as Figure 6.7.

It can thus be seen that it is only on the basis of a known reference rate (fairly safe level) that it is possible for agents to make their choices. If one wanted to interpret the curve of Figure 6.7 as a demand curve, it would be necessary to follow the lead of Adam Smith, and assume that the 'natural

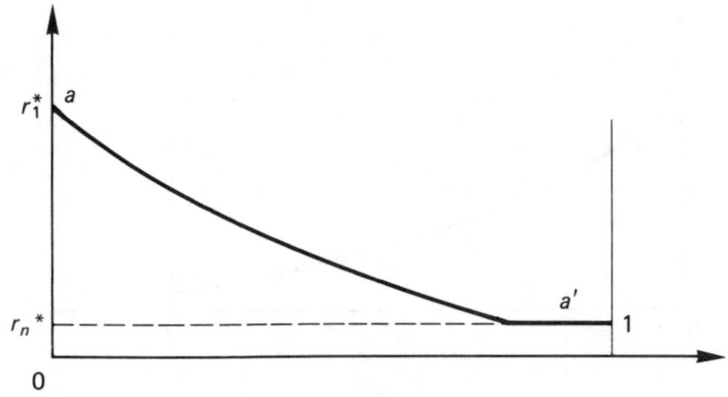

Figure 6.7

rate' exists independently of the market. Keynes expresses this in a different way: 'the rate of interest is a highly conventional, rather than a highly psychological, phenomenon. For its actual value is largely governed by the prevailing view as to what its value is expected to be' (*CW*, VII: p. 203).

The state of opinion (or of expectations) of the individual holders of the surplus may thus be figuratively expressed by the curve *aa'*, which does not represent a *functional demand curve* for money.

Now let us turn to the 'supply side'. It is impossible to express the 'supply of money' by means of a vertical or sloped curve, since it would be impossible to determine who would hold it. What is at issue, in fact, is the rate interest (or the rates) proposed by the individuals who possess the surplus.

The reference to the supply of money, with its inference of an open market, is equivalent in fact to the introduction of a centralised monetary policy which seeks to impose one particular rate. Let us suppose that $\bar{r}$, is this rate. (See Figure 6.8.) What is then determined is the fraction of the surplus held in liquid form, *OL*. *LC* represents the holding of bonds. Keynes's remark concerning the importance of the existence of a diversity of opinion for the success of the authorities' monetary policy evidently applies to this situation (*CW*, VII: p. 172).

The absence of such a centralised policy would seem to render the question of the structure of the surplus indeterminate. In these conditions we are left with a simple description of entrepreneur's opinions (i_j^*) weighted by their realised deficit (and not their expected deficits, which cannot be aggregated). But the intersection of the curves depends on the ranking of the i_j^*, and nothing precise can be said on this subject. The ratio of liquidity to assets remains indeterminate.

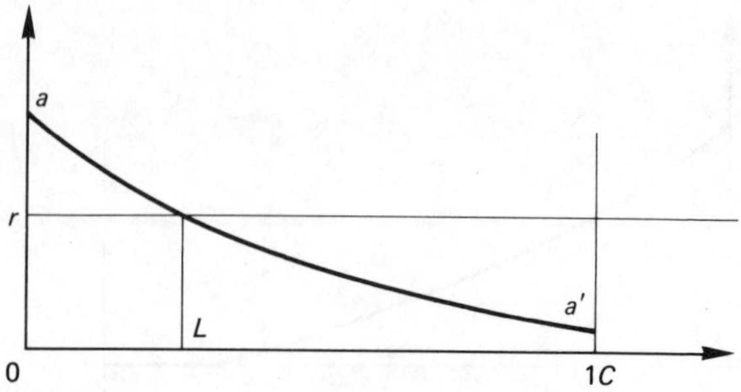

Figure 6.8

SOME CONCLUDING REMARKS

It is possible to summarise the findings that result from our examination of the two lines of reasoning that Keynes followed in the *General Theory* in explaining the rate of interest.

(1) To the extent that money possesses the characteristics mentioned by Keynes *it cannot be subordinated to effective demand.*

If such subordination were attempted, for whatever reason, it would be to no purpose since effective demand would become indeterminate.

But, above all, money cannot be the subject of production, that is, of *entrepreneurial* activity. It possesses its essential characteristics because it is the unit in which contracts are expressed: that is, it is not the result of the process of choice of economic units. The existence of money is logically anterior; indeed, it is the very condition for Keynes's economic interpretation.

It follows that *liquidity* is not the attribute of money as generally understood, but of anything other than money, but which is rapidly convertible into money. This is not a question of subtlety, but of the distinction money/capital which Keynes failed to develop. Money is not considered as the object of economic choice (effective demand, preservation of wealth), but rather as the means of obtaining objects, financial assets among them.

(2) *The properties of money are not of a nature such as to permit the determination of the rate of interest.* One of the possible reasons for Keynes's confusion on this point is that the essential properties, applied to an actual good – that is, a produced good – in fact define the classical standard commodity, whose conditions of production we know de-

termine the *rate of profit*. But nothing further can be said on this point because entrepreneurs are always considered in the aggregate.

(3) The 'money market' does not exist; rather, there are variable conditions for the *formation of financial assets*. If Keynes reasons in terms of a rate of interest it is because he takes a perpetual bond as the representative of financial assets, not because there is a *unique* money.

Considered in the context of the Keynesian circular flow, the analysis of liquidity preference takes on the following meaning: it concerns the *determination of the structure of financial assets formed in order to cover the deficits of the entrepreneurs.*

The study of the conditions for this determination leads to the conclusion that *the theory of liquidity preference does not determine the rate of interest*, but on the basis of the hypothesis of the existence of centralised policy for the rate of interest paid on financial assets, *it determines the structure of the assets formed in order to eliminate the deficit.*

(4) As a result, the simple recognition of the *identity* of the deficit and the surplus does not exhaust the description of the circular flow. It is necessary that this identity is accompanied by the process of elimination of the entrepreneur's deficits. The surplus held in money has to be transformed into a surplus held in financial assets. The identity should thus be associated with an explanation of the *formation of finance capital.*

Notes

1. *General Theory*, (*CW*, VII, 10; 73: p. 4). The quantity of employment is obtained as the quotient of two monetary magnitudes: $N = E/W$ where E is the wage bill, and W is the wage unit.
2. Another point is the assimilation of user costs in the expenditures on the output of other entrepreneurs.
3. This is the solution that is adopted in C. Benetti and J. Cartelier, *Marchands, salariat et capitalistes* (Paris: Maspéro, 1980).

Part II
Effective Demand and Time

7 The Role of Effective Demand in the Short Run and the Long Run

Lord Kaldor

The core of Keynesian theory can be summed up in two propositions. The first is that in a capitalist economy the level of production in general is not determined by the availability of resources but by effective demand which determines *how much* of potential resources are effectively utilised. The second is that demand is the sum of two components: an endogeneous component which varies *in proportion to* the costs incurred by entrepreneurs (which constitute the incomes of wage and salary earners), and an exogenous component which is financed out of capital – by borrowing, or by the sale of financial assets, which comes to the same thing – and which Keynes treated as a given factor in the short period, determined by expectations. The principle of effective demand asserts that there is an equilibrium level of output (or employment) at which the proceeds of entrepreneurs (as a group) are neither greater nor less than the proceeds the expectation of which is the necessary inducement to cause them (the entrepreneurs) to incur expenses on the scale required to produce that output. If we call the latter the 'aggregate supply price' (ASP) (consisting both of the costs incurred on hiring labour etc., and the profits necessary to induce entrepreneurs for incurring costs on that particular scale), the equilibrium level of output will be that at which the sum of endogenous ($D1$) and exogenous ($D2$) demand (which could be termed as the 'aggregate demand price', $\text{ADP} \equiv D1 + D2$) is equal to ASP.

Keynes identified exogenous demand with Investment (I) and endogenous demand with Consumption (C). If consumption is assumed to be a simple linear function of Income, Y

$$C = cY, \quad \text{with} \quad 0 < c < 1,$$

and Investment is regarded as given. $I = \bar{I}$, the equilibrium level of output, Y^* is given by

$$\bar{I} = Y^* - cY^*$$

subject to the constraint

$$Y^* \leqslant \hat{Y}$$

where $\hat{Y}$ is the maximum level of output in the short period which Keynes identified with the position of Full Employment.[1]

Professor Malinvaud published a number of papers[2] to the effect that effective demand is only one of a number of possible constraints on output in the short period; it is possible to have unemployment due to insufficient productive capacity, which causes 'classical' or 'Marxian' unemployment; or if capacity, as measured in terms of places of employment (*postes du travail*), is greater than the labour supply, it could be full employment. Depending one one's definition of what constitutes an 'economy' – whether it relates to a region, a sovereign political entity (like France), or an association of countries (like the European Community) or the world as a whole – there can also be a *third* type of constraint, determined by the economy's propensity to import in relation to its exports. In this case, exports play the role of the exogenous component in demand, while imports, investment and consumption of home-produced goods are all endogenous.

In Harrod's[3] original formulation of the theory of the 'foreign trade multiplier', exogenously given exports ($\bar{X}$) together with the propensity to import which is assumed to be a simple function of income ($M = mY$), determine the equilibrium level of output at the point at which exports and imports are equal, so that $\bar{X} = mY$, which can be expressed, in terms analogous to the Keynesian model as

$$Y^* = \frac{1}{m}\bar{X}$$

This is more likely to provide the critical constraint when we consider the problem not in the context of a short-period static equilibrium, but of the equilibrium of an 'economy' (which may be a region, a country, or a group of associated countries, etc.) in a state of steady growth where all components – the physical output potential, the labour potential (as determined by the sum of the rate of growth of employment and the rate of growth of productivity), exports and imports – grow at a steady rate (though not, or not necessarily, at the *same* rate). Under these conditions, investment must be treated as an endogenous factor, depending on the rate of change of demand (on the so-called 'accelerator principle') and so must imports, the growth-rate of which is given by the growth-rate of output multiplied by the income elasticity of demand for imported goods.

As was shown by A. P. Thirlwall,[4] the dynamic version of the original Harrod formula (given above) becomes

$$y^* = \frac{\bar{x}}{\pi}$$

where y^* is the growth-rate of Y^x over time and $\bar{x}$ the *growth*-rate of exogenous exports $\bar{X}$, while π is the *income* elasticity of imports. This model abstracts entirely from the possible effect of changes in relative prices (i.e., in the terms of trade) on either the growth-rate of exports or on the propensity to imports.[5] Nevertheless, it is capable of explaining the post-war differences in growth-rates among the *developed* countries remarkably closely (with the exception of Japan, whose predicted growth-rate was considerably higher at 13 per cent than her attained growth-rate of around 9 per cent a year),[6] though it is less successful in predicting the growth-rates of developing countries.[7]

The growth-rates derived from Harrod's 'foreign trade multiplier' are essentially demand-determined – they could not hold if the level of output and its rate of growth were supply-constrained. The question which we must now discuss is whether Professor Malinvaud's alternatives of supply-constrained equilibria which were put forward as short-run static concepts have corresponding dynamic or long-run equivalents.

Keynes was undoubtedly right in thinking that, given time, the production of pretty well everything responds to demand – on account of the fact that the growth of effective demand induces a higher rate of investment in increasing capacity. But the speed of response may be slower in some economic sectors than in others. For example, in primary products like minerals or fossil fuels, the enlargement of capacity may require enhanced investment in exploration or in the opening-up of new producing areas. Such investments have a long 'gestation period' and will only be undertaken when long-term expectations are favourable, which depends not only on the current rate of growth of demand but also on business confidence that the favourable 'conjuncture' is here to stay.

Professor Malinvaud was undoubtedly correct in suggesting that in the short period there are always *some* 'sectors' which are constrained by capacity shortages and therefore suffer from 'classical' unemployment; and these in turn may be responsible for Keynesian unemployment in other sectors – particularly where the two types of 'sector' are complementary and not in a substitute relationship with one another. (Complementarity which introduces a structural relationship in the 'product-mix' or 'output-mix' of commodities tends to be neglected by the general equilibrium approach which emphasises, as a universal feature, the substitutability of individual commodities in relation to others.) However, in relation to a particular trading area such as an individual country, or a particular region within the country, it is the function of external trade to eliminate the discrepancy between the attainable 'product-mix' on the supply side, and the required 'product-mix' on the side of demand. Each trading area exports those commodities of which it produces a structural surplus and imports those in which it is structurally deficient. Nevertheless, except for those countries which are capable of attaining full utilisation of resources (because their physical capacities are as great, or greater than that required for the full employment of its inhabitants, and because they are able to export in sufficient volume to pay for their imports of all those goods in which they are structurally deficient), the actual output and employment of individual regions or countries and their rate of growth over time, will be limited by their exports and by the imports which can be paid for by those exports. In normal circumstances, therefore, any difference between the desired 'product-mix' on the demand side, and the attainable 'product-mix' on the supply side will give rise to a situation in which exports are the main determining factor in the level of output and effective employment.[8]

However, when we consider the problem in the context of the world as a whole, a clear distinction emerges between a group of commodities which are likely to be capacity-constrained and *not* labour constrained, and another group which in the long run at any rate (if not in the short run) are likely to be constrained by demand (internal or external) or by lack of complementary goods. I would regard the former group as consisting of those sectors which exploit the natural environment and the production of which is dependent on the availability of natural resources as well as on capital investment necessary for their exploitation. I mean by the second group the industries which convert raw materials into finished goods (the industrial and manufacturing sectors) the physical capacity of which is entirely a matter of investment, and of services which are analogous to industry – they require investment in the form of labour training and the provision of facilities (hotels, restaurants, consultancy bureaux) necessary for their performance. In none of these sectors can we regard employment as the *constraining* factor – except in the short period, due to limited mobility and insufficient training. Over a longer period, any economic sector in which the demand for the various grades and kinds of labour threatens to exceed the locally available supply will become a centre of immigration, attracting labour from the vast reserves of the labour-surplus areas, which, under conditions obtaining now or likely to obtain in the foreseeable future, represent an unlimited source of labour ready to move (and be trained, if necessary) to any sector threatened by potential labour shortage. 'Full Employment' of an industrial region or country is therefore essentially a short-run concept, which ignores the long-run mobility of labour and the possibility of an increase in training which responds to demand in much the same way as capital investment.[9]

For these reasons, it is illegitimate to assume that there is a given long-run equilibrium 'growth path' for an individual country or even for the world as a whole, determined by the growth of population, the accumulation of capital and the rate of technical progress (all exogenously given). Since under the stimulus of growing demand capacity of all sectors will be expanded through additional investment, there are no long-run limits to growth on account of supply constraints; such constraints, whether due to capacity shortage or to local labour shortage, are essentially short-run phenomena – at any one time, they are a heritage of the past. The future path is likely to be constrained only by limitations on the speed of response to the stimulus of demand, which is likely to be faster in some directions than in others.

It follows from this, however, that the faster the growth of effective demand for goods in the aggregate, the more likely it is that expansion will meet temporary hold-ups due to the constraint imposed by the laggard sectors the expansion of which requires longer gestation periods.

The remarkable feature of the long post-war boom in the world economy (which undoubtedly owed a great deal to the policies of 'demand management' adopted by numerous governments under the influence of Keynesian ideas) was that it could continue for so long without being pulled up sharp by bottlenecks, in the shape of a worldwide shortage of basic foods, materials or energy. The main reason for this was that owing to land-saving or natural resource-saving technological progress, as well as to much larger investments, the growth of capacity for primary products taken generally, was, for the first fifteen years or so, more than adequate for satisfying the growth of requirements. The oft-prophesised world food shortage never materialised, and in the case of exhaustible resources, such as minerals, the increase in proven reserves and in extracting and refining capacity kept pace, by and large, with the increase in consumption.

In the pre-war, or rather pre-world-depression, circumstances such a tendency for commodity surpluses to emerge would, sooner or later, have brought the boom to an end through a collapse of prices – just as happened, as a result of changed expectations, in 1930–31, following a continued rise of end-of-season stocks of the main producing countries for a number of years prior to these events. It would have happened again but for the intervention of government-controlled marketing boards charged with the task of securing remunerative prices – which was a legacy of the new policies introduced during the pre-war depression as well as of post-war international agreements such as the Common Agricultural Policy of the EEC. This, in turn, involved the accumulation of stocks in government-owned stockpiles; and when these became too burdensome (in narrow financial terms) they gave rise to subsidies on consumption (through soft 'commodity loans' to the Third World), or to subsidies for *non*-production through acreage restrictions. As a result, the accumulated surpluses of wheat and other commodities were gradually liquidated during the latter part of the 1960s, so that when there was a sudden rise in world demand due to crop failures in China and Soviet Russia, stocks were cleared out and prices shot up rapidly. At the same time, the *formal* divorce of the dollar from gold in 1971 enhanced inflationary expectations which led to sharp rises in commodity prices for non-ferrous metals due to speculative 'movement trading'. And all this was capped by the fourfold increase in oil prices imposed by the OPEC cartel at the end of 1973. But as we now know, the OPEC cartel only became a feasible proposition when the world became dependent on Middle East oil for a disproportionate share in the annual increase in *total* energy requirements.

This rise in prices exerted a strong deflationary influence (in terms of *real* demand) in much the same manner as a one-sided addition to taxation. And for the industrial countries the inflationary problem was compounded by the accelerated rate of growth of wages – which started in 1968–9, first in France (after the '*évènements*' of June 1968) and was rapidly followed by a number of other countries, including Germany as well as Britain and Italy, and many others.

This again was very much a delayed reaction to the changed distribution of power between Capital and Labour under full employment – an 'incidental' consequence, which was much feared by *Keynesian* economists (including Keynes himself) long before Keynesian policies of demand management were put into practice, and which led to the early advocacy (by economists) of institutionalised, permanent income policies in place of free collective bargaining.

For many years it looked as if these initial fears of the consequences of enhanced trade-union bargaining power were much exaggerated. Thus in the latter part of the 1950s, the post-war 'creeping inflation' (which was itself a more moderate affair than feared) looked like petering out altogether, despite unprecedentedly low unemployment of 1–1.5 per cent both in Britain and in other European countries, and an excess of vacancies that could be filled only by the importation of labour from the less developed labour-surplus countries.

In both these aspects – in the 'physical' plane of commodity balance, as well as the 'social' plane of the distribution of income and power – forces of imbalance which built up gradually over the years came to a head suddenly, much in line with the new 'catastrophe theory' in mathematics, according to which seemingly stable situations become unstable after a certain number of years, which in principle should be predictable. But this potential instability would not have taken its actual forms were it not for the far-reaching ideological changes which emerged on an intellectual and political plane.

The causes of the wave of reaction against Keynesian economic policies that is now sweeping the western world must be sought more in terms of Marxian (or, if you prefer, Hegelian) philosophy than in Keynesian economics. Its intellectual expression is the spread of 'monetarist' doctrines which attribute most evils to inflation and attribute inflation to the rate of increase in the amount of 'money' in circulation. This view ignores the fact that in a credit-money economy there is no *unique* definition of 'money', since what is commonly regarded as 'money' is merely a part of a whole family of financial assets, issued by the government or by financial institutions, which represent transferable certificates of debt formally repayable on demand or at some stated future date, but which can only be 'repaid' in the sense of being exchanged for some other certificate of indebtedness. It also ignores the fact that a rise in costs consequential upon a rise in raw material prices or a rise in wages automatically causes an increase in the value of working capital which is normally financed by bank borrowing and a consequential increase in the amount of bank credit. Ignoring financial assets like bonds, not repayable on demand, any increase in the total public and private debt held by the non-banking private sector must have as its counterpart a corresponding increase in the 'money stock'. Hence the rise in the money stock (even when it is regarded as one of many forms of financial assets held by the non-banking public) is always the consequence, not the cause, of the rise in prices and wages.

At the present time, in the absence of a universally accepted monetary standard, no single government is in a position to follow Keynesian policies of demand management without thereby inducing an adverse balance of payments due to a consequential rise in imports relative to exports. Hence a revival of the growth-rates of the Keynesian era must await a general consensus on economic policies by the governments of the leading countries and their readiness to take co-ordinated action. It may also require the creation of new international institutions designed to stabilise commodity prices through the institution of internationally operated buffer stocks for the main commodities, and the creation of new instruments, inside each country, for preventing an excessive rate of increase in money wages relative to the rate of increase in productivity.

Notes

1. However, in a later paper, 'The Theory of the Rate of Interest', in *The Lessons of Monetary Experience, Essays in Honour of Irving Fisher* (London: Allen & Unwin, 1937), Keynes recognised that 'the condition in which the elasticity of supply for output as a whole is zero is, I now think, the most convenient criterion for defining full employment' (p. 150, now reprinted in *Collected Writings*, vol. XIV, p. 106).
2. Cf. *The Theory of Unemployment Reconsidered* (Oxford: Basil Blackwell, 1937); 'Macroeconomic Rationing of Employment', in Malinvaud and Fitoussi (eds), *Unemployment in Western Countries* (London: Macmillan, 1980) pp. 172–93.
3. Cf. R. F. Harrod, *International Economics* (Cambridge, 1933) pp. 104–20.
4. A. P. Thirlwall, 'The Balance of Payments Constraint as an Explanation of International Growth Rate Differences', *Banca Nazionale del Lavoro, Quarterly Review*, March 1979.
5. In other words, it neglects the *price* elasticities of both exports and imports, and shows both as single valued functions of income elasticities. The growth-rate of exports of any particular country is a reflection of the growth-rates of other countries and of their income elasticity for *j*-goods, whilst π is the income elasticity of the inhabitants of *j* country for foreign goods.
6. The figures relate to the period 1953–76. Japan's exceptionally high growth-rate was due both to her exceptional success as an exporter, with her export volume rising at 16 per cent a year, and her exceptionally low income elasticity of demand for imports (which was no doubt assisted by various forms of 'invisible restraints' on the import of manufactures).
7. Cf. Thirlwall and Hussain, 'The Balance of Payments Constraint, Capital Flows and Growth Rate Differences Between Developing Countries', *Oxford Economic Papers*, November 1982.
8. I use the term 'effective employment' to exclude 'ineffective employment' (work-sharing) or 'disguised unemployment' which is present to some degree in most countries but which is the dominant form of unemployment in the less developed countries with a large proportion of population formally occupied in agriculture and services – but who make no net contribution to output.
9. The immigration of labour into a country is normally inhibited by restrictions imposed by the host government in the interest of native workers. As post-war experience has shown, however, such restrictions are lifted whenever the demand for labour exceeds the supply of indigenous wokers – either by allowing immigration from overseas dependencies (as in the case of Britain or France) or from the less developed countries of southern Europe (as in the case of Germany, Holland, Switzerland, Austria, etc.).

8 The Short Period of Keynesian Analysis and the Time-Period of the Circuit

Frédéric Poulon

Keynes's preoccupation with the short period is not limited to the *General Theory*. Several years after his famous aphorism concerning the long run in his *Tract on Monetary Reform*, Keynes in his *Treatise on Money* reminds the reader, 'it is above all with short-period consequences that we are concerned' (p. 94). On the basis of this work it is possible to discover what meaning the short period had for Keynes at that time. Largely inspired by the Wicksellian tradition, the *Treatise* was concerned with the period of the credit cycle.

The *General Theory*, which from a number of points of view might be considered as an autocritique by the author of the *Treatise*, certainly did not deny this definition of the short period. It is true, however, that he does superimpose an apparently new definition. The *General Theory* conceives of the short period as the time for which expectations are held concerning the results of employing a certain quantity of labour, given the stock of capital. It no longer seems to concern either credit or money. But this is not correct. As we shall see, the period considered in the *General Theory* does correspond to the period of circulation of money flows, which we shall call the 'time-period of the circuit'.

Thus both the *Treatise* and the *General Theory* refer us to a sort of monetary cycle, which we shall investigate in section I. We then proceed in section II to an evaluation of the Keynesian short period within the framework of a suitably defined monetary circuit. Finally, we will briefly demonstrate, in section III, how we may be able to cast a new light on certain traditional aspects of Keynesian theory, such as the multiplier of the *General Theory* and the equilibrium condition of the *Treatise*, on the basis of this interpretation of the short period.

I THE CYCLE OF MONEY

Money's cycle is composed of the succession of different states that money assumes in the course of its circulation. It can be represented by the suitably ordered succession of monetary flows observed in the course of any period of time. The first of these flows is the net quantity of money created, which, as we know, can have three different sources. For simplification, let us suppose that there is no government, nor international trade. There is thus only one source for the quantity of money created: the credit of financial intermediaries to non-financial agents. These may be separated into two categories – firms and households. We will suppose that only firms receive credit, represented by L for the period under consideration. Following the lead given by Keynes in the initial chapters, and especially chapter 6, of the *General Theory*, we define the other flows as follows:

F, factor cost, is the amount of income transferred by firms to households, the owners of the factors of production, in exchange for services rendered.

U, user cost, is defined (chapter 3) as the amount paid by firms for the purchases that take place between them, including those which correspond to the costs involved with the operation of equipment. They comprise approximately what national accounts now define as intermediate consumption and consumption of fixed capital.

C, consumption, is the sum of expenditures made by households with firms during the period under consideration.

I, investment, is the value, net of user cost, of inter-firm purchases in the period under consideration. It concerns the addition to the value of capital equipment arising from the productive activity of the period; in national accounting terms this is called net fixed capital formation (if necessary, variations in inventory accumulation should be added to give the total net formation of capital).

The excess of factor cost over consumption is defined as *households' saving*, and is collected by financial intermediaries. It may be written: $S = F - C$. All these flows integrate three large groups of agents: entrepreneurs (E), households (H), and financial intermediaries (B). Their balance sheet positions (uses on the left, sources on the right) may be represented as follows:

E		H		B	
F	L	C	F	L	S
U	C	S			
I	U				
	I				

Graphically these accounts could be presented as in Figure 8.1.

Without doubt, the graphical representation of Figure 8.1 gives a better image of money's cycle than the balance sheets because it also indicates the hierarchy of flows, given the point of departure. As indicated above, this is the flow, L, of credit from the financial intermediaries to the firms to allow them to finance their investments, I, a part of which is effectively financed by the formation of debt to an amount L. The remaining portion, $I-L$, corresponds to the (possibly negative) incomes or profits of the firms and represents internal finance.

This represents the circuit of money which may be derived immediately from the initial indications given by Keynes in the *General Theory*. We shall see in the next section that it provides the basis for a precise evaluation of the duration of the short period in Keynesian analysis.

II THE EVALUATION OF THE KEYNESIAN SHORT PERIOD

At the beginning of the period, in Keynesian analysis, firms form expectations which determine the amount of credit requested from financial intermediaries to finance production. The expectations themselves are determined in particular by the results achieved in the preceding period. Yet, if one trusts the hierarchy of flows expressed in the representation of the circuit given in Figure 8.1, it appears that the end of the period corresponds to the savings of households. Consequently, the period itself is measured by the time that elapses between the moment of initial monetary creation and the moment when this money becomes the source of household savings.

It is not possible to evaluate the duration of the period on the basis of Figure 8.1, since all the flows observed in the course of the same arbitrary period are, so to speak, concomitant. The circuit of Figure 8.1, suitably transformed, does nevertheless yield the means of evaluating the short period of Keynesian analysis.

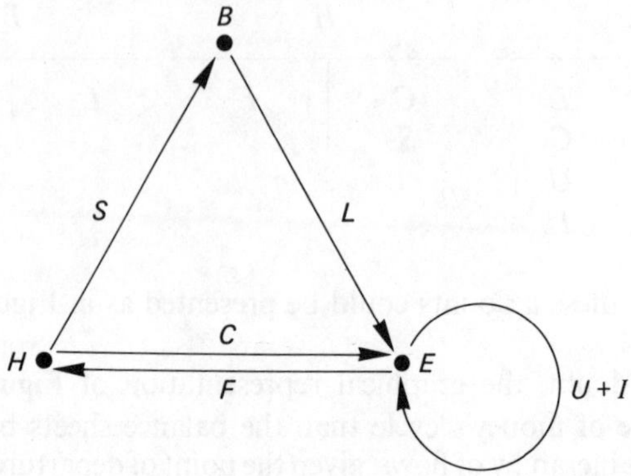

Figure 8.1

We imagine that at the initial moment the flow of money injected into circulation by financial intermediaries is one money unit ($L = 1$). We suppose that the propagation of this monetary unit between different poles of the circuit obeys the two following rules:

(1) the transitions from one pole to another are instantaneous, while money arriving at each pole remains for a constant time of finite duration independent of the particular pole;
(2) the monetary unit, 'single and indivisible', moves from one pole to another according to probabilities which reflect the structure of the flows represented in Figure 8.1.

Let us write P_{ij} as the probability that the money unit moves, in a period of transition, from pole i to pole j; (i or $j = B, E$ or H). By virtue of rule (2) above, given the necessity of an accounting equilibrium for each pole, the only non-zero probabilities in the process described above are:

$$P_{BE} = L/S = L/L = 1$$
$$P_{EH} = F/(L+C+U+I) = F/(F+U+I) = f$$
$$P_{EE} = (U+I)/(L+C+U+I) = U/(F+U+I) + I/(F+U+I) = u+i$$
$$P_{HE} = C/F = C/(C+S) = c$$
$$P_{HB} = S/F = S/(C+S) = s$$

Naturally this also implies: $f+u+i = 1$ and $c+s = 1$.

The circulation of the typical money unit can thus be represented by the graph of Figure 8.2.

Figure 8.2 makes clear that the money unit, having left pole B at a given moment, returns to this pole at the end of a finite period of time which is equal to the total duration of its stay at the poles E and H. During this period of time the money unit has served (see Figure 8.1) for diverse consumption expenditures (intermediate consumption or consumption of fixed capital by entrepreneurs, final consumption by households), for paying incomes to households (flow F), for capital accumulation (flow I), and *finally* for the constitution of savings (flow S) by households.

The moment in which money becomes the source of saving is crucial. This is because money, lent by the financial intermediaries to firms, here escapes from their control for an undetermined period of time and compromises their ability to repay credit. We will not here develop the consequences of this situation (the interested reader is referred to my book, *Macroéconomie Approfondie*, Cujas, Paris, 1982, pp. 340–5). Here we shall be content to simply indicate that at the moment indicated firms are pressed to attract the savings of households in the financial markets. The operation is easier when the results obtained by the firms in the period are profitable: when firms are profitable this allows the firms to substitute debt of households and other financial market investors with bank debt. When they are bad they lead to an aggravation of the firm's debt position with the banks, creating what has been defined as an 'overdraft economy'. But in either case there is a revision of expectations, optimistic or pessimistic, of the firms in the elaboration of their investment plans for the next period.

It thus appears that the constitution of saving really marks the end of the period of the monetary cycle. To the degree that this period corresponds to the period of the validity of expectations, we are dealing with the short run of Keynesian analysis. We only need to give a precise evaluation of its time-period. We shall do this on the basis of Figure 8.2.

The Keynesian short run is interpreted in Figure 8.2 as the total time that the monetary unit remains in either pole E or H, between the moment of its departure from B and the moment it returns to B. This total time is obtained as the product of the duration of the stay in any pole and the average number of passages between the poles E and H between the two moments considered. This average number is equal to the inverse, less unity, of the probability p_B that the monetary unit is at pole B at any moment far enough from the initial moment (stationary regime). This number may be represented as $(1/p_B) - 1$.

The calculation of p_B is made simultaneously with the calculation of the other stationary probabilities p_E and p_H concerning E and H respectively. The calculation in this case is very simple and results from

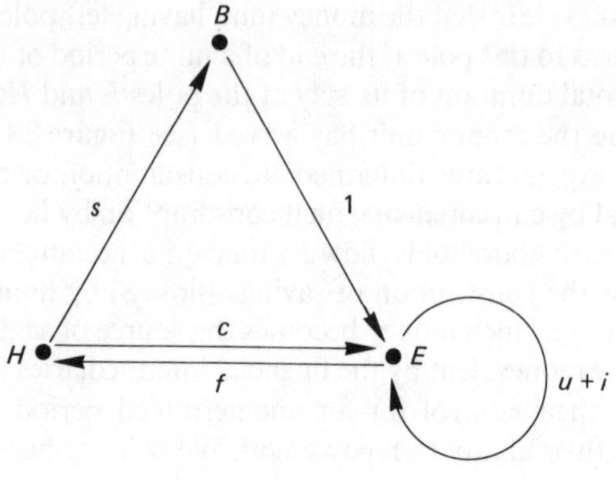

Figure 8.2

the resolution of the following system, the last two equations of which are immediately derived from the graph of Figure 8.2:

$$p_B + p_E + p_H = 1, \quad p_B = s \cdot p_H, \quad p_H = f \cdot p_E, \quad \text{which gives:}$$

$$p_B = s \cdot f/(1 + f + s \cdot f), \quad p_E = 1/(1 + f + s \cdot f),$$

$$p_H = f/(1 + f + s \cdot f) \quad \text{and} \quad (1/p_B) - 1 = (1/s)(1 + (1/f))$$

The number thus obtained is a pure number. To give it a dimension in real time it must be multiplied by the duration of presence in any pole. This means that we shall have a rather rough estimate because of the uniformity of the duration of stay assumed in rule (1) above. None the less, a plausible estimate may be achieved by noting from Figure 8.2 that the passage of the money unit from pole *E* to pole *H* corresponds first to the payment and then the expenditure of wages and in general takes place in a period of around one month. In this time the money unit has resided in each of the two poles, *E* and *H*, so that the duration in any pole cannot exceed two weeks on average. We may assume the following values, inspired by the French national accounts, for the coefficients *s* and *f*: $s = 0.14, f = 0.4$. The effective duration of the Keynesian short run is thus:

$$100/14 \times (1 + 10/4) = 25 \text{ fortnights, or about 1 year.}$$

The result that is obtained, which is of course only an order of magnitude, confirms the opinion generally held of the length of the short period. In any case, it is the duration which Keynes seems to have attributed to it, although he paid little attention to the subject. For example, we find in chapter 20 of the *Treatise on Money*, in the presentation of what we should today call a 'model' of the credit cycle, suggestion of a period of 50 weeks.

But, besides giving us a better idea of the Keynesian short period, the time-period of the circuit also allows new interpretations of some traditional aspects of Keynesian theory.

III THE TIME-PERIOD OF THE CIRCUIT IN KEYNESIAN ANALYSIS

One of the best-known aspects, but without doubt of slightly exaggerated importance, of Keynesian theory, is the multiplier ($1/s$) of the *General Theory*. It is not our intention to discuss its real importance, only to demonstrate how it may also be derived on the basis of the time-period of the circuit. The time-period for the circuit defined above may also be written:

$$1/p_B - 1 = (1 - p_B)/p_B = (p_E + p_H)/p_B = (p_E/p_B) + (p_H/p_B)$$

The ratio p_E/p_B represents the number of passages of the money unit in pole E in the period that elapses between two successive injections of the money unit starting from pole B.[1] The ratio p_H/p_B may be interpreted similarly. It should, however, be noted that each passage in H represents (see Figure 8.1 or 8.2) the payment of an income of 1 money unit to households. The number p_H/p_B thus represents the total income generated by each unit of money put into circulation, or the income multiplier. In fact, the ratio p_H/p_B is equal to $1/s$, as is easy to see from the preceding calculations.

Another aspect, which may however be less well known, of Keynesian theory, is the study of profit presented in the *Treatise on Money*. Profit is there defined (chapter 9) as the difference between I and S. From the 'fundamental equations' (chapter 10) Keynes concludes that a positive profit is associated with a rising price level of aggregate output, and that negative profit involves a fall in prices. The equilibrium condition is thus $I = S$. Without endorsing these conclusions, which were ultimately rejected by Keynes himself, we can use the preceding analysis of the time-period of the circuit to give new meaning to the equilibrium condition of the *Treatise on Money*.

We have noted that the ratio p_E/p_B indicates the average number of passages in pole E, between two successive injections of money starting from pole B. Moreover, Figure 8.2 suggests that a proportion i of these passages in E is followed by an accumulation of capital. We can thus calculate the value accumulated as a result of each money unit placed in circulation as $i \times p_E/p_B = i/s.f$. The definition of these coefficients (given above, p. 164 allows us to write:

$$i/s \cdot f = [\, I/(F+U+I) \times (F/S) \times (F+U+I)/F \,] = I/S$$

The equilibrium condition given in the *Treatise on Money*, $I = S$, thus appears to be equivalent to the condition $i/s \cdot f = 1$. We will briefly give a new interpretation of this condition. While firms try to attract households' savings by offering bonds or assets, it can be seen that they will only be able to succeed if their accumulated wealth in the period is at least equal to the value of the savings that they seek to attract. If, for each money unit saved, the accumulated value $i/s \cdot f$ is superior, savings will be spontaneously attracted and there will, in addition, be an increase in the price of assets. If, on the contrary, $i/s \cdot f < 1$, there will be a fall in the price of assets. The equilibrium condition for the price of assets is thus expressed in the equality $i/s \cdot f = 1$, that is, the equality $I = S$ of the *Treatise on Money*.

Between the *Treatise on Money* and the *General Theory*, Keynes, as he himself admits (see his *Collected Writings*, vol. XIII, pp. 275–89), accepted the criticisms of Hawtrey, Hayek and Robertson. He changed his definition of aggregate income to include profits, the savings of firms integrated into aggregate savings along with the savings of households. At a stroke, the equilibrium conditions, $I = S$, of the *Treatise on Money* becomes an identity, true at every moment of time, in the *General Theory*. This does not, however, prevent us from considering the equilibrium or disequilibrium conditions of the *General Theory* analogously to those of the *Treatise on Money*. Only the interpretation is different.

Notes

1. Between two successive injections of the monetary unit in the circuit, that is, between two successive departures from pole B, the average number of passages in all conditions is $(1/p_E - 1) + 1 = 1/p_B$, in order to take into account the passage in pole B as well. The average number of passages in E is thus the proportion p_E of this total number or p_E/p_B.

9 The Identity of Aggregate Supply and Demand in Time

Bernard Schmitt

Consider aggregate supply, p, and aggregate demand, q, both applying to the same period of production. There can be no doubt that p and q are the terms of a relation. Indeed, simple observation suggests that supply and demand 'go together'. Without knowledge of the exact relationship of p to q, we know that in the actual economy p supposes q and vice versa. But what is the precise nature of the relation between p and q? It is interesting to note that the responses that might be given *a priori* are in fact solutions that have already been proposed in the history of economic thought.

The relationship may be *causal:* aggregate supply is considered the cause of aggregate demand which it 'creates'. But it is also conceivable that the causality might be the reverse, with demand 'calling forth' supply. The hypothesis of causality running from p to q is, in fact, the basis of Classical theory from the Physiocrats to the Scottish and English Classical economists, and beyond them, to Marx. The causal influence of p on q is also the basis, especially in the United States, of a modern strain of thought: 'supply side economics'. The inverse causality, q determining p, is the basis of certain heterodox theories such as Malthus's *Principles*, and mediocre interpretations of Keynes's 'effective demand'.

Causality is not the only relationship that comes to mind. Indeed, it was abandoned for a period of several decades after the Walrasian revolution. In the general equilibrium relationship p is not the cause of q, nor is it the effect. Since Walras economists have learned to speak of co-determination, or more, of simultaneous determination, of all offers to supply and demand in all markets (for productive services, commodities and financial assets).

There is one last *a priori* possibility: it is conceivable that p and q might be identical actions. Despite the fact that the identity of supply and demand seems to contradict common sense, and appears to offer little theoretical prospect, it is the source of the theoretical originality of Keynes's two great books, *A Treatise on Money* and *The General Theory*.

How is the modern economist to decide, faced with the positions of Ricardo, Walras and Keynes? *The logical test offered by consideration of the passage of time suggests that the identity of supply and demand is the only possible position which is free from inconsistency.* This is examined in the first part of this chapter. Then we will investigate the deeper significance of the identity: it is not a tautology. We will verify that already in Keynes's work the identity of aggregate supply and demand plays a positive, even a central role (second section). Next we will show that the *permanence* of the identity of aggregate supply and demand allows, paradoxically, adjustment 'inside the identity'. In this way the economy obeys the logic of the market despite the identity of supply and demand being satisfied at each moment of time (third section).

Finally, we well confute an idea accepted by many who hesitate to recognise the logical implications of the argument because it appears to contradict the facts. Far from being an 'ideal truth', the identity of aggregate supply and demand is real and actual, admitting no exception. Although p and q are always the terms of an identity, we will show, in another apparent paradox, that q can be greater than p (inflation), and that p can be greater than q (unemployment). We will even be able to demonstrate the coexistence of the two disequilibria (fourth section).

I

Only by means of the identity of aggregate supply (p) and demand (q) can the relationship between p and q through time be rigorously identified.

Let us consider the three hypotheses mentioned above in order.

1. Hypothesis of a Causal Relationship Linking p and q, or q and p

It is unnecessary to quote textual evidence attributing the causality hypothesis to any particular authors. Every economist knows that during the Classical period (extending from 1750 to 1870 or even later) the causal link between supplies and demands, or vice versa, was, often explicitly, present at the core of the great works. Consider Say's Law, that supply creates its own demand, or Malthus's doctrine, that saving may produce a slump; 'the principle of supply and demand' was 'the first, greatest and most universal of the principles' of political economy.

But here we are not interested in an investigation of the history of economic thought; rather our goal is to use modern analytical methods to provide an answer to the still-unresolved question: Can a causal relationship between p and q or between q and p be obtained logically?

Let us consider the problem at its most general level. If p is in fact the cause of q, then four conditions are satisfied (cf. E. Nagel, *The Structure of Science*, London: Routledge & Kegan Paul, 1982, pp. 74–5):

Condition 1. Event p never occurs without producing event q.
Condition 2. Events p and q are contiguous in space.
Condition 3. Events p and q are contiguous in time.
Condition 4. The relation between p and q is asymmetric: p produces q, but q does not produce p.

Contiguity in space and time of cause and effect is a generally recognised condition (e.g. *The Fontana Dictionary of Modern Thought*, A. Bullock and O. Stallbrass, eds, London: Fontana/Collins, 1977, p. 91). We shall only retain condition 3, contiguity in time. Let us try to justify it by means of a simple argument.

The supposed cause (p) occurs at the moment of time t, while the effect (q) occurs at the moment t^+. If contiguity in time is not satisfied, then a *finite* period of time, let us call it P, separates t and t^+. The hypothesis of causality then signifies that the action observed at moment t produces no effect during the period P, until the very last moment, t^+. This implies that the effect *is not produced* by the passage of time from t to t^+, nor is it produced in the moment t^+. To say that the effect is produced at a later time means that it does not occur at all. Time can only transmit what it carries; since no effect occurs during P, no effect can arrive at t^+. The conclusion is equally negative if the cause is given a temporal dimension, duration in time. As soon as the effect is separated from the cause by a finite span of time it is formally impossible for it to occur: the supposed causal link is logically excluded.

Now, let us apply the contiguity condition to the economy. Supply p appears at moment t, but at this moment demand does not yet exist; it occurs at time t^+, which is contiguous with t, because it is assumed by hypothesis to be caused by supply. It is opportune to examine carefully the event which occurs at t. While it represents 'supply without demand', it is none the less fully realised since it will be followed in the next moment in time by its corresponding demand. Might it be possible to identify a condition of 'supply without demand', and if so, on which market? Neither the goods market nor the asset market provides examples, for on both of these markets realised supply defines a *simultaneous* demand (produced at moment t, not t^+). There remains the market in which the national economy pays its costs of production and creates its income. The payment of the social costs of production, aggregate supply, itself constitutes the incomes which will be spent at a 'later' time. In the interval it would be correct to say that the incomes created by aggregate supply produce no aggregate demand. It is thus possible to observe at moment t the existence of a positive supply corresponding to demand that does not yet exist.

It is thus possible to consider that supply is the cause of demand. But it is still necessary for the contiguity condition to be satisfied. There is no law which compels agents to spend their incomes immediately beginning in moment t^+, contiguous with t. Moreover, it is not even certain that all incomes created will be directed towards expenditure, whether present or future. Thus event q may never occur even if event p occurs, or if it does, it may be after an indefinite lag.

The causality hypothesis must thus be abandoned; aggregate supply cannot be the cause of aggregate demand. The converse is equally true for the same reasons. If a 'demand without supply' produces some influence on production it must necessarily be on future production; the contiguity condition would then not be satisfied.

Let us suppose that the reader still gives some credence to the idea that logic has just been invalidated. He may think, for example, that if the demand for cars increases, production will follow; how are we to deny, on the other hand, that the growth of incomes leads to an increase in expenditures? It is true that the production of a commodity is always linked to the demand for it. It is equally clear that the creation of incomes leads to their expenditure. But in no event should these platitudes be mistaken for causal laws. Indeed, one of the tasks of economic science is to discover and formulate the exact relationship between supply (p) and demand (q). This is in no way accomplished by pretending that p or q is the cause of q or p. Yet, there is a link between p and q, a relation which is an exact law. Might p and q be co-determinate?

2. The Hypothesis of the Co-determination of p and q

Without necessity of reference to particular authors, it is well known that the determination of price by means of the equations of supply and demand is neoclassical. It is true that this approach is represented by two opposed points of view: are prices determined by the exchange ratios of physical goods (in terms of a physical numeraire), or can equivalence be established only through the use of money in exchange? There is no need to make a choice. We just have to keep in mind two ideas: exchange takes place between goods, real or monetary; and in general equilibrium every exchange is the equation of its terms (the goods supplied and demanded).

Accepting the principle of general equilibrium, markets achieve the simultaneous equalisation of all existing supplies and demands. How then are we to test the hypothesis of co-determination? It depends on the verification of an essential condition: by means of *tâtonnement* or other means, it is necessary for transactions to yield a system of *equations*.

In fact, if the two sides of an exchange could not be written in the form of a mathematical equation, then neither the quantities supplied nor the quantities demanded could be definitely *measured*–they would remain indeterminate. There is no question but that this is an involved argument. When three kilos of tomatoes exchange for one kilo of pears (or for one unit of money), is it logically possible to define an equation in these quantities of tomatoes and pears? The equation, or the equality, signifies 'indifference' between the goods exchanged; pears or tomatoes could be replaced by tomatoes or pears without effect.

The problem is profound and it may be feared that it can only be resolved by means of an act of faith. Well, let us believe. We thus suppose that the exchange of goods (real or monetary) does define a system of equations. It would then seem to follow that the hypothesis of co-determination is confirmed, because if exchange represents the equalisation of its terms, then the quantities supplied and demanded are equal: one measures the other so they are simultaneously determined.

The time has come to apply the test of logic: does co-determination survive the introduction of time? In order to prepare the 'experiment' properly we must distinguish with great care the precise moment in which exchange takes place from all other moments in which exchange is prepared by means of adjustments of supply and demand. The supply–demand equations are defined by the realisation of exchanges; at every other moment the goods supplied and demanded remain 'estranged' from each other.

Logic thus imposes the following reasoning:

—By hypothesis (or by act of faith) realised exchange allows the formulation of equations or mathematical equalities of its two terms.
—As soon as the good supplied and the good demanded are equated (by means of the relation established between the physical quantities of each exchanged), the supply–demand equation becomes *numerical*. The

terms of the relation can be expressed in terms of *numbers*. The theorist is thus formally authorised to choose one of the terms (the quantity supplied, or if he prefers, demanded) to represent the 'number–numeraire'. Since one of the two goods is thus turned into a number, so is the other, since they are related by a numerical relation.

—It is clear that assigning numbers to goods is only legitimate in exchange, and only when the terms of exchange are an identity.

—Let us maintain our resolve to embrace the neoclassical faith: exchange is an equalisation. But let us be on our guard. The quantities exchanged would not be able to define the terms of any equations if they are not realised. *This means that outside exchange no numerical relation can exist between goods supplied and demanded.*

—A fundamental conclusion necessarily follows:

—All numerical relations established in exchange have but an instantaneous existence. Neither before nor after exchange takes place may goods be represented by numbers. Consequently it is certain that exchanges cannot be conceived: ratiocination cannot establish co-determination of supply and demand within the neoclassical framework.

—Co-determination could only be confirmed if the quantities supplied and demanded were comparable or commensurable *before* exchange takes place. But they are not, since this is only possible in realised exchange. The absurdity may be revealed in these terms: it is a question of equating the masses of two objects which have no mass, and which only acquire mass at the instant in which the equalisation of their masses takes place.

—The absurdity may also be represented in geometrical terms. Supply and demand are co-determined at the points of intersection of the two curves. But the curves can only be conceived *numerically* because geometry is a system of measure; it is , then, only possible to imagine the curves if supply and demand can be expressed in numbers, which is only the case at the points of intersection. The problem is thus to discover the points of intersection of curves which do not exist.

—The only reason that co-determination is of interest is because it pretends to bring about adjustment between magnitudes which logically cannot be measured until the adjustment is completed. Adjustment can thus only take place in the imagination.

—Theoreticians have not noted this enormous error because they have eliminated time and its effects from their analyses. But once attention is focused on the flow of time, it is clear that the numerical relations established in neoclassical theory have only instantaneous validity. This is an insufficient basis for the foundation of a science. Let us examine the last hypothesis.

3. Hypothesis of the Identify of *p* and *q*

Let us start by recalling that the question at issue in this first section is neither to establish nor to identify the identity of aggregate supply and demand. Our purpose is much more limited: the examination of the compatibility of the hypothesis with the fact of the passage of time. The two other hypotheses have been shown to be incapable of dealing with the flow of time: they thus cannot be applied to the world in which we live. If logic does not reveal any contradiction involved in a temporal description of the identity, our first goal will have been attained: the identity of aggregate supply (p) and demand (q) can exist in the real world while neither the causal nor the co-determinous relation can exist in any but a pure chimera.

The contiguity condition is too weak if p and q are the terms of an identity, for then aggregate demand must appear at the same instant as aggregate supply. Now, as we have already seen, the contiguity condition is too restrictive, for in the real world the incomes created by the payment of costs of production are not (necessarily) spent without delay, immediately after their creation. Since the identity condition is even more restrictive it seems that it should be rejected *a fortiori*. But reflection suggests that this is not the case, for as soon as aggregate demand is identified with aggregate supply it takes on a new meaning.

If p and q are distinct, the condition of contiguity of two events in time is already too restrictive. But given that p and q are inseparable, the condition of contiguity is logically insufficient and the stronger condition of the identity of aggregate supply and demand, and conforms to the facts. What, in fact, does the identity of p and q mean? It is verified if, and only if, payment of costs as incomes to the factors of production allows them to purchase the output of the economy as a whole.

Let us assume that aggregate supply, defined as the payment of the national costs of production, gives to agents the ownership in money of the newly produced physical output. It can thus be seen that aggregate supply is in the same moment aggregate demand since income recipients instantaneously attain, and thus demand without delay, the entire new output. The *creation* of money incomes is the first demand for the new output, the *expenditure* of money incomes is the second demand for the new output. According to the identity hypothesis the output of the economy is demanded twice, in money and in real terms.

If the new incomes are identical to the new output it would be inconsistent to pretend that the incomes created, but not yet spent, represent demand which is zero while it is waiting to be spent. In reality demand is immediately positive since the new output is already present in the money earned by the factors of production. Even though the period (t, t^+) has finite duration, several calendar days for example, demand is not forthcoming *after* supply because its first appearance occurs at moment t. Certainly the *physical* outputs only reach agents at moment t^+, but they had already received them *in money* at the moment t.

We have just shown that the simultaneity condition of p and q is realistic, while the contiguity condition over time is a chimera. The identity of aggregate supply and demand is thus not contradicted by the facts, at least with respect to the temporal order of events. It is logically possible for p and q to be produced simultaneously, while their contiguity in time is the purely imaginary effect of incomplete analysis.

We still have to examine the identity in the presence of the passage of time. It is understood that the two events, p and q, may arise simultaneously (the formal error of causality is avoided), but it still has to be proved that the two inseparable events have finite duration, for if p and q only exist for a moment of time aggregate supply and demand would be indeterminate (as is the case under the hypothesis of co-determination). Now, it is easy to show that the unique magnitude (p, and identically q) occurs in a finite moment of time (non-infinitesimal). Indeed, the identity indicates that the agents initially obtain the product in its money form. As long as incomes are not spent on final purchases, supply and demand remain unseparated.

Let us summarise in two points:

(1) According to the neo-classical explanation, supply and demand can only exist in a common unit of measurement for a peiod of time that is strictly equal to zero (at the instant of exchange). This is why p and q are never determined, for by hypothesis they are co-determined and their co-determination is not achieved in actual time which evolves and has duration. We live in a world in which events that do not occur in the passage of time simply do not exist.

(2) According to the explanation in terms of the identity of p and q, aggregate supply and demand exist in a common unit of measurement during a finite period of time: the identity of p and q thus finds

expression in reality, while this is impossible in the case of causality and co-determination. J. M. Keynes is the author whose work most precisely supports the identity of aggregate supply and demand.

II

In the work of J. M. Keynes the identity of aggregate supply (p) and demand (q) is a proposition of crucial importance: it is neither a tautology nor a truism.

The entire economics profession has long accepted that Keynes established the identity of *p* and *q*. The majority of economists no longer have the courage to contest this position even though the identity is presented as an equilibrium condition in classrooms throughout the world: supply and demand are identical on the assumption that they are perfectly adjusted one to the other. Thus in the ever-present *IS-LM* schema supply and demand finally produce the so-called Keynesian identity only after all necessary adjustments have taken place on the markets for savings and investment and the money markets. There is no doubt that every fundamental innovation experiences the same fate: first it is rejected, then resistance gives way to slow acceptance, but without anyone giving up their prior beliefs. Its essence is thus deeply absorbed into the pre-existing theory.

But, recognition of the importance of the passage of time exposes this duplicity. If adjustments were a reality, they would take place through time. But Keynes's identity (just as Say's identity) is permanent, valid for each 'point' of chronological time: when the Keynesian identity is obtained by means of adjustment it must either be the result of conscious or unconscious intellectual fraud.

The identity of *p* and *q* cannot be the result of an adjustment between *p* and *q*. Let us examine the antimony (identity and adjustment) only with respect to its essential relation to the passage of time:

(1) The measurement of supply supposes the measurement of demand (and conversely), but supply and demand can only be measured at moments when they are identical.
(2) The identity of *p* and *q* is either always true, or it is never true.
(3) Supply and demand must both be either real or monetary, otherwise they could never be compared. Expressed in physical terms supply and demand are not in themselves even measurable and at the moment in which supply or demand is in money, demand or supply is also, and they are identical.

(4) Under point (2) we examined the question of whether or not the identity existed. Here we take the identity for granted in order to analyse it in the passage of time. The identity of *p* and *q* does or does not have a positive duration in real time. If its duration is zero, the identity is not real (it does not exist); but if its duration is positive, it is true for all time, which excludes the possibility of adjustment between *p* and *q*.

A. The Antimony

Let us examine briefly four points.

(1) *Supply and demand can only be measured together.* Naively one might think that supply and demand could each be measured independently, just as one determines the mass of a certain number of tomatoes and, quite independently, the mass of a certain number of pears. Nevertheless, it is clear that the mass of tomatoes cannot be measured with the help of tomatoes; another mass is necessary, for example the kilo on the other side of the scales. We have to be able to formulate the equation between weights and tomatoes and, independently, the weight of the pears. That is to say, measure is a relation of equivalence. Supply can then only be measured if it exists in an equation. What is the other term of the equation? Supply itself? That would imply measuring tomatoes with tomatoes. Measurement is only effective when supply is equated to demand. It is true that the condition, though a necessary one, looks insufficient: isn't the equality of supply and demand the image of the equation of tomatoes and pears? We know that theory has resolved this problem, the equation of supply and demand is a numerical relation. On the basis of this relation the good supplied or demanded (at the choice of the observer) can be represented as a number. Ultimately, supply (demand) is measured by a number and not by demand (supply). *But it remains that neither supply not demand are measurable except in their equation.* The serious theoretician should therefore abstain from speaking of supply and demand: he can only speak of them as an identity. At every point in time when supply exists 'without demand', or demand exists 'without supply', neither supply nor demand are measurable: then *p* and *q* are only fantasy. The 'supply curve' is a unique point because a curve is a set of points located in measured space; equally, the 'demand curve' only exists at the point where demand is equated to supply. Each time they have real existence, supply and demand are combined in a single magnitude.

(2) *The identity of supply and demand always exists or it never exists.* If supply and demand were separate magnitudes they would remain so, even when they achieved equality. Inversely, if supply and demand are inseparable, then they always remain so.

(3) *When supply and demand are measurable it is necessarily in money; it is logically impossible that monetary supply or demand is not identically monetary demand or supply. Once supply exists, it is at the same time equal (identical) to demand.* In pure theory what does the term 'money' mean? Money is the number which expresses the measurement of supply and of demand. The equality, supply = demand, is thus the result of the two following identities:

supply = x units of the numeraire
demand = x units of the numeraire.

However, the equality of supply and the numeraire is given by *exchange*. It must thus be concluded that the good supplied is exchanged for the good demanded represented by the numeraire.

Now we shall discover the proof of this proposition. At the moment that supply appears it is constituted (measurable) if it is expressed in numeraire (or in money), but as soon as supply is expressed in money it is identical to demand, because it is identified by the quantity supplied and the number of units of money obtained in exchange. Any quantity supplied awaiting demand is thus formally excluded. But this means that the idea of a quantity demanded waiting for 'its supply' is just as specious, because demand is only measurable in relation to existing supply.

(4) *The identity of supply and demand exists over time; if it exists for zero time it would not exist. Consecutive p, q identities thus comprise the totality of chronological time.* Mathematicians have accustomed us to thinking of time in infinitely small durations. This is an ingenious mental construction. But we must not confuse quantities which tend to zero with those which are zero. The identity of supply and demand cannot be extended to an infinitesimally small period of time: the identity either occupies a finite period or no time at all. This is because the identity is not obtained 'in the limit': it is not a variation considered in an infinitely small period of time. The reason for this is already known: every separation, even infinitesimal, of supply and demand from the value given by their identity removes the quantity from its measure space. Movement through time does not then produce a 'tendency to' the identity: if it doesn't exist, it will never exist; if it is going to exist, it

already exists. It is thus necessary to reason along the lines of the following alternative. The identity has a finite duration (not infinitesimal) in time or it does not exist in any moment. As a consequence it is clear that the identity is verified in any period in which it occurs.

This is sufficient exploration of the antimony between the identity and the adjustment process. It remains to show that Keynes clearly defended the identity against adjustment while his commentators have sought to reconcile the irreconcilable.

B. Keynes and the Keynesians or the Identity and the Adjustment-Identity Antimony

By quoting unequivocal textual evidence we shall establish that Keynes excluded the concept of adjustment, even instantaneous, of aggregate supply and demand (negative argument). On the contrary, Keynes presumes the identity of aggregate supply and demand at all times (positive argument). Finally, we shall show that Keynes's identity is a crucial proposition, rather than a tautology or a truism. In each of these three steps we shall also evoke the general lines of the errors that must be attributed to Keynes's commentators.

1. According to Keynes, Aggregate Supply (p) and Demand (q) Never Adjust One to the Other

N, 'the price level of output is wholly governed by the three factors: (i) E, the volume of money earnings of the factors of production, (ii) O, the volume of current output, and (iii) I–S, the relation between the volume of saving and the value of investment' (*Treatise on Money*, *CW*, V: p. 231). The price level of output can thus be written as $N = E + (I - S)$. As soon as costs of production are paid (to the factors of production), the price of output as a whole is known: it is equal to E, the sum of the payments to factors. It is true that we should, as Keynes says, take the difference between I and S into account, *but neither investment (I), nor saving (S), are at any moment the result of a process of adjustment*. The three elements (E, I and S) can only be affected by three factors: the 'monetary factor', the 'investment factor' and the 'industrial factor' (ibid).

Monetary factors come into play when the supply of money is inadequate to meet firms' finance requirements: 'the supply of money available to entrepreneurs is no longer in equilibrium with the amount required by them' (ibid, p. 232). In this case, there is no question of adjusting the supply of, to the demand for, money. On the contrary, firms accept supply and 'adjust' their spending, in particular on investment. 'There will, therefore, be a tendency for a series of changes and adjustments to take place, of which a disturbance of the rate of investment is likely, as we shall see, to be the first stage' (ibid). In no case does the supply of money adjust to the demand for money (we are far from the *LM* curve); in no case does investment adjust to saving (we are far from the *IS* curve): adjustment of supply to demand is absent *at all times*.

Investment factors come into play when the 'market rate' of interest diverges from the 'natural rate' (ibid). To be sure, the divergence of these rates is not due to the behaviour of suppliers and demanders, nor will the interaction between supply and demand be capable of reducing the disparity. In fact, the market rate varies because of the new conditions created in the market for loanable funds by the monetary factors (ibid). On the other hand, the natural rate is sensitive to changes affecting the attractiveness of investment and saving (ibid). In brief, the two rates vary according to objective factors which are exogenously given to agents and which condition their behaviour. Again, logic excludes any idea of adjustment between supply and demand.

As for the *industrial factors*, they do not create any disequilibrium whose effects cannot be traced to consequences of the other two factors (ibid, p. 234).

In the *General Theory*, supply–demand adjustments are rejected with equal vigour. In chapter 19 Keynes denies the possibility of constructing an aggregate demand curve on the basis of particular industry curves, even if they could be identified for every industry:

> For the demand schedules for particular industries can only be constructed on some fixed assumption as to the nature of the demand and supply schedules of other industries and as to the amount of aggregate effective demand. It is invalid, therefore, to transfer our argument to industry as a whole unless we also transfer our assumption that the aggregate effective demand is fixed. Yet this assumption reduces the argument to an *ignoratio elenchi*.
>
> (*General Theory*, CW, VII: p. 259)

In chapter 21 of the *General Theory* Keynes suggests the particular importance to be attributed to the interaction between supply and demand in the economy:

> So long as economists are concerned with what is called the Theory of Value, they have been accustomed to teach that prices are governed by the conditions of supply and demand; . . . But when they pass in Volume II, or more often in a separate treatise, to the theory of money and prices, we hear no more of these homely but intelligible concepts and move into a world where prices are governed by the quantity of money, by its income-velocity, by the velocity of circulation relatively to the volume of transactions, by hoarding, by forced saving, by inflation and deflation *et hoc genus omne*. (ibid, p. 292)

Keynes does not reproach theoreticians who deal with the problem of value by means of supply and demand, nor does he criticise the completely different method used in the monetary sphere where supply and demand are inadequate concepts. The innovation lies in the choice of one of these approaches which, according to Keynes, should produce a general explanation of economic phenomena: the direct study of money, abandoning all consideration of supply and demand for different goods and assets.

In order to conform to a monetary economy the analysis should start with exchange between real goods and money. Thus, in chapter 21, which constitutes the real conclusion to the *General Theory*, Keynes rejects the division of economics into a Theory of Value and Distribution on the one hand, and a Theory of Money on the other. 'The right dichotomy is, I suggest, between the Theory of the Individual Industry . . . and the Theory of Output and Employment *as a whole*' (ibid, p. 293, italics supplied).

Yet, if we assume that the rates of remuneration of the different factors of production all change in the same proportion, 'it follows that the general price level (taking equipment and technique as given) depends partly on the wage unit and partly on the volume of employment' (ibid, p. 295). And the level of employment does not depend on supply and demand, but on the quantity of money: ' So long as there is unemployment, *employment* will change in the same proportion as the quantity of money; and when there is full employment, *prices* will change in the same proportion as the quantity of money' (ibid, p. 296, italics supplied).

Keynes sets aside the theoretical constructions elaborated by means of individual supplies and demands with such clarity and vigour that it is difficult to explain the persistence of the so-called Keynesian school of thought founded on the *IS–LM* diagram. How could a unified theory of money and value give even minimal attention to adjustments between supply and demand? It is inconceivable, because at all times aggregate supply and demand are the terms of an identity.

2. Keynes Shows the Permanent Identity of Aggregate Supply and Demand

In order to be convinced, it is only necessary to read chapter 3, the cornerstone of the *General Theory*: 'The Principle of Effective Demand'. Notwithstanding Hazlitt's lucid analysis, economists persist in talking about effective demand as if it concerned demand when it is expressly defined as a 'supply-demand': the theories of Keynes's commentators should all be fundamentally revised to replace effective demand with effective supply. There can be no doubt about the identity. Let N be national employment, Z the aggregate supply price, and D the receipts expected by firms from the sale of the output of N workers. 'The value of D at the point of the aggregate demand function, where it is intersected by the aggregate supply function, will be called the *effective demand*' (ibid, p. 25, italics supplied). Keynes immediately adds that this is 'the substance of the General Theory of Employment'. Effective demand is the point of intersection of two curves; it is thus as much a supply as a demand, indifferently one or the other, *identically*.

The identity forms the basis of chapters 6 and 7. National income is supplied and identically demanded because it is formed at the point of fusion of aggregate supply and demand. In Keynesian theory it is thus unthinkable that output supplied should not be completely demanded. It is thus with apprehension (and even with anger) that one thinks of those textbooks in which the '45 diagram' is supposed to represent Keynes's great contribution.

In neoclassical theory, income can exist without being spent and, what is even stranger, expenditures may exceed disposable incomes. The new theory is certainly more logical. All income which exists presumes an equivalent expenditure (if not, how would the income be created?). The determination of national income at the point of equilibrium of supply and demand is thus not simply an awkward formulation, it expresses the very nature of Keynes's thinking. And there is more. The supply–demand adjustment is non-existent, since neither supply nor demand are measurable except at their point of intersection.

Keynesian theory does not provide any other possibility which might be accepted or rejected. It brings to light the deep-seated vice of every analysis, which considers supply and demand independently one from the other. Economic theory makes no sense whatsoever if it does not respect the identity constraint; it is only consistent when it considers supply and demand as a unique reality, as a single piece representing one dual-faceted object.

Why then is this identity still misunderstood today? The reason is simple: theoreticians think that the identities are accepted and tautological definitions. From this point of view, causality and co-determination would be good hypotheses because their 'real content' is positive–they can be proved or disproved. A definition, on the other hand, could never have any real content. Nothing could be more false. The identity of p with q is a law even stronger than the presumed causality. The information drawn from the $p-q$ identity is not only positive, it is crucial, because it determines the entire body of economic science.

3. *The Identity of Aggregate Supply and Demand is the Fundamental Principle of All Economic Science*

At each moment in which supply and demand could be separated they would cease to be measurable. In the real world, supply and demand are at each moment perfectly defined quantities: it is thus patently clear that (neoclassical) analysis wrenches apart what fact reveals in union or fusion. The theory will only recover its usefulness when it recognises the internal coherence of the identity of aggregate supply and demand.

As Keynes stressed, economic theory is first of all *monetary* theory. What, indeed, is the fundamental importance of the $p-q$ identity? It can be expressed in three points:

(1) Supply is monetary because it is defined by the payment of the factors of production.
(2) Demand is monetary because the factors do not directly receive output in its physical form, but rather in the form of money income.
(3) Supply is instantaneously demand because the receipt of incomes transfers the ownership of the new output to the factors. Demand could only be separated from supply if the payment of incomes did not signify the appropriation of output *by the income recipients.*

The entire traditional conception of money is thus overturned. Neoclassical theory postulates the distinction between money and output; the producers of services receive an object which is distinct from real output. From such a standpoint failure is inevitable: thus separated one from the other supply and demand cannot be defined (or measured) except as an assumed premise of the analysis.

Keynes introduced the solution. Money is not a good, distinct from physical output. On the contrary, money and output emerge simultaneously in the act of production. The factors of production thus receive output through money; money is the form or the receptacle of which output is instantaneously its content. The income recipient is thus the owner of the *physical* output. Supply, the formation of income, is demand, possession of output in the form of income.

One imagines that money is an asset distinct from goods and assets, a 'nominal substance'. But the theory of a money-substance is metaphysical in the pejorative sense because it presumes what does not exist. In fact, money is a pure number assigned to the product. The association (or the 'identification') of money with output is the result of the process of production or, more precisely, the act of paying the factors of production. Once incomes have been created, the physical output is linked to the money-number, and the recipients of money incomes are thus the sole holders and owners of the new output. The sale of output is not demanding it for the first time; it is the dissolution of the link between number and output by substituting the purely physical output for the output-number; output is then demanded in physical form, although it was already demanded in money.

Here we are reasoning in terms of a completely new theory of the formation, the distribution and the end of the association between numbers and physical outputs. In this coherent framework it is impossible to discover, at any moment, the least separation between supply and demand. When money does not intervene, the entire output supplied is instantaneously demanded as *physical output* by those who have produced it. When money does intervene, output is instantaneously demanded *in money* by those who produce it. It is never possible for a good supplied not to be demanded. And it is equally impossible for a good that is demanded not to be supplied. In fact, to demand means to dispose of a sum of money, and all money is, by association, output: the buyer gives up an output (his *real* money) for a physical output.

Carrying out the analysis in terms of the pair supply–demand certainly is fraught with grave difficulties for the 'novice'. In the last two sections of this chapter we propose to show that the constraint is more flexible than it appears.

III

The permanence of the identity of aggregate supply and demand paradoxically permits adjustments 'within the identity'. The economy obeys the logic of the market despite the identity.

Let us recall the exact significance of the identity. Supply (p) is the event which allocates output in money to the factors of production. Demand (q) is the same event because output is instantaneously transmitted to the factors in money. The identity (p, q) thus holds until the time output is sold: supply and demand disappear at the same moment because output is consumed (or invested, but investment is a form of consumption) and thus no longer supplied nor demand since it is definitively distributed in physical form.

The identity (p, q) does have an unambiguous meaning: income recipients have access to output because they already possess it in the form of money. The exchange of money and output is thus, in the last analysis, an exchange of goods for goods.

According to the neoclassical school, money is a good distinct from real goods; it has a different nature. Yet, curiously, agents nevertheless have the option of exchanging money–a purely nominal good–for output composed of physical goods. To this end, they supply money and demand goods. As for the sellers, they supply goods and demand money (they give up real, physical goods in order to obtain fictitious, nominal goods). When the contracting parties reach an agreement, the supply of and the demand for money (or identically, demand for and supply of real goods) are equal and transactions can take place. In order to furnish an abstract definition of the point, or points, of equilibrium the theory launches into advanced mathematics to discern, without any observation of fact, whether or not these positions exist. Keynes had perfectly foreseen this new era of scholasticism:

> Too large a proportion of recent 'mathematical' economics are mere concoctions, as imprecise as the initial assumptions they rest on, which allow the author to lose sight of the complexities and interdependencies of the real world in a maze of pretentious and unhelpful symbols. (*CW*, VII: p. 298)

If the neoclassical writers applied the same rigour to the philosophical premises of their arguments as they do to their mathematical instruments, they would notice that the preparation for exchange according to their own theory takes place in a world that is totally unreal, void of any measurement space. Let us repeat that if exchange is in fact a relation of equivalence (which, in any case, can only be shown within Keynesian analysis), there is no equivalence in the preparatory period before exchange takes place; in the absence of equations there are no relations of equivalence: all reasoning is thus carried out in an absolute void. Yet, exchanges are in fact prepared in a world in which equivalence relations do exist: but only Keynesian analysis is capable of demonstrating this fact.

Incomes are only spent after their formation: a finite space of time necessarily separates the two events. Buyers and sellers can thus prepare their transactions. As soon as the market is open, no exchange having yet taken place, output and money confront each other *as equivalents* since money income is the definition of output. It is thus permitted – but only within the Keynesian logic of the identity of money and output – to speak of a space of common measure for output and income brought to different markets.

Here it is essential to understand that the money-output identity is established by the identity of two events: the creation, and destruction, of national income: 'the flow of the community's earnings or money-income . . . with its twofold division (1) into the parts which have been *earned* . . . and (2) into the parts which are *expended*' (*CW*, V: p. 121). It is because the identity (p, q) is ultimately derived from the identity 'creation–expenditure' of national income, that it permits the existence of adjustment between p and q. More insight into this question may be gained by means of a short historical summary of the (p, q) relation in economic analysis, from Ricardo to Walras, and up to Keynes.

For Ricardo, the (p, q) relation is causal: every cause has an effect, and every effect stems from a cause. If p (output) is the cause of q (the acquisition of output), the equivalence relation is satisfied for every individual output, the 'unity of causes' and the 'unity of effects' being equal in number. Every output must thus earn its 'natural' price, all deviations summing to zero. Demand is thus preconstrained by supply: this means that q does not possess a degree of freedom with respect to p.

With Walras the goods market and the market for productive services are complementary: they are joined to each other as if 'in a circle'. Thus the theorist could not determine the amount of factor incomes without knowing the sum of the actual expenditures on the goods market. The purchases of goods finance the payment of the services of the factors of production. The reverse is equally true. Expenditures on the purchase of goods cannot be determined unless the incomes of the factors of production are known. The event p (payment for the services of productive factors) is fulfilled as expenditure q (purchase of goods) and, at the same time, expenditure p is fulfilled as expenditure q. The two events form a unique action which could not be determined on the basis of just one of its components. In such conditions it is inconceivable that the demand for an output should deviate, even if only very little, from the supply of the same output. Productive services, being paid p, should logically receive, as q, an amount strictly equal to p. It is true that the theories of 'imputation' have demonstrated (notably on the basis of Euler's theorem) that the equality of p and q for each output is only rarely satisfied. But in every case in which it is not, the theory reveals its logical deficiency because it is found twice wanting, unable to provide an explanation of either prices or incomes.

Finally, there is Keynes's theory, which is realistic. Demand has one degree of freedom with respect to supply. Supply is not the cause of demand (cf. *CW*, VII: pp. 25–6) and supply and demand are no longer mutually complementary (cf. *CW*, V: p. 121, especially the passage quoted above). The (p, q) relation is conceived in a new way, in the distinction concerning the *sign* of the operations: the output *creates* income and demand *destroys* it. Thus demand can differ from supply for each individual output. It is true, none the less, that all income destroyed is (or has been) indeed destroyed. But logic does not require that incomes created by production of output n are fully spent by households, without excess or shortfall, on the flow of output of n: $q(n)$ can be inferior, superior, or equal to $p(n)$. If $q(n)$ is inferior to $p(n)$ the difference represents income lost by firms to the benefit of households. The opposite case is more frequent, providing profits for firms defined by the positive difference $q(n)-p(n)$. The households who have received the output n in money, purchase it in its physical form for a sum of money $q(n)$, greater than $p(n)$. Profit is the income of households transferred to firms. Keynes adopts this analysis from the time of his *Treatise*, where profit was 'earned at the expense of the consumer' (*CW*, V: pp. 270, 281, 284).

As a result of Keynes's theoretical contribution, the deviation between supply and demand no longer represents a serious logical problem. Supply $p(n)$ occurs at moment t. The demand for *physical* output occurs at moment t^+. But the demand for output in *money* is realised at t. How is it possible that these two demands for the same output do not exactly coincide? In fact, they coincide perfectly. As soon as demand for *physical* output differs from demand *in money*, the supply of n, $p(n)$ absorbs the difference. From moment t, households only receive in money the amout that they spend in order to purchase output,

n, in its *physical* form. Keynes's theory in fact supposes the retroactive effect of demand (exercised at moment t^+) on supply (occurring at the earlier moment t). This is the case for the reason set out above: the formation and destruction of incomes are complementary components of a single unique action.

The last part of this chapter will discuss an even more important advance produced by Keynes's work: although aggregate demand is constantly identical to aggregate supply, it may exceed it (inflation) or fall short of it (unemployment). These two inequalities may even co-exist, which is often the case in the real world.

IV

The identity of aggregate supply (p) and demand (q) permits two inequalities: q greater (inflation) or smaller (unemployment) than p. The two inequalities may even co-exist.

If the identity (p, q) were a tautology, any inequality between p and q would be absurd. But we know that the identity does not mean that p is p or that q is q. On the contrary, it conveys the crucial information that money incomes define the *physical output* incorporated in the money. In all non-Keynesian theory and even in certain contemporary interpretations of Keynes, money income is a nominal asset (which, it should be remarked, is a clear contradiction of terms) which meets another asset, this one real or physical, stored in the firms. The identity (p, q) shows reality in a completely different light: once the remuneration of the factors of production takes place the physical product has already reached the households. In fact, as in the aphorism of the wine in the wineskin, the physical product is contained in the money paid out as incomes: closely associated, incomes (in wage units) and the physical outputs constitute the identity or the union of the container-form (the money wage-units created) and the contained-essence (the physical product).

But why does the identity form–essence permit such inequalities? It would seem, on the contrary, that since the same action, the remuneration of the factors of production, defines the two quantities (nominal and real), the nominal form and the real content could only co-exist over time as an identity. This is true. We have insisted on this point from the beginning: it is inconceivable that aggregate supply and demand should not be continuously identical, from their creation to their simultaneous annihilation. The answer can already be found in Keynes's *Treatise*.

Before quoting the relevant passage, let us try to find an *a priori* explanation by means of logical reflection.

In a monetary economy, the payment of factors of production incorporates the output in money. If firms do not have access to part of the new output, the incomes created will remain with the households until final purchase and sale of consumption goods. In reality, however, firms 'earn' a positive portion of current output. This portion of output is tautologically withdrawn from households, but what is more, it is withdrawn *in money*. Reason imposes this conclusion. What is the action that gives access to physical output? It is the conversion of money income into a purely physical output, that is, the final expenditure of money income. The portion $p(r)$ of output earned by firms is thus *bought* by them: $p(r)$ is thus obtained by an expenditure of money income. The only difficulty is to 'isolate' this expenditure from the observed streams of income. The difficulty is due to the fact that firms create *household* incomes. It is thus hard to imagine how they can themselves spend part of the incomes they create. However, it is naive to presume that payment of income cannot *include* the final purchases of a portion of current output. If the firms recover all of the money they pay out as money incomes from the sale of only two-thirds of the physical product, then payment of incomes implies purchase of the remaining one-third of the current output by the firms for their own uses. The firms' purchases of the portion of new output which accrues to them thus takes place via the payment of income to the households. Thus, supply p, reduced by the portion $p(r)$, confronts demand q, which is identical to p, *and not to* q-$p(r)$.

Before pursuing investigation of the inequality (p-$p(r)$, q), let us provide textual support for the accuracy of the analysis proposed. Let S be the amount of savings, that part of *households*' income which is not consumed. Let I be the value of new investment in the period. Finally, define Q as the total profit, realised in industry as a whole. This gives the following equation (*CW*, V: p. 124): $Q = I-S$. 'Thus the profits on the production and sale of consumption goods are equal to the differences between the *cost* of new investment and savings' (ibid).

If the difference ($I-S$) were zero, all revenues accruing to households would be spent by them, and all current output would be consumed. But any positive difference between I and S implies an equivalent reduction in the incomes of households and an equivalent increase in the profits of firms. The flow of incomes is thus threefold:

(1) households receive E, the total amount of the nation's money income;

(2) households lose part $(I-S)$ of their incomes and thus receive the *value* $E-(I-S)$;
(3) firms, recipients of the *value* $(I-S)$ *never spend this amount on the goods market*, because – and this is the basis of the *Treatise* – *'windfall' profit is not a part of national income.*

Logically we note that profit is *already spent* in the reduction of the value of incomes in the hands of households who no longer dispose of the value $(E-Q)$ because they have lost the value $(I-S)$. *This means that profit,* Q, *is spent within the confines of the flow* E, i.e. in the creation, and not in the expenditure, of household incomes.

Although supply p (E in Keynes's notation) and demand q (the expenditure of E) are terms of an identity, part $(I-S)$ of p is directly absorbed by the creation of new fixed capital accumulated by firms. The money sum E, whose *value* is diminished by $(I-S)$, is thus left to the households. Thus, the difference $(I-S)$, the definition of profit, is equally the definition of inflation, because the numerical amount of incomes is E and because their *value* is $E-(I-S)$. 'We may have a rise or fall of Q, the total profits above or below zero, due to an inequality between saving and the value of investment. We shall call this *profit inflation* (or *deflation*)' (ibid, p. 140).

The lessons to be drawn from an attentive reading of the *Treatise*, written more than fifty years ago, are far from exhausted. In the 'fundamental equations' commentators have seen but banal exercises in algebraic manipulation, while in fact they represent purely conceptual relationships. The *General Theory* does not go much further. In his two great contributions Keynes imposed a method which is little followed today (with the consequence of the stagnation of knowledge) on the entirety of economic science. It consisted of *starting* from the study of money flows. The equilibria constructed in the 'real sector' by supply–demand adjustments are thus put in their true perspective as mental exercises which are logically inconsistent (for their components cannot be measured except in equations) and destitute of any application to the world in which we live.

It is time that we took Keynes seriously. One single decision would be necessary and sufficient to do this: orthodox thought must finally recognise, no matter the intellectual difficulty, the permanent identity of aggregate supply and demand. If, as we have shown by rational and textual evidence, aggregate demand (q) is superior to aggregate supply (p), two essential remarks are sufficient to establish that, despite the divergence, the identity is maintained in the creation of the flow of incomes and permanently until the final purchase of national output.

(1) The creation of incomes instantaneously difines the identity of p (supply of output in every sector of the economy) and of q (demand of output arising from all sectors of the economy). The identity signifies that the whole output gives rise to the monetary remuneration of factors of production who dispose of the output in money, i.e. a disposition which represents the national income.
(2) A portion of current output is directly withdrawn from money to be added to firms' accumulated fixed capital. The *value* of q is diminished but, in terms of its definition in *money units*, q remains unchanged. To be precise, q exceeds p to the extent of the consumable portion of p. The total of the sum, q, is necessary for the portion of p which is received by households.

In conclusion, inflation is the positive difference between the numerical value of aggregate demand and its real value (purchasing power). Households, disposing of q, can only obtain a part $(p\text{-}p(r))$, of q. When 'profits inflation' is zero, inflation is eliminated and households receive the total national product, including the part that is saved, and eventually invested. But whether inflation is zero or positive, aggregate demand is always equal to aggregate supply. The only difference between the two cases is whether households buy (inflation), or do not buy (equilibrium), a portion of output representing the profits of firms.

The opposite case still remains to be discussed: supply in excess of demand. Let us note immediately that the 'crisis' in no way contradicts the identity (p, q). This would betray insufficient clarity of mind: to believe that the identity is an ideal is contradicted by the events of the real world. We have sufficiently repeated that the identity of aggregate supply and demand is the alpha and omega of economic science and economic reality. Nevertheless, aggregate supply can exceed aggregate demand and, sadly, countries nowadays do experience such conditions which are considered as the expression of crisis. How is this possible? It is only possible within conditions which strictly respect the identity (p, q). The crisis supposes inflation: a portion $p(r)$ of national income is directly accumulated by firms. If accumulation is composed of machines and other equipment then only inflation occurs. But inflation is accompanied by unemployment as soon as $p(r)$ is composed of consumption goods destined for households. Let us follow closely Keynes's profound reasoning. A part $p(r)$ of output is sold *before any expenditure of national income*. Households thus can only dispose of purchasing power over the goods *non-accumulated* in $p(r)$. Now, when firms try to sell the entire output, including the portion accumulated, *households' incomes will not be sufficient to buy it*. The economy produces enough purchasing power, but the accumulation of $p(r)$ withdraws a part of it. As long as accumulation is made up of capital goods, this will not lead to unemployment, but if part of $p(r)$ is made up of consumption goods, there will be unemployment or underemployment because in any case households can only dispose of purchasing power over the portion $(p\text{-}p(r))$ of national output.

If Keynes's message had been heeded (rather than the vulgar opposition to fiscal and monetary policies), societies would be able to control inflation and unemployment. The identity of aggregate supply and demand would exclude all general disequilibria from the day that 'profit inflation' was eliminated. The remedy is at hand, *given that the diagnosis is correct*. Without inflation, unemployment will be non-existent. By means of a Monetary Reform, Keynes's message could thus transform Says's Law into a Positive Law (see *Etiologie de l'inflation et du chômage: les malformations du capital*, Editions Universitaires de Fribourg and Castella, 1983).

Part III
Effective Demand and the Process of Production

10 Capital and Effective Demand[1]

Pierangelo Garegnani

I INTRODUCTION

1. Today's economic theory appears to be unable to provide a generally accepted answer to some of the most basic questions one can raise about the working of a market economy. Among these questions there undoubtedly is the question concerning the relation between decisions to save and decisions to invest. On this question there is a traditional answer according to which, fundamentally, the decisions to save out of full employment income (i.e. the difference between full employment income and the decisions to consume out of that income) determine the amount of investment. Keynes's criticism has shown the weakness of that answer, but the position has remained uncertain with respect to long-period tendencies. Discussions of Keynes's theory conducted on the assumption of money wages being flexible relative to the money supply have in fact created a climate of professional opinion favourable to the traditional answer, though they have been by no means sufficient to restore the unanimity and confidence which it once enjoyed.

We shall here contend that the origin of this uncertainty – and of the fact that the Keynesian controversy persists after nearly fifty years – lies largely in the composite character of Keynes's thought. In the *General Theory* it is as if two fundamentally heterogeneous strands of thought were mixed. The first strand centres on the novel idea from which the book originated: the idea that it is principally variations in the level of aggregate output that equilibrate investment and saving in a capitalist economy. However, this innovatory strand is imposed as if by force upon a conceptual basis which remains to a large extent the traditional one. And this traditional basis deeply affects Keynes's theory: in particular, it affects his theory of investment and the rate of interest.

In fact, Keynes's innovatory theory of aggregate output, and its corollary, the possibility of equilibrium with unemployment, conflicted with the generally accepted theory of distribution on both the latter's flanks. It conflicted with it on the flank of the labour market, where Keynes had to deny that wages would be determined by the equilibrium between the demand for and supply of labour. It also conflicted with traditional theory on the flank of the capital market; where Keynes had similarly to deny that the rate of interest would be determined by the equilibrium between the demand for savings and their supply out of full employment income (that is, the demand for, and supply of, capital, cf. para. 20 below). In order to develop his initial idea and to get it accepted, Keynes had therefore to work out a criticism of the traditional theory of distribution and in particular a criticism of the traditional theory of interest: and it is in the way in which he effected, or did not effect, this criticism, that the traditional strand of thought becomes pre-eminent.

We shall accordingly argue that in Keynes we find a theoretical structure which bears the signs of a compromise: a compromise between his innovatory theory of aggregate output and the traditional elements which are present above all in his theory of investment and interest. Now, a characteristic of compromises is that they lend themselves to divergent interpretations and that they are unstable.

2. The divergence of interpretation I am referring to is that between Keynes and most of the subsequent literature. It centres on whether the rigidity of money wages is or is not necessary for Keynes's denial of a tendency to full employment. As is well known, Keynes generally denied that the flexibility of wages in the face of unemployment would have led to full employment of labour. Keynes, who is still struggling to 'escape from habitual modes of thought', relies on the innovatory strand of his analysis, where basically investment is viewed as an independent variable. Thus, he tends to the conclusion that the flexibility of money wages can provide no tendency to full employment. The role of the assumed comparative rigidity of money wages is then, for him, that of preventing an absurd indefinite deflation of wages and prices. This position is held even at the cost of exerting some violence on his own theory of the rate of interest and investment. As we shall see, he seems in fact to have viewed this second part of his theory as provisional when compared with the determination of aggregate output – as something, that is, which he would be ready to re-examine if it turned out to be incompatible with the other more essential part of his thought.

The position is basically different in most of the later literature, where Keynes's 'struggle to escape' is absent. There, on the contrary, the many problems which Keynes had opened up without arriving at a satisfactory solution provided a strong incentive for a return to traditional theory. Hence, the reliance of this literature on Keynes's theory of interest and investment – or, more exactly, on the traditional basis of his theory – in order to argue the dependence of labour unemployment upon rigid money wages.

3. The presence of these two conflicting strands of thought may also explain the instability of the Keynesian compromise. If rigid money wages are essential to the existence of unemployment, the attempt to re-absorb Keynes in traditional theory does not meet great obstacles: in Hicks's well-known words, Keynes would only have laid 'enormous emphasis' on qualifications of traditional theory that had already been admitted before him (Hicks, 1937, pp. 472, 465). And since what would be involved would be the *ratio* between money wages and quantity of money, the effects on employment of rigid money wages could be corrected by a flexible monetary policy.

4. We have referred to a distinction in Keynes between his innovatory theory of aggregate output and his more traditional and provisional theory of the rate of interest and of investment. Keynes himself comes close to this distinction in an important passage concerning the *General Theory*:

> the initial novelty lies in my maintaining that it is not the rate of interest, but the level of incomes which ensures equality between saving and investment. The arguments which lead up to this initial conclusion are independent of my subsequent theory of the rate of interest, and in fact I reached it before I had reached the latter theory. But the result of it was to leave the rate of interest in the air. If the rate of interest is not determined by saving and investment in the same way in which price is determined by supply and demand, how is it determined? . . . It was only when [attempts in other directions failed] . . . that I hit on what I now think to be the true explanation.

and he continues: 'It would be true to say that [the liquidity preference theory] does not carry us very far. But it gives us firm and intelligible ground from which to proceed' (Keynes, 1937, p. 250).

or, a few pages later, 'To speak of the Liquidity Preference Theory of the Rate of interest is indeed to dignify it too much . . . I am simply stating what it is, the significant Theories on the subject being subsequent.'

Here we have the distinction between the innovatory strand, 'the initial novelty' of Keynes's first passage, and a theory of interest which is explicitly admitted to be provisional and which came later to explain that variable left 'in the air' by the rejection of its traditional explanation.

5. This distinction between two conflicting strands in Keynes's thought, between his theory of aggregate output and his theory of investment and interest, seems particularly important at the present moment. The traditional concepts which underlie the second part of Keynes's theory, and in particular the idea of a regular decreasing functional relation between the rate of interest and the demand for investment, are, in fact, those which the criticism of the traditional notion of capital has thrown into doubt in the last twenty years.

If this criticism is well founded, it cannot but set free the innovatory part of Keynes's theory from the weight of the traditional part, which in the meantime has nearly succeeded in smothering it. In what follows it will be argued that that criticism allows the overcoming of the Keynesian compromise in a direction opposite to that in which the orthodox resurgence has attempted to overcome it. It may thus provide a more solid basis to the Keynesian conclusions on labour employment, taken as an essential part of a wider change which implies abandoning the theory of distribution dominant for nearly a century, in favour of a return to the earlier approach to such problems by Adam Smith, Malthus and Ricardo.

6. The aim of this chapter will be to support and develop what has been asserted in this introduction. In section II we shall focus our attention on the divergence between Keynes and most of the subsequent literature concerning the role of the assumption of rigid wages. The comparison with Wicksell's monetary theory will allow us to bring out the novelty of Keynes's theory and its dependence on the rejection of the traditional theory of interest.

In section III the attention will turn towards Keynes's criticism of the traditional theory of interest. The deficiencies of this criticism, we shall there contend, have opened the way to the idea that the flexibility of money wages, or an elastic monetary policy, would lead the economy to full employment.

Finally we shall see, in section IV, how the criticism raised against the traditional notion of capital may allow us to overcome the 'Keynesian compromise'. There we shall also indicate how the classical approach to distribution may provide a basis for solving the problems raised by a long-period application of the principle of effective demand.

II THE ROLE OF RIGID WAGES

7. Keynes says that the 'initial novelty' in the *General Theory* consisted of arguing 'that it is not the rate of interest, but the level of incomes which ensures equality between saving and investment' (Keynes, 1937, p. 250). To see the implications of this statement we must consider first of all in what way the interest rate was traditionally seen to be determined by the equality between investment and full employment savings.

A problem one meets in this respect is the contrast Keynes himself noticed (Keynes, 1936, p. 175) between the general acceptance of this idea and the difficulty of finding a detailed treatment of the problem before Keynes. The fact is that this theory of interest was seen as being entailed in the application to capital of a general theory where distribution, i.e. the prices of the services of factors of production, was determined by the demand and supply of such factors. However, the rate of interest emerges in the market for *money* loans and the question arises therefore of the relation between savings and money loans.

It is to Wicksell's monetary theory that we must turn for the most important pre-Keynesian attempt to ground by means of a systematic analysis of the money loan market (the market in which the rate of interest is actually observed), the marginalist[2] concept of interest as the supply-and-demand-determined price of the productive factor 'capital'.

Moreover, Wicksell's analysis is akin to that of the *General Theory*, in that it is focused on the source and the effects of variations in *aggregate* monetary expenditure, and his 'orthodox' theory of such phenomena provides a good basis for bringing out the exact point where Keynes's heterodoxy lies.

8. Fundamental to Wicksell's theory is the concept of an interest rate referred to as 'natural', 'normal' or 'real': the rate, that is, at which '*the demand for loan capital and the supply of savings* exactly agree' (Wicksell, 1935, p. 193).[3] The 'natural' rate, Wicksell writes, 'more or less corresponds to the expected yield on the newly created capital' or as he puts it elsewhere, to the return on capital which becomes 'free' in the course of the period considered, and can thus be 'invested' in the most profitable physical form. Since the expected return on 'newly created capital' will tend to coincide, under normal conditions, with the return that will be realised, the 'natural' rate of interest is the rate of interest which Wicksell had related, in the real part of his theory, to the data concerning the available quantity of factors, technical knowledge and the tastes of the consumers (cf. Wicksell, 1935, pp. 205–6). It follows that the natural rate of interest is liable to vary as a result of changes in any of these data. The explanation of variations in the price level can then be found, Wicksell argues, in the slowness with which the banks adjust their lending rates of interest to variations in the natural rate.

There are two aspects of Wicksell's argument that are important for us here. The first is the assertion that the market rate of interest can differ from the 'natural' rate for non-negligible periods of time. The second is that the possibility of this is attributed to the existence of the banking system. Wicksell maintains, in fact, that if money loans were to take place directly, from person to person, their supply would be largely determined by money savings.[4] The forces of demand for, and supply of, savings could then act *directly* on the market for money loans and bring the rate of interest back to the level of the natural rate, as soon as the former began to diverge from the latter. Thus if, for example, there was an increase in the profitability of investment, the increased 'demand for loan capital' would encounter the limit to the supply of loans set by the flow of savings: an increase in the market rate of interest, towards the new level of the 'natural' rate, would result. The situation is quite different when there is a developed banking system. Indeed, the volume of bank loans is independent of the flow of money savings: 'By the concentration in their hands of private cash holdings . . . [the banks] possess a fund for loans which is always elastic and, on certain assumptions, inexhaustible' (Wicksell, 1935, p. 194). Hence the banks can accommodate any variation in the demand for loans without changing their rates of interest, and can thus sever the link between the market rate of interest and the 'natural' rate which would otherwise have operated through demand and supply in the loan market.

Yet if this direct link between the two rates is broken, Wicksell continues, another far less rigid link will continue to hold good and will act via the price level. Let us consider an initial situation of real and monetary equilibrium, in which there occurs an increase in the profitability of investment, and suppose that the banks meet the increased demand for loans by an expansion of credit, leaving the rate of interest unchanged. As the loans come to be used for the purchase of means of production, the flow of aggregate money expenditure will increase: to an initially unchanged consumption expenditure there will be added the increased investment expenditure.

This increased aggregate expenditure, meeting a virtually unchanged volume of output, will lead to an increase in money prices: the increase will at first be in the prices of investment goods, but then, when the increased money income thus generated permits increases in consumption expenditure, the prices of consumer goods will also increase – and this latter increase may be contributed to by transfers of resources from the production of consumer goods to that of investment goods (see Wicksell, 1935, p. 194).[5] If we assume that the money rates of payment to primary factors tend to increase in the same proportion as prices, the profitability of investments will continue to exceed the market rate of interest and, as long as this condition holds good, the inflationary process will continue (ibid, pp. 195–7). An analogous process will take place, but in the opposite direction, when the 'natural' rate of interest falls and the banks keep the market rate unchanged (ibid, p. 200). But, Wicksell concludes, it will be these very cumulative processes of inflation or deflation which will compel the banks eventually to raise, or lower, the market rate of interest towards its 'natural' level (ibid, p. 201), the only level at which there will be price stability.

9. The theory briefly set out above brings to light the (often implicit) grounds on which the marginalist theorists maintained that the separation between savings decisions and investment decisions – or the influence of monetary factors in the loan market – could not endanger, other than temporarily, the claimed tendency to the full employment of the factors of production. At the basis of their argument there lay *the* *postulate of the elasticity of the demand for capital with respect to the rate of interest.*[6] This elasticity, it was thought, would make it possible for the rate of interest to adjust planned investment to planned savings through the play of demand and supply in the market for money loans. But if this first demand-and-supply mechanism were seriously hampered by monetary factors, that same elasticity would ensure that changes in the rate of interest would suffice to re-establish equilibrium in the face of variations of aggregate expenditure due to inequality between planned savings and investment. It is to Wicksell's merit that he provides a systematic and rigorous version of this line of thought; even though he shows that the link between saving and investment decisions must often be the indirect one.[7]

It is not surprising, therefore, that Wicksell did not find, in his analysis of the loan market, any factors which might bring into question the conclusions of the 'real' theory on the tendency to full employment of factors: variations of monetary expenditure are seen to have effects on the level of prices, but not on the levels of production and of factor employment. The assumption that unemployment of primary factors would make their money-rates of remuneration fall, allowing money prices to fall in step with monetary expenditure, did not entail admitting an absurd process of unending deflation or inflation of prices: the elasticity of demand for investible funds ensured the existence of a 'natural' rate of interest to which the banks would be able, and eventually compelled, to bring back the money rate of interest. It was thus natural for Wicksell to suppose that any underutilisation of productive equipment and primary factors could only be temporary, and could therefore be neglected in an analysis of value and distribution conducted at the level of general principles.[8]

10. What we must now consider is why Keynes, although starting from premises not unlike those of Wicksell, arrives at radically different conclusions. The picture which Keynes's *General Theory* draws is well known. As in Wicksell, the system of interest rates is proximately determined by monetary factors. Keynes approaches the problem of the rate of interest from the angle of the demand for and supply of the stock of money. The demand for money, or 'liquidity preference', is explained in terms not only of the two traditional 'transactions' and 'precautionary' motives, but also in terms of the 'speculative motive', which expresses the preference for money, as a means of holding wealth, of those who expect falls in the value of bonds (= increases in the rate of interest). According to Keynes, the demand for money due to this third motive must be elastic with respect to the rate of interest, since the lower is that rate, the greater is the risk that it will rise, and the smaller is the compensation for such risk provided by the interest rate (Keynes, 1936, pp. 201–2). The rate of interest is thus the price which will bring into equality not the demand for and supply of saving, but rather the desire to hold wealth in the form of money and the quantity of money made available by the monetary authorities. It is therefore determined once 'liquidity preference' and the quantity of money are known. Planned investment, on the other hand, depends on the rate of interest in the manner shown by the 'marginal efficiency of capital schedule'. Once the rate of interest is determined, therefore, the volume of planned investment is also determined when expressed in 'real' terms, i.e. in wage-units.[9]

There is thus no reason why the amount of investment should coincide with the amount of saving out of full employment income. Yet equilibrium requires equality between planned investment and planned saving: if that equality is not satisfied, aggregate monetary expenditure will tend to change over time.

It is necessary to distinguish, at this point, between the case in which planned investment exceeds full employment savings and the opposite case. In the former, equilibrium would be reached, according to Keynes, via an inflationary process not unlike that found in Wicksell: because of the increase of prices and money wages, the money value of national income (and thus the 'transactions' demand for money) would increase until it caused a rise in the rate of interest great enough to eliminate the cause of inflation (see, for example, ibid, p. 202). For the analysis of the second case, however, Keynes introduces the 'propensity to consume' and, therewith, the most original part of his analysis. It is assumed that, other things being equal, when employment increases the community will increase aggregate consumption, but by less than income has increased. It is then shown how, when planned investment falls short of planned saving, equality between investment and saving will be achieved through a contraction of the national product. The possibility of 'equilibria' characterised by unemployment of labour and under-capacity working of equipment is thus asserted.[10]

11. Keynes's conclusions concerning his second case stand sharply in contrast to those which Wicksell had reached for the analogous case. The search for the source of this difference cannot but start from the most obvious difference between the two analyses: the high flexibility of money wages assumed by Wicksell but denied by Keynes. Wicksell assumed a tendency for prices and wages to fall in the same proportion as aggregate expenditure; it was precisely this process of price and wage deflation that would eventually oblige the banks to bring the rate of interest down to its 'natural' level. By contrast, Keynes assumes that any shortfall of planned investment relative to planned saving is followed by decreases in total expenditure *measured in wage-units*: he assumes, that is, that money wages do not fall or, more exactly, do not fall in the same proportion as money expenditure has fallen. Given this assumption, there most be a shrinking of output, since the entrepreneurs will not continue to produce at below normal profits. It must now be asked to what extent Keynes's thesis would remain valid were we to admit, with Wicksell, that competition amongst unemployed workers would give rise to a continuous fall in the money wage.

As is well known, Keynes denied that the novelty of his conclusions turned on the hypothesis of money wage rigidity and chapter 19 of the *General Theory* is devoted to this question. The argument develops in two stages. Keynes assumes at first that the fall in the money wage rate will cause a shift in neither the consumption function nor the marginal efficiency of capital schedule. He also assumes that it will not affect the rate of interest. In this case, the fall in wages could not lead to permanent increases of employment and real income (Keynes, 1936, pp. 261–2). Thus, Keynes concludes, the fall in wages could affect employment *only* through its effects on the propensity to consume, on the marginal efficiency of capital schedule, and on the rate of interest.

Keynes then proceeds to the second stage of his argument and considers the effects of a fall in wages on the consumption function and on the marginal efficiency of capital schedule. He concludes that, in a closed economy, these effects will be negative, rather than positive, in their implications for employment. He therefore turns to consider the effects on the rate of interest, remarking that it is to these effects alone that reference can be made by those who claim that wage flexibility will lead to full employment. Yet if the available quantity of money contracts in step with money income, 'there is . . . nothing to hope for in this direction'. If the quantity of money remains approximately constant, however, Keynes continues, there will be effects on the rate of interest analogous to those which the monetary authorities can achieve by purchasing bonds on the 'open market'. In either case the quantity of money increases relative to money income: a greater quantity of money thus becomes available to meet the demand for money deriving from the 'speculative motive' and, given the speculative demand schedule, the interest rate must fall. It follows, says Keynes, that, leaving aside the disadvantages specific to this particular method of increasing the relative supply of money, decreases in money wages encounter limits to their effect on the rate of interest analogous to those specific to open-market operations. Just as open-market operations can have but a limited influence on long-term rates of interest when the increase in the quantity of money is moderate, whereas they can have unfavourable effects on the state of confidence when the increase is large, so a moderate fall in money wage rates will prove insufficient, whereas a large fall could shatter the state of confidence. Keynes thus concludes by asserting firmly that: 'There is, therefore, no ground for belief that a flexible wage policy is capable of maintaining a state of continuous full employment – any more than for the belief that an open-market monetary policy is capable, unaided, of achieving this result' (Keynes, 1936, p. 267; but see also ibid., p. 27; and our footnote no. 12 below).

We shall have reason to return to this argument of Keynes later on and to discuss its limitations. Here we need only note that the hypothesis of money wage rigidity does not suffice to explain the difference between Keynes's conclusions and those of the traditional economists; the flexibility of prices and wages would lead to the full employment of factors *only if* the resulting decrease in the rate of interest could so affect planned investment as to make it equal to full employment savings. Keynes denied that the rate of interest could play that equilibrating role and it is *here*, in the theory of the rate of interest, that he diverges from Wicksell and the other 'orthodox' economists.

12. Thus two results begin to emerge from this preliminary discussion of Keynes's analysis. The first result is that the source of the difference between Keynes and the orthodox economists is to be sought in the theory of the rate of interest. The second concerns the precise *nature* of this difference in the theory of the rate of interest. Keynes's conclusions rest in fact, not so much on the particular theory of the rate of interest which he put forward, as on his rejection of the traditional theory, which determined the rate of interest by the demand for and the supply of savings.

It is then in the *criticism* of the traditional theory of interest, rather than in the hypothesis of money wage rigidity, that the roots of Keynes's conclusions are to be sought. It is to that criticism, contained in chapter 14 of the *General Theory*, that we must now direct our attention. If the criticism were well founded, the assumption of money wage rigidity would appear to be a consequence, and not a premise, of the thesis that there exists no tendency to the full employment of factors. To assume wage flexibility, in the absence of a rate of interest capable of adjusting planned investment to full employment saving, would compel us to allow for the possibility of an absurd process of unending deflation of prices and wages.[11]

III KEYNES'S CRITICISM OF THE TRADITIONAL THEORY OF INTEREST AND THE REHABILITATION OF THE ORTHODOX THEORY

13. Keynes's criticism of the traditional theory of interest contain two strands. On the one hand, there is the charge that the theory is indeterminate. To each level of utilisation of productive capacity there corresponds a different real income and hence a different supply of savings schedule: given the marginal efficiency of capital schedule, there are therefore not one but many rates of interest at which planned investment and planned saving are equal – one for each level of real income (Keynes, 1936, pp. 179–82). This first criticism does not seem to be well founded. If the rate of interest tended to equalise investment to the savings corresponding to *any* given level of real income, any initial increase in employment would tend to validate itself and the fall in money wages could then bring the economy back to full employment (cf. Garegnani, 1979, p. 71). As a result, the full-employment supply schedule of savings is the *only* supply of savings to which the theory under examination need refer in the determination of the equilibrium rate of interest: the dependence of the supply of savings on the level of employment does not warrant the charge of indeterminacy laid by Keynes.[12]

14. We may therefore confine our attention to the second strand of Keynes's criticism of the received theory of interest. This may be summarised by saying that the traditional theory of interest ignored the effects deriving from the role of money as a store of value. When this role is given due weight, Keynes states, one must recognise that the aggregate demand for money depends on the rate of interest, as well as on the total money volume of transactions. For a given money value of output, the demand for money will be greater the lower the rate of interest: the latter will then have the role of bringing about equality between the quantity of money made available by the monetary authorities and the demand for money, not that of equating the demand for and the supply of saving (see, for example, Keynes, 1936, p. 167).

In this second criticism, Keynes confines himself to counterposing his own theory of interest to the traditional one, and the force of his argument is merely that of the theory which he puts forward. The idea that the demand for money depends on the rate of interest – which is quite in accord with marginalist principles when it is presented in terms of equality, at the margin, between the sacrifice of liquidity and the payment therefore – has been generally accepted in subsequent literature. The same has not occurred for the criticism of the traditional theory of interest which Keynes wished to base on that idea. Indeed we shall see below how it has been argued that the rate of interest can equalise *both* the demand for and supply of the stock of money *and* the demand for and supply of savings.

15. These attempts to reinstate the traditional analysis were undoubtedly encouraged by the feeling that Keynes's theory of interest need not conflict with orthodox theory properly interpreted. As Wicksell says, the orthodox theory of interest was only meant to refer to long-run tendencies, destined to assert themselves against the short-term obstacles raised by a number of other factors.

When examined from this standpoint, Keynes's theory of interest appears to be unsatisfactory. The quantity of money demanded on account of the speculative motive depends, Keynes says, not on the absolute level of the rate of interest but, rather, on the extent to which that rate lies below the rates which the various holders of wealth expect in the future (see ibid., p. 201). The position of the speculative demand for money schedule, and hence the rate of interest, thus come to depend on expectations about the future course of the latter. However, in the absence of their ulterior explanation, these expectations introduce a serious element of indeterminacy into the theory. Thus if it were assumed that expected rates of interest tend, albeit with a certain lag, to move parallel to the actual rate of interest, the principle reason advanced by Keynes for the interest-elasticity of the speculative demand for money – the growing divergence between expected rates and the current rate when the latter falls – would lapse. This point is reinforced when it is noted that the supply of money which is to satisfy the speculative demand can only change due to *either* changes in the money value of aggregate output *or* the policy of the monetary authorities: and it is difficult to imagine, in either case, that there will not be the same effect on expected interest rates. Keynes does in fact recognise this possible instability of the expectations on which the market rate of interest depends, and he takes it into account by admitting the possibility of shifts in the speculative demand for money schedule in the face of, for example, a central bank policy of monetary expansion (see, for example, ibid., pp. 197–8). Yet it is clear that, in so far as it is probable that speculative demand shifts as the supply of money changes, Keynes's analysis loses much of its force: like any other analysis in the terms of demand and supply, it presupposes a sufficient mutual independence of the two schedules.

Keynes's theory appears therefore to rest on the assumption of a considerable degree of stability of the expectations concerning the rate of interest: a stability which can only be based on stable views, on the part of the owners of wealth, as to what constitutes a 'normal' level of the interest rate. This seems in fact to be Keynes's rationale for the 'speculative' demand for money. Yet when it is interpreted in this way, the inadequacy of the liquidity-preference theory as a long-period analysis of the rate of interest becomes even clearer; the average value, over time, of the rate of interest on long-term loans proves to be largely determined by views about the 'normal' rate of interest, views which the theory does not explain (cf. ibid., p. 201).

It seems therefore that a *lacuna* was left by Keynes in his long-period analysis of the rate of interest; a *lacuna* which had to be filled, either by a return to the traditional theory or by its more radical rejection.[13]

16. If the *General Theory* left the theory of interest at this parting of the ways, Keynes's concept of the marginal efficiency of capital made it easy to return to the traditional theory. Keynes had already considered this possibility when he affirmed that those believing in the re-equilibrating tendencies of the economic system must base their argument on the effects which falls in money wages and prices, or open-market operations of the central bank, could have in increasing the quantity of money available for meeting the speculative demand. As was seen in section II, Keynes had denied that one could thus reach full employment. However, his arguments to this effect – based principally on the negative effects which significant falls in money wages or increases in the quantity of money would have on the 'state of confidence' – lose much of their force when the issue is, not the recovery of the economy from a situation of cyclical depression, but rather keeping the average level of investment sufficiently close to the full employment volume of savings over a long period of time. In this latter context, once it is admitted (on the basis of marginalist principles) that the marginal efficiency of capital schedule is highly elastic with respect to the rate of interest, the decreases in money wages, or increases in the quantity of money, required to ensure a sufficiently high average level of employment no longer appear drastic, as they can now be spread out over a long period of time. Besides, in the long period, the psychological factors summed up in the 'state of confidence' lose much of their force by comparison with the objective factors on which the real profitability of investment is supposed to depend.

This is in fact the line of argument taken in the attempts to rehabilitate traditional theory, which we referred to above.[14] The dominant concern of these authors with long-period tendencies[15] allowed them to ignore the negative psychological effects of falls in wages and prices, or increases in the quantity of money. That same concern explains, in part, a subtle but important shift in the interpretation of the 'speculative' demand for money. This demand is now made to depend not so much on views of what constitutes a normal level of the rate of interest, but rather on the convenience and security deriving from the holding of one's wealth in the form of money; the security in question is relative to those risks of changes in the value of bonds, entirely due to uncertainty, which would exist even when a rise in the rate of interest appeared no more probable than an equal fall.[16] By this change in the interpretation of liquidity preference, a sufficient stability is attributed to the demand for money without having recourse to views about a 'normal' rate of interest, which are not explained within the theory. Moreover, one thereby avoids consideration of the possibility of a high elasticity of the demand for money, with respect to the rate of interest, at rates above the minimum level to which we shall refer below; a possibility to which Keynes had attached considerable importance[17] and which can be explained only in terms of sufficiently unanimous views of wealth-holders about what constitutes the normal level of the interest rate. Given these premises, it is not difficult to conclude that, if unemployment of labour leads to the continuous fall of money wages, one will eventually reach – subject to the exception to be considered shortly – a state of equilibrium.

The significance of this argument does not depend on the assumption of a high flexibility of money wages, an assumption generally held to be of doubtful applicability. If the flexibility of money wages would permit the achievement of full employment in the way just described, then the same result can be obtained with an expansionary monetary policy. As Modigliani puts it: 'It is the fact that money wages are too high *relative to the quantity of money* that explains why it is unprofitable to expand employment to the "full employment" level'; and the remedy can take the form of *either* a decrease in money wages *or* an increase in the quantity of money, money wages being constant or a combination of the two (cf. Modigliani, 1944, p. 225; and Hicks, 1937, p. 465, and pp. 473–5).

We referred above to an exception to those conclusions. The authors in question admit only one situation in which money wage flexibility, or an expansionary monetary policy, cannot lead the economy back to full employment. This is the so-called 'Keynesian case' or 'liquidity trap': a situation in which the rate of interest required to ensure full employment is negative, or at least lower than that rate of interest which, in the view of the majority of wealth-holders, would be barely sufficient to compensate for the risk and inconvenience of holding any part of their wealth in any form other than money. At this level of the interest rate the elasticity of the demand for money would become infinite (cf. Modigliani, 1944, p. 222n; Hicks, 1937, pp. 470–72), and decreases in money wages or increases in the quantity of money could not lead to any further fall in the rate of interest. However, these authors attribute limited importance to this possibility – and here we find, yet again, the basic marginalist idea of a demand for capital which is, under normal conditions, highly elastic with respect to the rate of interest. The inelasticity and position of the schedule of marginal efficiency of capital which would be needed to explain a full-employment rate of interest lying below that minimum level, are held to be possible only in deep depressions, when they would be due to the subjective, temporary conditions of uncertainty and over-estimation of risks characteristic of such situations. These authors in fact maintain, agreeing here with Keynes, that a situation in which the preceding accumulation of capital has reduced the actual yield of capital almost to zero has never yet occurred (Modigliani, 1944, p. 222n; Keynes, 1936, p. 207).

The relevance of the 'Keynesian case' is thus confined to the analysis of short-period phenomena and the same is true for the importance of the psychological factors to which Keynes had referred in chapter 19 of the *General Theory*, in order to deny the possibility of reaching full employment through falls in money wages or increases in the quantity of money. In the former as in the latter context, the psychological state of lack of confidence characteristic of depressions would, as long as it persisted, constitute the obstacle preventing a return to the full employment of factors, following an argument not unlike that which had been put forward by Marshall long before.[18]

17. The line of argument considered in the previous section thus leads to a substantial rehabilitation of traditional theory for the long period and, in particular, for accumulation. The schema of the long-run interrelation between 'real' and monetary forces which the argument presents does not differ essentially from that which Wicksell had presented earlier. In the former, as in the latter, it is admitted that monetary factors can, temporarily, keep the market rate of interest at a level other than the full employment rate[19] – equivalent to the 'natural' rate in Wicksell's theory. In both schemata, however, the full-employment – or 'natural' – rate of interest continues to be the equilibrium one towards which the market rate of interest tends to gravitate. The divergence between the two rates would cause inflationary or deflationary tendencies, whether the latter consist principally of falls in prices and wages or mainly of unemployment of labour; these tendencies would then induce the monetary authorities, who are credited, in both arguments, with proximate control over the rate of interest, to adjust the ruling rate to its 'natural', or full-employment, level.

When compared with these similarities in the conclusions, the concepts of liquidity preference and of the consumption function – the specifically Keynesian elements in the above rehabilitations of the traditional theory – are of relatively minor importance. These elements are accorded a dominant role only for the analysis of the short period and the trade cycle. In this more limited context, the effects of the rate of interest on the demand for money highlight an obstacle capable of retarding the action of the 'real forces' on the rate of interest, particularly in the case of deflation. The consumption function then allows a theoretical treatment of the effects on real income and employment of decreases in money expenditure in the presence of rigid money wages. Thus, according to Hicks, Keynes's theory appears to be 'the Economics of Depression'; and, as mentioned in the introduction,

Keynes's specific contribution consisted of laying 'enormous emphasis' on the qualifications to traditional theory, the need for which had already been admitted by Marshall or his successors (Hicks, 1937).

We have clearly moved far from the meaning which Keynes himself attributed to his theory, when he contrasted it with the traditional theory, which he held to be applicable only in the 'special case' of full employment. And what is most remarkable is that this reversal of meanings is achieved without rejecting the basic assumptions of the *General Theory*, but, on the contrary, by moving within its conceptual framework. To note that the theory had been formulated by Keynes on the basis of short-period assumptions, and thus left open problems concerning long-period tendencies, does not appear to go to the root of the matter. Indeed, it remains to be explained why Keynes restricted to the short period an argument whose implications would, he thought, reach far beyond the theory of cyclical phenomena.[20] Above all, we have to explain why the long-period implications which Keynes thought he could deduce have proved to be open to contradiction within his own theoretical framework.

The root of this ambivalence has in fact to be sought in the two heterogeneous strands of thought present in the *General Theory*, which we mentioned in the Introduction. This root lies, in particular, in the traditional strand which seriously hampers the criticism of the orthodox theory of interest, essential to Keynes's conclusions regarding the possibility of permanent unemployment. Two successive logical stages may in fact be distinguished in the traditional analysis of distribution (cf. para. 18 below). In the first, from the marginalist premises concerning production and consumption one derives the idea that, given the quantities employed of all factors but one, the quantity employed of this latter factor increases as its real rate of remuneration falls. In the next step, it is maintained that, as a result of competition both amongst the entrepreneurs and amongst the owners of factors, there will be a tendency towards rates of remuneration at which the quantity employed will equal the quantity supplied for each factor. Now, in his criticism, Keynes accepts the first stage of the argument: in this way he inherits the traditional part of his theory, which is epitomised by the two schedules of the marginal efficiency of capital and of the marginal product of labour. His criticism has then to turn exclusively on the second stage of the argument. And at the second stage – with the conclusions from the first stage having already been admitted – the capacity of traditional theory to resist attack proved to be greater than Keynes had thought.

This traditional strand of Keynes's thought does not, of course, merely represent a remnant of received modes of thought which can readily be separated from the remainder of his theory, leaving the latter unaffected. Indeed, it is the schedules of the marginal product of labour and of the marginal efficiency of capital which determine the level of real wages and the volume of investment within the system. One may perhaps wonder how acceptable these determinations are and, above all, how consistent they are with the other parts of Keynes's theory, as soon as problems which are not strictly confined to the short period have to be confronted.[21] The fact remains, nevertheless, that it is thanks to this particular conjunction of traditional elements and short-period assumptions that Keynes is able to develop, to some extent, the novel strand of his thought, without having simultaneously to face the fundamental problems of value and distribution.

However, the price which Keynes has to pay for the traditional strand in his thought becomes clear with respect to the schedule of the marginal efficiency of capital.[22] As was seen in section II, the conflict with traditional theory over the tendency to an equilibrium between demand and supply in the labour market is, in effect, reducible to that over the determination of the rate of interest. The criticism of the traditional theory of interest becomes then the key to an acceptance of Keynes's arguments—and the concept of the marginal efficiency of capital proves to be the Achilles' heel of that very criticism. Keynes sees the rate of interest as determined by monetary factors: but, as Wicksell's earlier analysis had shown, the idea of an investment demand schedule constitutes an obstacle which a monetary theory of interest cannot easily overcome. Indeed, admitting an elastic investment demand schedule leads to maintaining, on the one hand, the existence of a full-employment level of the rate of interest and, on the other, the presence of inflation, or deflation and unemployment, when the actual rate of interest is not the full employment one; the idea that the market rate of interest tends to gravitate towards its full employment level then acquires plausibility.

So it seems that the origin of the contrasting meanings attributed to Keynes's theory is to be sought in the doubtful compatibility, from the standpoint of an analysis of long-period tendencies, between the concept of the marginal efficiency of capital and the argument that the level of output plays the leading role in equilibrating planned savings and planned investment. Once the former idea is accepted, it is difficult not to confine the importance of the latter argument to the explanation of the trade cycle and other short-period phenomena. On the other hand, the different conclusions to which Keynes was pointing can be sustained if investment is assumed to be insensitive to the rate of interest, even in the long period. But this assumption is in conflict with the presuppositions of the traditional theory of distribution and cannot find a firm foundation until the criticism of that theory has undermined those presuppositions.

The question which we must therefore ask ourselves at this point is whether the first of the two successive logical stages of the orthodox argument recalled above – the increase in the quantity demanded of a factor as its service price decreases (in particular the demand for capital = investment as the interest rate falls) – is as solid as Keynes supposed. In particular, we must ask if we have valid reasons to suppose that the average level of investment over a sufficiently long period of time would vary inversely with the rate of interest in such a way that this level could always be adapted to that of full employment savings by appropriate changes in the rate of interest. If the answer were to be negative, the conclusions Keynes was aiming at could be supported independently of his arguments concerning expectations and liquidity preference, which have proved indecisive in the light of subsequent discussion.

To this question we must now turn, starting from a closer examination of the way in which the notion of a regular long-run inverse relation between level of investment and rate of interest – expressed in Keynes's concept of the marginal efficiency of capital – was derived from the marginalist premises.

IV PERMANENT UNEMPLOYMENT AND THE CRITICISM OF THE MARGINALIST NOTION OF CAPITAL

18. The premises from which the marginalist authors derived the principle of a tendency to the full employment of factors are well known. They can be traced back to a particular conception of the social process of production. In this conception the elements required for production are treated as 'factors of production' which can be employed in the economic system in proportions that vary as the relative prices of their services vary. This is, in turn, the result of the two characteristics of the economic system as envisaged in the marginalist theories. First, we have the 'substitutability' in consumption between goods which will generally require different proportions of the factors for their production. Second, we have, for any given level of technical knowledge, the possibility of producing any commodity with different proportions of the factors; under the assumption of continuous variability of factor proportions, this leads to the well-known conditions of profit maximisation in terms of the 'marginal products' of the factors. By either route we arrive at an inverse relation between the price of the service of the factor and the quantity in which the factor would be employed in equilibrium, given the quantities of the other factors employed.

As we noticed above (para. 17), the way is then open for a second proposition according to which competition among the owners of a factor will modify the price of its service until the entire supply will be employed. With this second proposition, the inverse relation between the employment of a factor and the price of its service can be legitimately envisaged as a 'demand function' which, in conjunction with a 'supply function' of the same service, will give rise to the competititve tendency to an 'equilibrium' between such demand and supply.

The reasoning leading to a negatively elastic demand for the factor was based on the assumption that the quantity employed of the other factors remained constant, or generally equal to their supply (assumed not to fall drastically as their remuneration rises). But this assumption can now be seen to have been justified, for the same process which is at work in the market for the variable factor, assuming an equality between the quantity demanded and supplied of the other factors, will be at work in the market for the latter factors and will secure that very equality.

19. Thus the marginalist theory of distribution hinges on the notion of factors of production which may be employed in variable proportions in the economic system. Capital goods have to find a place among these factors. However, the application to capital goods of the notion of a factor, or factors, of production raises special problems. Capital goods, like other produced goods, have values which tend to equality with their supply prices. But free competition entails that the share of national income attributed to owners of such goods, over and above what is necessary for their replacement, tends to be distributed in proportion to the value of those goods, so as to give rise to a uniform rate of return on all kinds of capital goods. If we consider this uniform rate of return from the viewpoint of these theories, in which each rate of remuneration is the price of the service of a factor of production, the various capital goods will *ultimately* have to appear as quantities, measured by their values, of a single factor of production, 'capital', and the net rate of return on capital goods, or rate of interest will have to be determined[23] by referring to the conditions of demand and supply of this special factor.

But, as an amount of value, 'capital' is not defined until we have specified the standard in which that value is to be measured. Behind the variety and, at times, the vagueness of the indications given in this respect by the marginalist theorists, there lies a common idea. The capital goods, and hence the quantity of capital they represent, result from investment; since investment is seen as the demand for savings, 'capital' emerges as something which is homogeneous with saving. Its natural unit is therefore the same as we would use for saving, i.e. some composite unit of consumption goods capable of measuring the subjective satisfactions from which (according to these theorists) consumers abstain when they save.

Marginalist theorists then proceeded to apply the argument described above with this special factor now included alongside the others,[24] and in particular they thought it possible to state that, given the quantities employed of the other factors, entrepreneurs would find it profitable to use a larger 'quantity of capital' the lower the rate of interest falls.

20. For the application of this principle to the theory of distribution, we shall here focus on authors like J. B. Clark, Böhm-Bawerk or Wicksell, who expressly aim at a general solution to the problem of distribution. These authors refer to an equilibrium situation in which the condition of a uniform net rate of return on the various capital goods *is realised*. Given this condition, it becomes impossible to take the physical capital stock, i.e. the available quantities of the various capital goods, as given.[25] The 'capital' incorporated in such goods, i.e. their value, has instead to be taken as given. Capital is thus allowed to change its 'form' – though not its quantity – in order to acquire the physical composition compatible with equilibrium conditions.[26] The theory of distribution then follows along the lines already indicated in section III. It may be described in terms of the forces envisaged to be at work in the capital market. We shall have a *total* demand for capital – for capital *as a stock*, as distinguished from the demand for investment – i.e. for capital *as a flow*. This 'total' demand function gives the quantity of capital which the system would employ at the various rates of interest, assuming that the markets for products and for other factors are all in the equilibrium corresponding to the rate of interest considered.[27] Given the amount of capital available, the rate of interest will be determined together with the rest of the system (cf. Clark, 1907, ch. 9; Böhm-Bawerk, 1930; Wicksell, 1934).

We thus find a demand function for capital which is elastic with respect to the rate of interest, but we do not immediately find a demand function for *investment* which is elastic with respect to the rate of interest. The latter is, however, implied by the former; or, more exactly, the former represents, in the form of a demand for a stock, a time-sequence of demands for investment through which alone that stock-demand can be manifested and can determine the rate of interest. This relation between demand for capital as a stock and demand for investment can be seen in its most simple form if it is assumed that, in each industry, production takes place in an annual cycle and all capital is circulating capital (i.e. is entirely used up in the course of one year). If the wage rate and product prices are assumed to adapt without appreciable delay to the equilibrium compatible with the new rate of interest, the investment demand function at the end of each year will be nothing other than the demand function for capital as a stock. When there is fixed capital the analogous relation between demand for investment and demand for capital as a stock will be less simple but no less strict.

The theory implies that such circumstances as delayed adjustment in the markets for labour and products, or irregularity in the age distribution of fixed capital, do not fundamentally alter the terms of the question. As a result, the interest elasticity of the sequence of demands for investment would reflect, on average, the elasticity of the demand for capital as stock. Hence the significance of a demand for capital as a stock which exhibits, in a clear form, the basic tendencies which must emerge from the multiplicity of forces acting at any given moment of time.

21. It was in that way that the marginalist theory provided the basis of the idea of an inverse relation between the amount of investment and the rate of interest and hence for the first of the two propositions which we distinguished above (para. 18) in the traditional theory of interest.

That relation once admitted, it was easy to suppose a sensitivity of the rate of interest to a divergence between planned investment and planned savings sufficient to tend to eliminate that divergence, and this was in fact done when the rate of interest was considered (sometimes more explicitly, sometimes less so) as the price for the service of 'capital', determined by the conditions of demand for and supply of that factor simultaneously with the prices for the use of the other factors.

Since the *General Theory*, it has been widely recognised that this second step hid serious and perhaps decisive difficulties for the traditional theory of distribution. As Keynes showed, money in its role as a store of value may deprive the rate of interest of a sensitivity sufficient to adjust decisions to invest to decisions to save. And the controversy concerning the validity of the traditional thesis of the tendency to full employment has in fact been centred principally on problems related to the sensitivity of the rate of interest.

The basic idea of a demand function for investible resources has not been questioned, however. Nor is it surprising that criticism of the full employment thesis took this particular course. When, in the period between the two wars, the contrast between this thesis and the fact of large unemployment in the chief capitalist economies was particularly acute, criticism of the received theory naturally turned to the more empirical and less thoroughly explored monetary side of the theory, rather than to premises of pure theory which had by then acquired unchallenged acceptance.

22. The difficulties of the notion of such an inverse relation have however come to light in the course of the recent controversies concerning the concept of capital. These difficulties arise from the fact that the introduction of the factor 'capital' is incompatible with the logical basis on which the marginalist schema of factors of production rests. The principle that the proportions in which the factors are employed vary with the prices of their services, so as to give rise to demand functions of these services, can in fact be deduced from the conditions of equilibrium in production only if the quantities of the factors can all be defined independently of the system of prices. But this cannot be done when one of the factors is a value magnitude, 'capital'. As the rate of interest and the wage rate vary, the switch of techniques or the change in the relative outputs of consumption goods might well change the proportion between the two factors in a direction contrary to that asserted in marginalist theory. (See the 'Symposium' in the *Quarterly Journal of Economics*, 1966; and Garegnani, 1970.)

In fact, when we recognise the dependence of the value of capital goods on distribution, it becomes meaningless to compare the proportions of capital to labour required by different techniques and by different lines of production – or to refer to changes in the proportions of the two factors as distribution changes – in the unqualified way characteristic of traditional theory. Thus, the order in which the alternative techniques for a commodity, or the techniques for the production of alternative commodities, are placed with reference to their proportions of capital to labour will depend on the system of relative prices, and thus on the rate of interest or wages at which the comparison is made. And with respect to the change which the ratio of capital to labour in each line of production, or in the economy as a whole, undergoes as the rate of interest changes, the very direction of this change will depend on the commodity in terms of which the value of the capital goods is measured. (The assumed change in the rate of interest may indeed change the relative value of two alternative standards of value in such a way that, when using one standard we have an *increase* in the ratio of capital to labour, whereas the use of the other standard will give a *decrease* in that ratio.)

If the marginalist principle concerning the way in which the proportions of factors change with distribution is incorrect, we may ask what theoretical basis, if any, remains for the notion of demand functions for factors. We examined above the relation between the price of the service of a factor and the quantity of it employed with a constant quantity of the other factor. We then considered how the *negative slope* of that function, and the analogous form of the corresponding relation for the other factor, allowed these relations to be viewed as 'demand functions' capable of determining, in conjunction with the 'supply functions' of the factors, the prices of their services. Let us now follow the same line of argument, assuming that the two factors are 'capital' and labour.

Consider first the relation between the rate of interest and the value of the capital goods in use, assuming a constant quantity of labour employed and the equilibrium in the markets for the products.[28] The value of the capital goods employed will vary with the rate of interest for two different reasons, which we must now attempt to distinguish.

In the first place, we have changes in the value of the physical capital employed to which there corresponds no physical change in capital: these changes will be due purely to a change in the value of the capital goods relative to the commodity used as the standard of value.

In the second place, we have those changes in the value of physical capital to which there correspond *physical changes* in capital, which are due either to changes in the techniques adopted for producing the commodities, or to changes in the proportions in which those commodities are produced. The traditional thesis was that these changes in physical capital would ensure a *rise* in the value of the capital goods employed as the rate of interest falls, and vice versa. However, we now know that the analysis underlying this conclusion is invalid and that there is no reason why this second kind of change should have one sign rather than the other.

When we combine the two kinds of value changes that we have just considered separately, it seems that little or nothing of general validity can be said concerning the form of the relationship between the value of physical capital and the rate of interest. If we represent the relationship on a diagram, with the rate of interest on the vertical axis, the curve may just as well slope up to the right as down to the right, and it may alternate such slopes any number of times. Moreover, the form of the curve will depend on which commodity is used as the standard of value.

It seems, then, that even if the initial hypothesis of a constancy in the quantity of labour employed were well founded, the form that the relationship between the value of the capital goods and the rate of interest could assume would make it difficult to envisage it as a 'demand function' for capital – i.e. as the basis of a demand function for investible resources, capable of determining, together with a supply function of such resources, the rate of interest.

Yet the considerations which make this true of the relation between the rate of interest and the quantity of capital also undermine the validity of the assumption of constancy in the quantity of labour employed. As we have seen above, the traditional theory assumed a mechanism which equalised the quantity of labour demanded and supplied and thus ensured that the quantity employed would remain constant – or that it would change in accordance with the supply function of labour, if this had some elasticity. But this equilibrating mechanism of demand and supply can no longer be assumed: *the relation between the real wage and the labour employed would show the same characteristics as the relationship between the quantity of capital and the rate of interest*, and hence it could not be interpreted as a demand function, any more than could the first relationship.

What we have argued shows the weakness of the premises underlying the notion of demand function for investment which is elastic with respect to the rate of interest. Thus deprived of its theoretical foundation, that notion cannot, on the other hand, find genuine support on any purely empirical ground.[29]

It therefore seems possible to assert that, even if money wages and money prices could decrease in the presence of unemployment and cause a fall in the rate of interest, this could not set up a tendency to the full utilisation of capacity (to the full employment of labour). Some rigidity of money wages has thus to be admitted simply in order to explain why the presence of unemployment does not lead to an absurd cumulative process of deflation. (A similar rigidity was in fact implicitly assumed by the classical economists who always admitted the possibility of what we would now call 'structural unemployment': cf. para. 24 below.) The innovatory part of Keynes, the idea that it is the level of aggregate output that equalises decisions to save and decisions to invest, comes then into its own as the explanation of the way in which the decisions to invest are made consistent with the independent decisions to save.

23. We have just mentioned the attitude of the classical economists with respect to the behaviour of money wages in the face of labour unemployment. In fact, what we said above, like any argument validating the theory of Keynes in the long period, opens up the entire problem of distribution.

In this connection we may notice the relevance here of the relation, often used in this chapter, between the wage and the rate of profits which, asserted by Ricardo, has recently been taken up again, overcoming the problems encountered by both Ricardo and Marx for its exact formulation. This relation may in fact provide a basis for the necessary work of reconstruction. Thus, given such a relation, Keynes's suggestion that the average level of the rate of interest on long-term loans will be determined by conventional factors, ultimately subject to the policy of the monetary authorities (Keynes, 1936, pp. 203–4), would suffice to constitute the nucleus of a theory of distribution. Indeed, it seems reasonable to suppose that, as a result of competition in product markets, the average rate of profit and the average rate of interest on long-term loans will tend, over a sufficiently long period of time, to move in step with one another. If, then, the rate of interest depends on the policy of the monetary authorities, both the long-term movement of the average rate of profit[30] and, through the relation just mentioned, that of real wages, are explained by that policy. This does not entail maintaining afresh that the wage bargain has no power to change real wages: the policy of the monetary authorities is not conducted in a vacuum, and the movement of prices and of money wages determined in the wage bargain will be amongst the most important considerations in policy formulation.

24. This appeal to the Classical economists for the necessary work of reconstruction may seem to contrast sharply with the fact that Keynes had considered Ricardo and the old Classical economists as the originators of the school claiming the tendency to the full employment of labour which he intended to criticise. In that school, which he dubbed 'classical', Keynes had in fact included Ricardo besides 'the *followers* of Ricardo . . . who adopted and perfected the theory of the Ricardian economics, including (for example) J. S. Mill, Marshall, Edgeworth and Professor Pigou' (Keynes, 1936, p. 3).

Here Keynes seems, however, to fall victim to Marshall's tendency to present his own doctrines as a continuation of Ricardian theory. As I contended elsewhere (Garegnani, 1978, pp. 338–40) it is true that in his controversy with Malthus (who, however, in the proper original sense, was a 'classical economist' no less than Ricardo), Ricardo, like the 'orthodox' contemporaries of Keynes, denied that aggregate demand could set a limit to production. But it would be an error to move from acknowledging a similarity in the *question* under discussion to asserting a similarity in the *analysis* of the question. In particular, it would be an error to attribute to Malthus and Ricardo something akin to the theoretical core of the controversy between Keynes and the orthodox economists, i.e. the question whether the rate of interest can ensure that decisions to invest will adjust to decisions to save.[31]

The most evident deficiency of such an attribution is that both Malthus and Ricardo always identified decisions to save with decisions to invest:[32] there could therefore be no disagreement between them concerning the existence of factors capable of equilibrating decisions to invest and decisions to save. In Ricardo and Malthus, as in Smith before them, the question of a possible divergence between the two magnitudes had not been posed. They took it as a *fact* that anyone who had saved would have used his savings to employ productive labourers, or would have lent it to others who would have so used it.[33]

It would perhaps be possible to assert that, in this respect, Ricardo's theory of distribution is open, in the sense that it neither provides premises capable of justifying the tendency of investment to adjust to saving, nor depends on the existence of such a tendency.[34] This 'open' character sharply distinguishes the Ricardian theory from the subsequent marginalist theory which, as we saw above, provided the premises from which the role of the rate of interest as the equilibrator of decisions to invest and decisions to save was originally derived. At the same time, by determining distribution in terms of the equality between demand for and supply of factors of production, these theories depend for their validity on the absence of any long-run limits to aggregate production stemming from demand.

In fact, the absence from Ricardo's work of the notion of demands for the factors, elastic with respect to their prices, deserves to be stressed here, because it makes clear how little Keynes's 'classical school' has in common with Ricardo. We have seen that the 'classical' proposition criticised by Keynes concerned the existence of forces leading to the full employment of labour. But 'Say's law' did not lead Ricardo to any such proposition; it only led him to deny that demand could prevent the system from achieving that level of employment which was compatible with past accumulation, whether this level allowed for the employment of the entire labour force or only a part of it. Thus Ricardo admitted the possibility of the unemployment of labour and thought that it could only be eliminated by further accumulation of capital, or by a decrease in the population. Lower wage rates could therefore reduce unemployment only through higher profits and faster accumulation of capital, or through a slower increase of population – and not, as marginalist theories were later to maintain, by causing such changes in the methods of production, or in the relative outputs of consumption goods, as would permit the employment of the entire labour force with an unchanged 'quantity of capital'.[35]

When we have, with Keynes's short-period theory of capacity utilisation, and with that flexible 'classical approach' for long-period analysis, a satisfactory long-run theory of outputs, recognising the possible role of deficiencies of aggregate demand does not seem to require much more than (a) an analysis of how investment determines saving through changes in the level of productive capacity (and not only through changes in the *level of utilisation* of productive capacity); (b) a study of the factors affecting the long-run levels of investment; (c) a study of the partly irreversible increases which consumption expenditure undergoes as aggregate income increases (cf. Garegnani, 1983, pp. 77–5; 76–8). Theoretical and applied studies have already prepared a considerable amount of material in the last two fields.

Notes

1. This chapter derives much material from Garegnani (1978, 1979), to which the reader is referred for a more detailed treatment of questions raised.
2. The adjective 'marginal' or 'marginalist' has here been preferred to 'neoclassical', in order to designate the dominant theory. The latter appears in fact to imply a basic continuity with the 'classical' approach of Smith, Ricardo (and Malthus), which we have strong reasons to doubt after Sraffa's edition of Ricardo's *Works*. The reference to substitution at the 'margin' (which need not imply differentiality of the relevant functions) seems on the other hand to point to the basic element on which the dominant conception of demand functions for factors of production rests together with the corresponding attempt to explain the distribution of the product among social classes by demand and supply.

3. Savings, the supply of which is referred to by Wicksell in the above passage, should be understood to be the planned gross savings (on the definition of 'planned savings' and 'planned investment' or, equivalently, 'decisions to save' and 'decisions to invest', cf. Garegnani, 1978, p. 343n.) given by the difference between gross income and consumption under the assumption of full employment of resources with equilibrium relative prices and distribution on the prices assumed (cf. n.4 below). In what follows, a closed economy will be assumed and further we shall abstract from all state economic activity other than monetary policy. As usual, productive equipment is assumed to be appropriate to the composition of aggregate demand at its full employment level. By 'productive equipment' we shall here refer to fixed capital goods of sufficiently long duration: the quantity of other capital goods can be assumed to adapt rapidly to changes in the level of activity. A closed economy assumed; we shall also abstract from all state economic activity other than monetary policy.
4. On more difficulties in the Wicksell conception of 'free capital' and its evolution (cf. Garegnani, 1979, p. 65n.) what is of interest here is to note how this concept of Wicksell marks the fact that, in so far as the decisions in question were *correctly foreseen in the past*, the relevant sums of money may be spent on capital goods of any type whatever. The qualification concerning the necessity that the current saving and investment decisions were correctly foreseen in the past is important: demand for, and supply of, saving involve the decisions of *three* groups of people and not just of two, as might appear at first sight. The idea of a 'supply of savings' presupposes the coincidence of the savings decisions of income recipients and the decisions of producers concerning the divisions of aggregate supply between consumption and capital goods. Similarly, the idea of a demand for saving or investment presupposes that the producers of capital goods correctly foresee the physical composition of the investment demand.
5. To the extent that monetary expansion transfers resources from the production of consumption goods to the production of investment goods, real accumulation will be higher than it would have been at the 'natural' rate. To this extent, the 'natural' rate itself would tend to fall and approach the market rate. Wicksell admits this effect, but considers it to be of secondary importance (evidently because of his implicit assumption of a highly elastic demand for capital) (cf. Wicksell, 1935, pp. 198–9).
6. In *Geldzins und Güterpreise*, Wicksell seems to explain the increase in the demand for 'loan capital' that results from a decrease in the rate of interest in terms of the incentive that the growing difference between the rate of profits obtainable in production (equal to the 'natural' rate of interest) and the market rate of interest gives entrepreneurs to expand the *scale* of aggregate output (cf. Wicksell, 1965, pp. 89–90, and 1935, pp. 195–6).

   This explanation brings us to the question hinted at above concerning the relative prices and distribution underlying the schedules of the demand for and the supply of saving in traditional theory. Two alternative assumptions are conceivable: (a) that relative prices and factor remunerations are those ruling in the given situation and do not change as we move along the schedules; (b) that wages, the rents of natural resources and the relative product prices are those which would obtain in the equilibrium situation corresponding to the rate of interest assumed for the loan market (as assumed in n. 2 above). According to assumption (a), used in *Geldzins*, the rate of profits obtainable in production being given, independently of the assumed rate of interest on loans, the search for maximum profits would lead not only to changes in production methods adopted (factor proportions), but also to changes in the *scale* of every line of production. This explanation of the demand for investible funds does not, however, appear to be acceptable. The consequences of the change in the rate of interest on relative prices and wages are likely to react on the decisions to invest before these have had time to be carried out. Competition is likely to drive the rate of profits down in line with the new long-term rate of interest. This effect would seem to be particularly quick when, with the traditional theory we assume that labour and natural resources always tend to be fully utilised; the tendency to increase the scale of production in the aggregate could only lead to changes in the real remuneration of labour and natural resources. The investment planned to change the scale of production would thus be countermanded when, as it began to be carried out, distribution and relative prices adapt themselves to the rate of interest ruling in the loan market. The demand for investible funds will then in fact turn out to be determined exclusively by the tendency to change the ratio of capital to 'original' factors, i.e. according to assumption (b). Similar considerations hold for the supply of savings, which will also be influenced by changes in distribution and relative prices.

In the *Lectures*, Wicksell seems to take account of this and to modify somewhat his earlier position (cf., for example, the reference in Wicksell, 1935, p. 195, to 'increasing roundaboutness which is undoubtedly invoked by a fall in interest rates'). Wicksell's reluctance to adopt this second point of view exclusively is probably due to the difficulty of admitting a rapid adjustment of distribution and relative prices to the rate of interest on loans or, alternatively, of assuming entrepreneurs' forecasts of such effects which are sufficiently correct. But since assumption (a) is even less acceptable, it would seem that this difficulty is inseparable from the idea of supply and demand schedules for savings.

7. Similar suggestions were frequent in other marginalist writers. Consider, for example, Marshall's argument in *Money, Credit and Commerce* that an influx of precious metals would initially produce a fall in the rates of interest, which would then rise again as a result of the rise in prices that that influx had brought about (Marshall, 1965, IV, II, 2, p. 255).
8. The possibility is mentioned in the *Lectures* that increases in money demand might be satisfied, in part, by increases in output made possible by the presence of previously unemployed productive resources. Such a possibility is judged to be of secondary importance and is ignored in the rest of Wicksell's discussion (Wicksell, 1935, p. 195).
9. Keynes reduces the different qualities of labour to homogeneity by multiplying the quantity of each by the ratio which its wages bears to that of a standard type of labour. These ratios are assumed to be constant (Keynes, 1936, p. 41).
10. On the assumption given above concerning the behaviour of consumption, the aggregate demand function will intersect the aggregate supply function from above and the equilibrium can be supposed to be stable. Thus, if employment happened to be higher than is indicated by the equilibrium point, entrepreneurs would have an incentive to reduce the number of workers employed, since the aggregate expenditure in wage units would be *less* than the 'aggregate supply price' of that output. This would be so *if* this

expenditure were that shown by the aggregate demand function, i.e. that which would obtain with a disposable income equal to the supply price; *a fortiori*, expenditure will be less than supply price if, as a result of the failure to realise the full supply price, the disposable income is itself less than the 'supply price'. Similarly, entrepreneurs would have an incentive to increase output whenever employment was initially below the equilibrium level.

11. Keynes's conclusions concerning the effects of money wage decreases on the propensity to consume have been questioned in terms of the so-called 'Pigou effect': the significance of the latter for our argument will be discussed in n. 16 below.
12. Keynes himself appears at times to imply that variations in money wages could justify the traditional theory of interest when this refers to a full employment income for defining the supply schedule of saving. Thus he writes, 'the position could only be saved by some complicated assumption providing for an automatic change in the wage-unit of an amount just sufficient in its effect on liquidity-preference to establish a rate of interest which would just offset the supposed shift of the marginal efficiency of capital, so as to leave output at the same level as before' (Keynes, 1936, pp. 179–80). But in introducing the idea of 'liquidity preference', Keynes here forces his own theory on the traditional one. More relevant to the latter would seem to be another passage: 'If, however, there is a negligible demand for cash from the speculative-motive except for a short transitional interval, an increase in the quantity of money will have to lower the rate of interest almost forthwith, in whatever degree is necessary to raise employment and the wage-unit sufficiently to cause the additional cash to be absorbed by the transactions-motive and the precautionary-motive' (ibid., p. 171). Keynes is here referring to increases in the quantity of money, but the same conclusions hold for reductions in the money wage, given the quantity of money; it is then difficult to see how this position can be reconciled with the assertion that the traditional theory is indeterminate.
13. There are hints in this latter direction in the *General Theory*. Keynes, in fact, asserts the 'conventional' character of the rate of interest, and hence the capacity of the monetary authorities to control the average level of the interest rates on long-term loans, if they act with sufficient 'persistence and consistency of purpose' (cf. Keynes, 1936, p. 204). This idea which, if consistently developed, would lead to a theory of value and distribution radically different from the marginalist theory (see below, para. 23) does not seem to have been taken up in the subsequent literature.
14. Hicks (1937) seems to have opened up this line of argument by distinguishing between Keynes's 'special theory' and his 'general theory'. In the former, one would not consider the effect of changes in the money value of output on the demand for money; in the latter, admitting this influence, one would, by contrast, reach 'appreciably more orthodox' conclusions – amongst others, the possibility of increasing employment via money wage reductions, as well as by increases in the quantity of money (Hicks, 1937, pp. 467–70; and p. 465 for the effects of money wage flexibility). The argument was then taken up and rendered more explicit by Modigliani (1944), Haberler (1939), ch. 8, and 1964, pp. 240–43, Tobin (1955), etc. The conclusions of this line of argument have provided the theoretical basis of the numerous theories of economic growth on traditional lines (see, for example, Solow, 1956, pp. 91–3; Swan, 1956, p. 335; Meade, 1961, pp. 3–5).

15. Thus in Modigliani (1944, p. 187) the analysis is said to be conducted 'under "static" assumptions', since its object is the 'determinants of equilibrium and not . . . the explanation of business cycles'.
16. On the distinction between these two interpretations of 'liquidity preference', see Robertson (1963, pp. 382–3). For the tendency to adopt the second interpretation of 'liquidity preference' in these rehabilitations, see Hicks (1937, p. 467) and Modigliani (1944, p. 193).
17. Cf., for example, 'opinion about the future of the rate of interest may be so unanimous that a small change in present rates may cause a mass movement into cash' (Keynes, 1936, p. 172; see also p. 203).
18. A different, well-known attempt to rehabilitate the principle of the tendency to full employment is that based on the so-called 'Pigou Effect'. When money wages and prices fall, the aggregate net credit of the private sector of the economy – equal to the total net debt of the government and the central bank (banknotes and government stock) in a closed economy – will increase in real terms. The propensity to save of wealth-holders will consequently fall until the full employment level of savings equals the level of investment forthcoming in the situation under consideration (cf. Pigou, 1947, pp. 249–51; Haberler, 1939, pp. 483–9; Patinkin, 1948, pp. 258–70). One comment on this: it is reasonable to suppose that the greater part of saving comes from high-income recipients and that this group will also hold a large fraction of both the public debt and idle money balances. Thus what the 'Pigou Effect' implies is an increase in wealth of high-income recipients (whose incomes will also increase in real terms at the expense of tax-payers so long as the state pays a constant rate of interest on its debt) such as to lead them to reduce their savings by the required amount. Now – even admitting that the redistribution of wealth and income against private debtors and the redistribution of income through the government's interest payments do not impede the reduction in the propensity to save – it seems hard not to conclude that long before the community comes to accept such a redistribution of wealth, other methods of solving the problem of unemployment will become inevitable, which will be of more direct and less uncertain effect.
19. It is interesting to note how the concept of a full-employment rate of interest, though a corollary of the idea of a marginal-efficiency-of-capital, is given very little prominence in the *General Theory*. It just crops up here and there almost accidentally (e.g., Keynes, 1936, pp. 202, 236, 375)
20. For the long-period consequences that Keynes drew from his theory, consider Keynes (1936, pp. 203–4, 372–3) as well as, more generally, the first two sections of ch. 24 of the *General Theory*.
21. On these difficulties of Keynes's conceptions cf. Garegnani (1979, p. 77n).
22. An opinion about the nature of the 'marginal efficiency of capital' different from that in the text – and from that of Keynes, who saw his notion as a version of the traditional one (cf., e.g., Keynes, 1936, pp. 139–40) – is advanced by L. Pasinetti, when he writes that such a Keynesian concept reveals a 'different origin' than marginal economic analysis (1974, p. 43). Pasinetti assumes in fact that the prospective yields of capital assets are *independent* of the rate of interest ruling in the loan market (cf., e.g., p. 37). The investment projects could then be always ordered according to a decreasing rate of profitability, independent of the interest rate, thus ensuring the existence of a decreasing relation between the interest rate, and the volume of investment.

We have, however, seen in n. 4 above, that there are some arguments for which the assumption of prospective yields and prices independent of the ruling interest rate does not seem acceptable. We may now add that Keynes himself allowed for the effect of the interest rate on prospective yields (e.g., Keynes, 1936, p. 143). We may also observe that the dependence of prospective yields on the ruling interest rate follows from Pasinetti's own analogy between the marginal efficiency of capital and 'Ricardo's ranking of all lands in a decreasing order of fertility' (Pasinetti, 1974, p. 43): the ordering of lands according to fertility must in fact take into account the changes in interest and prices associated with the extension of cultivation.

Now, when we admit that the prospective yields of capital assets and the ruling interest rate can, and sooner or later will, adjust to each other, it does not seem that a generalised inverse relation between the rate of interest and the volume of investment can find a theoretical basis other than the marginalist notion of an increase in the proportion of capital to other factors as the rate of interest falls. In particular, there seems to be no general reason why the construction of new plant for previously unemployed workers (to which Pasinetti refers on p. 43) should be permanently favoured by a fall of the interest rate rather than by its rise (a rise might indeed raise the long-term profitability of investment and thus provide an incentive for it).

23. Cf. para. 20 and n. 25 below.
24. Some marginalist theorists, such as J. B. Clark and, ultimately, also Marshall and his school, seem to have thought that the case in which a factor of production, 'capital', is conceived as an amount of value, could be treated similarly to that in which all factors are measurable in physical terms. A more interesting, indirect procedure was that adopted by theorists such as Böhm-Bawerk and Wicksell, who conceived of capital as a 'subsistence fund', used in order to 'advance' the remuneration to the 'original' factors of production (land and labour) during the time elapsing before completion of the consumption goods produced by them. In any given instant, this 'fund' would be 'embodied' in the capital goods, and it would be measured by their value in terms of consumption goods. As the rate of interest decreased (the wage increased), the 'time structure' of production was supposed to change so as to require a larger 'subsistence fund' in order to employ the same quantities of the 'original factors'. (Cf. note 20 below for Walras's still different approach.)
25. A demonstration of the inconsistency between a uniform rate of return on the supply price of capital goods and the treatment of the quantities of the various kinds of capital goods as data, has been given by the present author (Garegnani, 1960, part II, chs 2, 3 and appendix G). The problem is there considered as a criticism of Walras's theory of distribution which suffers from this very inconsistency.
26. For the different approach adopted by Marshall and the marginalist tradition he originated, cf. Garegnani (1978, pp. 346–8). It is there argued that 'The different starting point – i.e. the physically specified equipment – and the apparent realism of the second group of theories appears to have obscured but not altered the basis on which the supposed inverse relation between investment and interest . . . must rest in the last analysis', and this basis is that expounded by the authors referred to in the text.
27. Under more general assumptions, the 'demand function' for capital described in the text would result from the following procedure. We take as

data: (a) the preferences of the consumers; (b) the techniques of production; (c) the available quantities of all factors except capital; (d) the criteria determining the distribution of ownership of capital goods (the quantities of which are among the unknowns of the equations) among the individuals; (e) the criteria determining the age distribution of fixed capital. For any level of the rate of interest – *the independent variable* in this system – the equations concerning the conditions of equilibrium in the markets for the products and for the factors *other than* capital will determine, in addition to the usual unknowns of a general equilibrium system, the physical quantities of the capital goods of the different kinds in use in the assumed equilibrium position. The prices of these capital goods being also determined by the equations, the quantity of capital employed in equilibrium for the given rate of interest can easily be obtained. By repeating this procedure for other rates of interest, we obtain the corresponding points of the demand function for capital. In short, we subtract from the usual equations of general equilibrium the one requiring equality between the quantity of capital employed and the quantity available; the degree of freedom which the system acquires permits the definition of the relationship between the quantity of capital employed and the rate of interest.

28. This relationship between the value of the capital goods and the rate of interest results from the procedure indicated in note 24 above.
29. The changes in the rate of interest discussed here would imply changes in most of the variables of the system (the relative prices of the products, the levels of output, the labour employed, etc.), each of which may in turn react on the level of investment. It would therefore seem that the question of the influence of interest on investment can only be meaningfully discussed within a theoretical scheme which accounts for the relations between these variables. It seems unlikely that all these interrelationships could be accounted for in an empirical study. As it happens, the results of the numerous empirical investigations concerning the *direct* influence of the rate of interest on entrepreneurs' decisions to invest are known to be negative (cf. Andrews, 1938; Sayers, 1940; Ebersole, 1938–9; Brockie and Grey, 1956).
30. Cf. the hint in this direction given by Sraffa (1960, p. 33).
31. For more detailed treatment of the question cf. Garegnani, 1978, pp. 338–41.
32. See, for example, Malthus's acceptance of Ricardo's assertion that an increase of £10,000 in the income of an individual would bring about an increase in the demand for commodities of the same value, whether this increase were saved or consumed (Malthus, 1958, pp. 322–3). The fact that Malthus, like the other classical economists, tended to identify savings and investment, has been noted by R. L. Meek (1950–51, p. 156, n. ii), L. Robbins (1958, p. 248) and J. A. Schumpeter (1954, p. 641), and has been used by B. A. Corry (1959) for a more general criticism of the prevailing idea that Malthus was a precursor of Keynes.
33. Nor can we find in these authors an analysis of the possible changes in the intervals of time elapsing between the acts of purchase and sale; an analysis that would have led, by another route, to the admission of a possible divergence between planned savings and investment as they are defined today. A few decades after Ricardo's *Principles*, this kind of analysis caused Marx to reject 'Say's law' and the Ricardian position on the subject (cf., for example, Marx, 1969, pp. 493–9).

34. Thus Marx had no difficulty in rejecting 'Say's law' while sharing the basic elements of Ricardo's theory of value and distribution (cf. no. 27 above). The Ricardian theory of distribution, while it excludes the possibility of permanent effects of aggregate demand on the *nominal* rate of profits (the rate of profits corresponding to a nominal degree of utilisation of equipment) is not incompatible with effects of that demand on aggregate output or the speed of accumulation.
35. Of the numerous passages of the *Principles*, the following, which summarizes the conclusion of his famous ch. 31, 'On Machinery', may suffice here: 'the discovery and use of machinery may be attended with a diminution of gross produce; and whenever that is the case, it will be injurious to the labouring class, as some of their number will be thrown out of employment, and the population will become redundant, compared with the funds which are to employ it', and, a few lines above, 'But with every *increase* of capital he would employ more labourers; and, therefore, a portion of the people thrown out of work in the first instance, would be subsequently employed' (Ricardo, 1951, p. 390; our italics). An interesting expression of the contrast between the Ricardian and the marginalist theories on the employment of labour is provided by Wicksell's criticism of Ricardo's thesis on the effects of the introduction of machinery. Wicksell argues that production will not decrease because 'as soon as a number of labourers have been made superfluous by these changes, and wages have accordingly fallen, then, as Ricardo failed to see, [other] methods of production . . . will become more profitable . . . and absorb the surplus of idle labourers' (Wicksell, 1934, p. 137).

Bibliography

Andrews, P. S. (1983) 'Summary of replies to questions on effects of interest rates', *Oxford Economic Papers*.

Böhm-Bawerk, E. (1930) *The Positive Theory of Capital* (New York: Stechert).

Brockie, M. D. and Grey, A. (1956) 'The marginal efficiency of capital and investment programming', *Economic Journal*.

Clark, J. B. (1907) *Essentials of Economic Theory* (New York: Macmillan).

Corry, B. A. (1959) 'Malthus and Keynes', *Economic Journal*.

Ebersole, J. E. (1938–9) 'The influence of interest rates upon entrepreneurial decisions in business', *Harvard Business Review*.

Garegnani, P. (1960) *Il Capitale nelle Teorie della Distribuzione* (Milan: Giuffre).

Garegnani, P. (1970) 'Heterogeneous capital, the production function and the theory of distribution', *Review of Economic Studies*.

Garegnani, P. (1978, 1979) 'Notes on consumption, investment and effective demand', *Cambridge Journal of Economics*, part I, vol. 2, n. 4; part II, vol. 3, n. 1, as reprinted in Eatwell J. and Milgate M. (1983).

Garegnani, P. (1983) 'Two routes to effective demand' in J. Kregel (ed.) *Distribution, Effective Demand and International Economic Relations* (London: Macmillan).

Haberler, G. (1939) *Prosperity and Depression*, 2nd edn (Geneva: League of Nations).

Haberler, G. (1964) *Prosperity and Depression*, 4th edn (London: Allen & Unwin).

Hicks, J. R. (1937) 'Mr Keynes and the classics: a suggested interpretation', *Econometrica*, as reprinted in *Readings in the Theory of Income Distribution* (Toronto, 1946).
Keynes, J. M. (1936) *The General Theory of Employment, Interest and Money* (London: Macmillan).
Keynes, J. M. (1937) 'Alternative theories of the rate of interest', *Economic Journal*, June.
Malthus, T. R. (1958) *Principles of Political Economy*, 2nd edn (New York: Kelley) (first printed 1836).
Marshall, A. (1965) *Money, Credit and Commerce* (New York: Kelley) (first published, 1923).
Marx, K. (1969) *Theories of Surplus Value*, vol. 2 (London: Lawrence & Wishart).
Meade, J. (1961) *A Neo-Classical Theory of Economic Growth* (London: Allen & Unwin).
Meek, R. L. (1950–1) 'Thomas Joplin and the theory of interest', *Review of Economic Studies*.
Modigliani, F. (1944) 'Liquidity preference and the theory of interest and money', *Econometrica*, as reprinted in *Readings in Monetary Theory* (London: Unwin, 1952).
Pasinetti, L. (1974) *Growth and Income Distribution: Essays in Economic Theory* (Cambridge, CUP).
Patinkin, D. (1948) 'Price flexibility and full-employment', *American Economic Review*, as reprinted in *Readings in Monetary Theory* (London: Unwin, 1952).
Pigou, A. C. (1947) 'Economic progress in stable environment', *Economica*, as reprinted in *Readings in Monetary Theory* (London: Unwin, 1952).
Ricardo, D. (1951) *Principles of Political Economy and Taxation*, vol. I of *Works and Correspondence of David Ricardo*, ed. P. Sraffa (Cambridge: CUP).
Robbins, L. (1958) *Robert Torrens and the Evolution of Classical Economics* (London: Macmillan).
Robertson, D. H. (1963) *Lectures on Economic Principles* (London: Fontana) (first published 1957–9).
Sayers, R. S. (1940) 'Business men and the terms of borrowing', *Oxford Economic Papers*.
Schumpeter, J. A. (1954) *History of Economic Analysis* (New York: OUP).
Solow, R. (1956) 'A contribution to the theory of economic growth', *Quarterly Journal of Economics*, February.
Sraffa, P. (1960). *Production of Commodities by Means of Commodities* (Cambridge: CUP).
Swan, T. (1956) 'Economic growth and capital accumulation', *Economic Record*, November.
Symposium (1966) Symposium on paradoxes in capital theory, *Quarterly Journal of Economics*.
Tobin, J. (1955) 'A dynamic aggregative model', *Journal of Political Economy*.
Wicksell, K. (1934) *Lectures on Political Economy*, vol. I (London: Routledge).
Wicksell, K. (1935) *Lectures on Political Economy*, vol. II (London: Routledge & Kegan Paul).
Wicksell, K. (1965) *Interest and Prices* (New York: Kelly) (first published 1898).

11 The Multiplier and Liquidity Preference: Two Sides of the Theory of Effective Demand

J. A. Kregel

I INTRODUCTION

One of the most perplexing facts in interpreting post-war developments of Keynes's theory is his comment on Hicks's now-famous 'Mr Keynes and the Classics'. Although Hicks himself has in recent years become critical of the uses to which his *IS–LM* apparatus has been put, he still stands by it as representing the essence of Keynes's theory and supports his contention by reference to what he interprets as Keynes's tacit agreement with the contents of his 1937 paper: 'Keynes accepted the *IS–LM* diagram as a fair statement of his position' (Hicks, 1977, p. 146).

The present chapter has two goals. The first is to assess Keynes's pointed criticism of the representation of the rate of interest upon which Hicks's 1937 paper was based. The second is to attempt an explanation of *IS–LM* which might be interpreted as a 'fair_ representation' of Keynes's theory. These two goals permit discussion of what I believe to be the most often overlooked aspect of Keynes's theory, the indissoluble relation between the multiplier and the liquidity preference explanation of money prices.

II KEYNES'S CRITICISM OF 'MR KEYNES AND THE CLASSICS'

The careful reader of Keynes's comments in his exchange of letters with Hicks (*CW*, XIV: pp. 74ff.) will note two points. Hicks centred his comparison of Keynes and the Classics on the effect of an increase in expenditure on the rate of interest. What Hicks calls 'Mr Keynes's special theory', 'yields the startling conclusion that an increase in the inducement to invest, or in the propensity to consume, will not tend to raise the rate of interest, but only to increase employment' (Hicks, 1982, p. 107). Keynes comments on this characterisation of his position:

> From my point of view it is important to insist that my remark is to the effect that an increase in the inducement to invest *need* not raise the rate of interest. I should agree that, unless the monetary policy is appropriate, it is quite likely to. In this respect I consider that the difference between myself and the classicals lies in the fact that they regard the rate of interest as a non-monetary phenomenon, so that an increase in the inducement to invest would raise the rate of interest irrespective of monetary policy, – though they might concede that monetary policy was capable of producing a temporary evaporating effect. (*CW*, XIV: p. 80).[1]

Keynes thus rejects the *shape* of the *LM* curve as the focal point of difference between his theory and the classics. Had Hicks accepted this point he should not have insisted 'the most important thing in Mr Keynes's book' is that 'it is also possible to say something about the shape of the [*LM*] curve. It will probably tend to be nearly horizontal on the left, and nearly vertical on the right' (Hicks, 1982, p. 109).[2] Indeed, he could not have found any distinctive feature in Keynes's theory, for without this possibility 'Mr Keynes takes a big step back to Marshallian orthodoxy, and his theory becomes hard to distinguish from the revised and qualified Marshallian theories, which, as we have seen, are not new' (ibid, p. 108).[3]

Keynes concludes his commentary on the 1937 paper by returning to Hicks's interpretation of his theory of the rate of interest:

> I am just about to write a lecture on the question of the relation between my theory of the rate of interest and a theory based, as the Swedish one is, on the demand and supply for loans. In this connection I shall be referring to what you wrote in your review of my book. But you dealt with this very briefly, and I do not really understand what you were driving at. In particular, where you say 'It is a perfectly legitimate method, but it does not prove other methods to be wrong', what exactly are the other methods which you have in mind? (*CW*, XIV: p. 81)

Keynes may have had 'next to nothing to say by way of criticism' of Hicks's 1937 paper, yet he questioned the very point upon which Hicks had centred his comparison of Keynes with the classics and suggested that Hicks had already misunderstood his position on this very point – the theory of the rate of interest – in his earlier review of the *General Theory*. Keynes further promises a formal criticism of the point in what became 'Alternative Theories of the Rate of Interest' (*CW*, XIV: pp. 201 ff.).[4]

In his letter of reply Hicks notes that Townshend (1937) had already pointed out an error in the presentation of Keynes's theory of interest in the review. At the same time as Hicks suggests a correction he attempts to clarify the meaning of his earlier statements on the rate of interest.[5] Hicks concludes, 'Of course what lies behind this rather silly business is a desire to separate the essential content of your theory from its formal arrangement. I am a convinced liquidity preference man, but I do covet some freedom of choice about the way (or ways) the doctrine shall be expressed' (*CW*, XIV: p. 83). Keynes remains unconvinced, and writes in his 1937 *Economic Journal* article of the approach of Ohlin, Robertson and Hicks: 'Some of the writers . . . believe that my theory is on the whole the same as theirs and mainly amounts to expressing it in a somewhat different way. Nevertheless the theories are, I believe, radically opposed to one another' (*CW*, XIV: p. 202). There clearly was no freedom of choice possible in the presentation of Keynes's theory of the rate of interest.

If Keynes had any hesitation concerning Hicks's *IS–LM* representation we must look for it not in the polite comments of Keynes's private correspondence, but in his clearly enunciated public criticism of the point upon which he felt he differed fundamentally from the interpretation given by Hicks in his review of the *General Theory*, and which is the centre about which the comparison of Mr Keynes and the classics is built: the exposition of the rate of interest. Although Keynes's article deals with Hicks as one of a group of proponents of a similar position, Townshend's short note (1937) deals directly with Hicks's exposition of the rate of interest. Keynes's subsequent correspondence with Townshend (*CW*, XXIX: pp. 255ff.) concerning the 'basic postulate' of the Classical theory is also of interest in confirming Keynes's position on the fundamental difference between his theory and the classics as the rate of interest.

What Hicks intended by 'freedom of choice' can be simply summarised (cf. also Kregel, 1982b). If one interprets Keynes's three fundamental psychological variables – the propensity to consume, liquidity preference and the efficiency of capital – as representing 'bundles' or aggregations of individuals' decisions in 'three markets' for goods, money and loans, then there are three equations to 'determine' the prices of goods and the rate of interest in terms of money as the numeraire.

> Thus two of the equations, as you would say, are operative equations, one is a check equation. But it is possible to select any one of the three equations as a check equation, and distribute the operative equations among prices and interest as we choose. Thus there are six possible alternative 'theories'; but if they are correctly stated, they all mean the same thing, and are equally right. (*CW*, XIV: p. 82)

Hicks interpreted the equality of savings and investment (the supply and demand for loans, in Hicks's terminology) as Keynes's choice of the 'check' equation, leaving the supply and demand for goods to determine their prices and the supply and demand for money to determine the rate of interest. But it was also possible to use, for example, the supply and demand for money as the 'check' equation, producing one of the other five 'alternative theories', with the rate of interest determined by the supply and demand for loans (saving and investment) and goods prices determined by the supply and demand for goods.[6] Hicks considered these two formulations identical 'monetary' explanations of the rate of interest and built his comparison of Keynes's theory and the classics via *IS–LM* on the basis of these similar 'alternative' formulations.

Keynes clearly objected to this contention of similarity, for Hicks's alternative theory implied that the rate of interest was determined by savings and investment, and that the 'price' of money was the inverse of goods prices, which appears to be a very precise representation of Say's Law and the Quantity Theory of Money![7] Accepting such an equivalence Hicks could only produce Keynes's result of unemployment equilibrium by means of arbitrarily fixing prices or interest rates. In the *IS–LM* formulation it is the last possibility that is chosen in the horizontal *LM* curve representation of the 'liquidity trap', and which allows Hicks to identify Keynes's 'special theory' as implying that expenditure can change without affecting the rate of interest (indeed, Hicks never provides a citation for this contention). It is, as already noted, precisely this point to which Keynes objects, and to which he returns in a more detailed fashion in his public criticism of the possibility of 'alternative' monetary theories of the rate of interest, insisting on the distinctive nature of his own 'liquidity preference' approach. Had Keynes not considered this point fundamental to understanding of his theory he certainly would not have taken such pains to correct misunderstanding with those few economists who were most receptive, at least superficially, to his theory through their acceptance of the necessity of a 'monetary' explanation of the rate of interest.

III KEYNES'S CRITICISM OF THE ALTERNATIVE MONETARY THEORIES OF INTEREST

Keynes's 1937 criticism of these 'alternative' monetary theories of the supply and demand for credit or the supply and demand for loans, is that they all reduce supply to 'exactly the same thing as the quantity of saving' and reduce demand to 'exactly the same thing as the quantity of net investment', so that 'we are completely back again at the classical doctrine . . . that the rate of interest is fixed at the level where the supply of credit, in the shape of saving, is equal to the demand for credit, in the shape of investment' (*CW*, XIV: pp. 205–6).

Keynes was right to suspect that Hicks's position fell into this category, for one of Hicks's six alternative combinations of three markets is precisely this case, and it is on the basis of this three-market representation that Hicks represented Keynes's theory in the two market-equilibrium curves, one equation being redundant as the check equation. If Keynes could not accept the horizontal *LM* curve as representative of his 'special theory' then his theory became one of the six variants in Hicks's 'General' theory and was formally equivalent to the traditional approach, as Hicks had already noted.

Accepting Hicks's framework, the argument between Hicks and Keynes then turns on whether one can be 'indifferent' to the choice of which equations determine which variables. Hicks notes that mathematically there can be no difference, while Keynes contends that economically his theory has not been understood. Recall what Hicks calls the 'ordinary method of economic theory'. Here the check equation is the supply and demand for money which determines the price *level*, while the demand and supply for goods determines *relative* prices and savings and investment the interest rate. This implies that changes in the demand for money relative to supply will determine the general price level and be independent of relative prices. Now, Keynes repeatedly insists that his theory differs from the traditional theory in treating money as a 'real' factor (*CW*, XIV: pp. 202–3, note 2), while he considers the rate of interest as a 'monetary' factor (ibid, p. 80), or that money has no 'direct' effect on prices. Rather Keynes insists that it is the rate of interest that determines prices through its effect on the rate of return to assets, i.e. on the relation of their demand prices to their supply prices:

> In so far as [money] has been noticed, the essential nature of the phenomenon has been misdescribed. For what has attracted attention has been the *quantity* of money which has been hoarded; and importance has been attached to this because it has been supposed to have a direct proportionate effect on the price level through affecting the velocity of circulation. But the *quantity* of hoards can only be altered either if the total quantity of money is changed or if the quantity of current money income . . . is changed; whereas fluctuations in the degree of confidence are capable of having quite a different effect, namely, in modifying not the amount that is actually hoarded, but the amount of the premium which has to be offered to induce people not to hoard. And changes in the propensity to hoard, or in the state of liquidity preference as I have called it, primarily affect, not prices, but the rate of interest; any effect on prices being produced by repercussion as an ultimate consequence of a change in the rate of interest. (*CW*, XIV: p. 116)[8]

This emphasis on money as a 'real' factor, and the rate of interest as a 'monetary' factor, may cause perplexity to those who believe that Keynes's sole contribution to economic theory was the income multiplier (which he adapted from Richard Kahn's employment multiplier), or have only noticed those passages in Keynes's correspondence – with Harrod, Hawtrey and Robertson – where he states repeatedly: 'The novelty in my treatment of savings and investment consists, not in my maintaining their necessary aggregate equality, but in the proposition that it is, not the rate of interest, but the level of incomes which (in conjunction with certain other factors) ensures this equality' (*CW*, XIV: p. 211), or 'As I have said above, the initial novelty lies in my maintaining that it is not the rate of interest, but the level of incomes which ensures equality between savings and investment' and 'the result . . . was to leave the rate of interest in the air. If the rate of interest is not determined by savings and investment in the same way in which price is determined by supply and demand, how is it determined?' (*CW*, XIV: p. 212).

In Keynes's comments on the possibility of 'alternative' theories, instead of insisting on savings and investment being brought into equality via the multiplier Keynes emphasises his rejection of the view that the 'price' of money is the inverse of the price of goods, denying any direct influence of changes in the demand for money or the velocity of circulation on prices. As Townshend puts it, 'the volume of money is not a directly determining factor . . . of any prices' (1937, p. 158). Instead, Keynes emphasises that it is changes in liquidity preference that will bring changes in the rate of interest; it is the change in the rates of interest which affect the prices of capital assets and their marginal efficiencies, the change in marginal efficiency leading to decisions to increase or decrease holdings of capital goods, i.e. to investment decisions. Changes in investment in their turn affect the rates of return on capital assets as they set in motion the multiplier process which produces the savings required to balance the changes in investment. It is in this sense that money is a 'real' phenomenon: changes in the price of money, the rate of interest, will bring about changes in the rates of return on capital goods and thus cause investment and income to adjust. At the same time, this argument shows clearly that Keynes's theory of interest is simply the other side of the multiplier medal.

Hicks's alternative formulations approach may aid in seeing this interrelation, for if one accepts the 'ordinary method of economic theory' it is formally equivalent to object to the rate of interest being determined by savings and investment and to the supply and demand for money directly setting the level of prices. Rejecting one means rejecting the other. At the same time, insisting that money is a real phenomenon and the rate of interest is a monetary phenomenon means that the money market determines the rate of interest. Savings and investment becomes the check equation, and effective demand determines the *level* of output. The theory of interest and the multiplier thus replace Say's Law and the Quantity Theory of Money. But, in this version it is relative prices which are left hanging in the air. The insistence that money is a real phenomenon that affects prices via the rate of interest means that it is left to liquidity preference to determine *money* prices. The end result may be the same in equilibrium no matter which of Hicks's alternatives is chosen; the process of adjustment to the equilibrium position is not.

Further, Keynes insists that in such a process a change in liquidity preference may affect prices without *any* change in aggregate money holdings. Hicks might better have interpreted Keynes's 'special theory' as proposing that an increase in the inducement to invest may occur without any change in the quantity of money demanded rather than without any change in the rate of interest.[9]

As Keynes reiterates in his contribution to the Irving Fisher *Festschrift* – Keynes credited Fisher with leading him to this position[10] – this is the basic difference from traditional theory:

Put shortly, the orthodox theory maintains that the forces which determine the common value of the marginal efficiency of various assets are independent of money, which has, so to speak, no autonomous influence, and that prices move until the marginal efficiency of money, i.e. the rate of interest, falls into line with the common value of the marginal efficiency of other assets as determined by other forces. My theory, on the other hand, maintains that this is a special case and that over a wide range of possible cases almost the opposite is true, namely, that the marginal efficiency of money is determined by forces partly appropriate to itself, and that prices move until the marginal efficiency of other assets fall into line with the rate of interest. (*CW*, XIV: p. 101)

Thus Keynes's insistence, in his discussions with Hicks, that the distinctive feature of his theory compared with the classics was to be found in treating money as a 'real' factor (*CW*, XIV: p. 203), and that the rate of interest is not determined by 'real' factors such as the productivity of real capital, but is a monetary phenomenon (*CW*, XIV: p. 80, 206; *CW*, VII: pp. 214–15), leading to his position that the money rate of interest as determined by liquidity preference sets the rate of return on real assets, which is just the opposite of Wicksell's theory, for example. This, of course, is the basis of Keynes's theory that the money rate of interest rules the roost, spelled out in chapters 16 and 17 of the *General Theory*.

It is important to note that Keynes's insistence on the importance of the rate of interest comes from his repeated denial that money enters the determination of prices and demand for goods via changes in the demand for money (or changes in hoarding, or changes in the velocity of circulation) affecting the effective quantity of money. This further testifies that Keynes did not consider his theory of liquidity preference as an improved specification of the demand-for-money function. Yet it is precisely this point that Hicks emphasises in his 1937 characterisation (although not in 1936) and which is now commonly accepted by both neoclassical and post-Keynesian writers. At best, Keynes's position might be described as a theory of shifts in the demand for money. What Hicks and others have interpreted as an improvement in the specification of the demand for money Keynes considered to be a revolutionary approach to the determination of money prices via the influence of money on the rate of interest.

IV THE MULTIPLIER, LIQUIDITY PREFERENCE AND MONEY PRICES

There can then be no difference between Keynes's insistence that it is the level of income via the multiplier that equates savings and investment and his insistence that it is the degree of liquidity preference which determines the rate of interest. Placing emphasis on the latter 'equation' leads more clearly to what Keynes called the main point of difference with the classical theory: that money is a *real* phenomenon, for if the rate of interest is a monetary phenomenon then money enters the determination of prices via the rate of interest. As Fisher had emphasised, every rate of interest can be conceived of as two prices, present and future. Thus, Keynes's theory implied not a 'time preference' explanation of prices, but a 'liquidity preference' theory of *money* prices, or as Townshend (1937, p. 160) suggested in his note, a correction of the marginal theory of value.

It is now easy to see that if the multiplier and liquidity preference are two sides of the same coin, then the liquidity preference theory of money prices must be an integral part of the explanation of the changes in the demand for investment goods which is necessary to bring about the adjusting action of income on saving via the multiplier. To split the multiplier from liquidity preference is to deprive the income adjustment mechanism of its motor force – profit opportunities caused by movements in relative money prices.

The impossibility of separating liquidity preference from the multiplier was already suggested in a note in Hicks's 1937 article (1982, p. 107, note 4). Hicks rewrites his representation of Keynes's theory, retaining the Quantity Theory demand for money equation. The famous three equations thus become: $M = kY$; $I = f(i)$; $I = S(Y)$. Hicks notes that now the 'multiplier is shorn of its wings. For since Y still depends only on M, I now depends only on M, and it is impossible to increase investment without increasing the willingness to save or the quantity of money. The system thus generated is therefore identical with that which, a few years ago, used to be called the "Treasury View". But Liquidity Preference transports us from the "Treasury View" to the "General Theory of Employment".'

Keynes's theory replaced not just Say's Law, but Say's Law *and* the Quantity Theory which formed a unified whole (cf. Kregel, 1983, pp. 52 ff.). It thus had to replace *both* if it were to be creditable. And just as Say's Law and the Quantity Theory formed a unified system, the theory of income adjustment and liquidity preference formed a unified whole.

Keynes was further concerned (especially in his post-1936 writings) to point out not only the equivalence of income equating saving and investment and his monetary theory of the rate of interest producing real effects; he also stressed that this latter was not simply an alternative explanation of changes in the level of hoarding (or the velocity of circulation, or the quantity of money demanded). This was because traditional theory had argued that an increase in the demand for money would reduce the velocity of circulation, the reduced effective money supply leading to lower prices, leaving saving, investment and the rate of interest unchanged.

Thus Keynes argued the extreme case that a change in liquidity preference could cause a change in prices and output without any change in the quantity of money. As Townshend puts it:

> Any quantity of money, however small, will in theory support any price, however high, provided it circulates fast enough. And any quantity of money, however large, is consistent with zero prices, provided it does not circulate at all, or with indefinitely low prices if it circulates slowly enough. Thus the limitations, whatever they may be, of the stock of money cannot suffice to prevent expectations from raising (or lowering) the money-prices of all durable goods and assets (not, of course, equally) without limit of speed – that is to say, to an arbitrary extent even in the shortest period. (Townshend, 1937, p. 161)

The change in prices in Keynes's approach comes instead from the effect of a change in liquidity preference on the rate of interest relative to the rates of return on other durable assets. Following Fisher, Keynes defines the rate of interest in terms of two prices, for present and future delivery. It is to emphasise this point that Keynes starts his criticism of the alternative monetary theories of interest by stating 'The liquidity-preference theory of the rate of interest which I have set forth . . . makes the rate of interest to depend on the present supply of *money* and the demand schedule for a present claim on money *in terms of a deferred claim on money*' (*CW*, XIV: p. 202, italics added), or 'Interest on money *means* precisely what the books on arithmetic say that it means; that is to say, it is simply the premium obtainable on current cash over deferred cash, so that it measures the marginal preference (for the community as a whole) for holding cash in hand over cash for deferred delivery' (*CW*, XIV: p. 101).

In chapter 17 of the *General Theory*, Keynes had put it: 'The money-rate of interest – we may remind the reader – is nothing more than the percentage excess of a sum of money contracted for forward delivery, e.g. a year hence, over what we may call the "spot" or cash price of the sum thus contracted for forward delivery' (*CW*, VII: p. 222). The rate of interest is thus the difference between two prices, the spot price and the price for forward delivery per cent. Keynes goes on to note, 'It would seem, therefore, that for every kind of capital-asset there must be an analoque of the rate of interest on money' (ibid) each involving the spot and forward price of the asset or good in question. On the basis of Sraffa's (1932) suggestions, Keynes works out the analysis of this point in terms of what he called the 'own rates of own interest' (or the marginal efficiency in terms of the asset) which are defined in terms of spot and forward (or demand and supply) prices.

Changes in liquidity preference will thus change the relation between spot and forward prices of all assets: 'it would seem that it is essential to take liquidity into account in order to discuss *any money* prices. For even if certain assets have so little liquidity-premium that changes in it do not affect their money-prices, variations in the (large) liquidity-premium of money will do so – operating of course on the conditions of new production of the assets' (Townshend, 1937, p. 161). The relation of the spot to forward price of all durable goods are thus seen to be determined by the rate of interest: 'The function of the rate of interest is to modify the money prices of other capital assets in such a way as to equalise the attraction of holding them and holding cash' (*CW*, XIV: p. 213). Keynes's 'novelty' could thus be expressed as a theory of money relative prices determined by the rate of interest. Townshend correctly concludes, 'Now, if Mr. Keynes' views . . . be accepted, it would seem that the considerations governing the prices of monetary assets must also, pro tanto, apply to determine the prices of other durable assets. For the latter have, as Mr. Keynes puts it, "monetary attributes in a varying degree". A kind of liquidity-premium attaches to them also' (Townshend, 1937, p. 159).

Thus relative money price changes lead to profitable investment opportunities and to new investment decisions which produce income adjustment via the multiplier. At the same time as the multiplier adjusts income to equate savings and investment, it adjusts the relation of present to future prices so as to produce 'net balance in the minds of wealth-owners between the conflicting desires to retain purchasing-power (in any form) and to exercise it' (ibid), or to equate the marginal efficiency of all durable stores of value with the marginal efficiency of money: the rate of interest (Keynes development of this theory is more fully spelled out in Kregel, 1982a).

In chapter 14 of the *General Theory*, Keynes criticises those theories 'which attempt to make the rate of interest depend on the "marginal efficiency of capital"' (*CW*, VII: p. 184), noting that although they will be equal in equilibrium, the correct calculation of the latter depends on the former. The factor which determines their equality is the level of income, and it is thus the same adjustment process that equates savings and investment which operates to adjust relative prices and thus brings the rate of return of capital investments (the marginal efficiency of capital) and the rate of interest into equality. A change in liquidity preference is thus capable of changing prices and output independently of any change in the quantity of money held by the public, as the multiplier process equates saving and investment at the same time as it adjusts present to future prices so as to equate the marginal efficiency of capital to the new rate of interest resulting from the initial change in liquidity preference.

Keynes's theory thus substitutes both Say's Law and the Quantity Theory with his Liquidity-Preference–Income-multiplier theory. Much of the post-war literature has emphasised *only* the income-expenditure adjustment process, substituting a traditional demand for money formulation for the theory of liquidity preference. Ironically, although this is how Hicks represented liquidity preference, he was also the first to recognise that it was inappropriate to split that theory from the multiplier.[11] The theory of liquidity-preference-determined money prices cannot be separated from the 'novelty' of income adjusting saving to investment, because they are part of one and the same process.[12]

I have elsewhere (Kregel, 1983) argued that the money prices so determined will, in stationary equilibrium, be compatible with what have come to be called 'Sraffa prices'. Whether or not this view is accepted, we must conclude that the novelty of the multiplier cannot be separated from the theory of liquidity preference without losing what Keynes considered to be his main difference from the traditional theory – the determination of the rate of interest by monetary factors representing the direct influence of money on real factors, rather than vice versa. As Hicks saw, divorcing liquidity preference from the multiplier and adding a simple demand for money function leads back to the Treasury View (or forward to modern monetarism).

The recognition that liquidity preference and the multiplier are but different sides of the same coin also provides an explanation for those who have been bothered by the aggregate representation of demand, enquiring how individual entrepreneurs can be expected to formulate (or why they should be expected to formulate) a schedule of aggregate demand for output as a whole. What the individual entrepreneur faces is a series of supply prices for different levels of activity, and what he formulates is a series of anticipated prices or marginal efficiencies, and he acts in order to bring them into equality. Keynes's effective demand is an attempt to give an economy-wide representation of this fact. For a discussion of the idea that prices lie behind the idea of aggregate demand, cf. Parrinello (1980).

V REINTERPRETING *IS–LM*

It is the relation between money, the money rate of interest and money prices which will distinguish Keynes's theory from Hicks's representation of it. It is thus interesting to go back to Hicks's initial 'three market' model to see how his 1937 rendering of Keynes was developed. His 1935 attempt to dynamise his *Theory of Wages* (1932) dealt with the markets for labour, loans, and goods (bread). If bread is taken as the standard, there are three market equilibrium relations to determine the wage rate and the rate of interest. 'Of these three equations (as in the system of Walras) one follows from the other two. But it is completely indifferent which of the three equations we strike out in this way; convenience seems to dictate that we should strike out the equation relating to loans' (1982, p. 77). Within this framework Hicks presumes that 'bread' wages increase. The result is that 'the total demand for bread will rise, and the rate of interest will rise' (ibid, p. 78). This causes a reduction in the demand for labour, the expected response to an increase in the 'price' of labour.

Hicks notes the fact that the rate of interest and the wage rate moving in the same direction is unusual. This occurs because the bread rate of interest is determined by the equations for the supply and demand for bread. There is no independent 'price' of bread in the model; since bread is the numeraire,

> the world that we have been analysing is a world in which wages are paid in bread, and the rate of interest is a 'bread' rate of interest; in the real world wages are paid in money, and the rate of interest is a money rate. This affects our analysis in two ways. On the one hand, since the

> enterprise does its calculations in money . . . we have to take into account . . . the current price of the product, and the expected movement of that price. . . . On the other hand, since money is now taken as the standard of value, it is the equation of demand and supply for money which is available to determine the rate of interest. The 'consumption-good' equation which we used before is now no longer available, for it is fully occupied in determining the prices of consumption goods. This means that the reactions through interest are monetary reactions, and will depend in practice on the monetary system. (ibid, pp. 78–9)

This seems very like Keynes's theory.

As Hicks points out, at this stage he had not yet seen the *General Theory*, but 'I must certainly have heard that Keynes was determining the rate of interest by the supply of money. I was curious to test out this doctrine on the model with which I was working' (1982, p. 10). Let us follow the adjustments suggested by Hicks. To account for 'money' there will now be four 'markets' – loans, bread, labour and money–to determine interest rates, prices and wages, money now serving as numeraire. As in the orginal analysis the equation for loans is dropped, leaving the supply and demand for bread to determine the price of bread, the demand and supply of labour to determine the wage rate, and the demand and supply of money to determine the interest rate. In this framework a change in wages affects the demand for bread *and* the costs of producing bread; the rate of interest rises as the nominal value of bread increases if this raises the demand for (transactions balances) money given the supply. The effect on employment depends on the effect of the change in wages relative to prices on bread output, and the effect of the rate of interest on future bread production plans; or on the positive effect of higher wages on consumption relative to the negative effect of the higher interest rate on investment on the demand side, and the negative effect of the change in relative prices on current production and expected profits.

Hicks later explained that such a mechanism might be called 'orthodox Keynesian':

> If there is not enough money to support full employment at the enhanced level of money wages, the rate of interest will rise, employment will *therefore* fall, and (probably) real wages will rise, since a smaller volume of labour is being applied to an unchanged capital stock. This is not so very far away from the classical analysis of

> the same problem; after all, it is a rather 'classical' problem, with which classical theory ought to be better able to cope. Both are agreed that the rise in money wages will now lead to a rise in real wages and a fall in employment. (Hicks, 1965, pp. 360–1)

On the other hand, if Hicks's 'monetised' 1935 bread model takes wage units as the numeraire and drops the labour market equation, this leaves three equations to determine the prices of goods, the rate of interest and the price of money. Since the latter is the 'purchasing power of money' or the inverse of the price of goods, there are just two unknowns to be determined by three equations. This seems to be the formulation that Hicks had in mind when he wrote the review (Hicks, 1936) of Keynes's book, rather than the suggested 1935 adjustments. The difference is the introduction of the wage-unit as numeraire, something which Hicks could not have foreseen in 1935.

Problems arise, however, in equating Keynes's scheme with this one, for as Hicks notes, Keynes's two 'prices' were rather different: 'Keynes also appeared to have two parameters – his Y (income in terms of wage units) and r, the rate of interest' (1982, pp. 320–1). As noted, reference to wage-units as numeraire allowed the elimination of the labour market. The rate of interest posed no problem as it appeared in Hicks's earlier version of the model determined by the money market. But income did not fit in, for in Hicks's bread model the output of bread was assumed to be given within the 'period'. Thus, in order to adapt his scheme, Hicks was forced to substitute income for goods prices. This, in fact, involved taking physical output as given; money income was thus determined by the supply and demand for goods determining prices. The equilibrium relations in the money, loans, and goods markets were thus available to determine the interest rate and the 'price' of a physically given aggregate output (Hicks might have referred to Keynes's aggregate demand price, but did not). Given Keynes's assumption that savings equal investment, the loans market became the check equation, leaving supply and demand for money to determine the rate of interest and the supply and demand for output to determine the level of income: *LM* and *IS*.

It is in elaborating this latter relation that Hicks, as he now recognises (Hicks, 1980–1), ran into trouble. Instead of adopting Keynes's aggregate supply and demand structure of effective demand, this market becomes completely demand-determined, physical supply being given within the period. Since demand was composed of consumption and investment, and saving is the inverse of consumption, the equality of savings and investment for any level of income would also determine aggregate demand for that level of income. Thus the multiplier relation could be represented by means of two equations, one linking investment to the marginal efficiency of capital and the other linking saving to the level of income. Since in equilibrium the marginal efficiency of capital equals the rate of interest, different values of the rate of interest (equal to the marginal efficiency of capital) will then produce different levels of consumption and investment and different equilibrium levels of income. It would be possible to derive from this equilibrium a relation between the rate of interest rate (marginal efficiency of capital) and the level of income.[13] The *LM* curve would then show the relation between income and the money rate of interest. The *IS–LM* diagram will then have the money-rate of interest (always equal to the marginal efficiency of capital) on the vertical axis and the level of income on the horizontal axis. Equilibrium is described by the level of income at which the rate of interest which produces equilibrium in the money market is equal to the marginal efficiency of capital. To the left of the intersection of the *IS* and *LM* curves the rate of interest is below the marginal efficiency, profitable opportunities for investment lead entrepreneurs to increase their demand for investment goods, and the multiplier adjusts income to the level at which savings equals investment and prices have adjusted so as to eliminate further profit opportunities to entrepreneurs.

A change in liquidity preference, given the supply of money, will shift the *LM* curve. Since the *IS* curve is drawn up on the assumption that interest equals the marginal efficiency and saving responds to the rate of interest as well as the level of income, the *IS* curve will also shift. A reduction in liquidity preference shifts the *LM* curve to the right. Since the effects of lower interest rates will also affect the investment for any level of income, the *IS* curve will also shift to the right. Thus income will expand until the marginal efficiency read off the *IS* curve equals the rate of interest determined in the money market. If the shifts are equiproportional we have precisely the case that Hicks described as Keynes's 'special theory': Income expands at an unchanged rate of interest. At the same time, Keynes's requirement that income and prices are affected without a change in money holdings initiating the change, is also satisfied. Keynes could hardly have objected to *IS–LM* had he interpreted it in this way.

But this is not what Hicks presented in his 1937 paper. In his 1936 review he had already warned: 'This monetary character of interest is, of course, no novelty; it has been generally recognised at least since the time of Wicksell. But the way of expressing it used by Wicksell and his followers has, of course, to be abandoned by Mr Keynes – since a "natural rate" of interest would be a concept foreign to the whole present trend of his ideas' (1982, p. 92). Yet, in his 1937 presentation, Hicks makes no distinction between the rate of interest which equates saving and investment – the 'investment rate of interest' –and the rate of interest determined in the money market, until his concluding summary where he notes: 'When generalised in this way, Mr Keynes's theory begins to look very like Wicksell's . . . if *IS* is horizontal, we do have a perfectly Wicksellian construction; the investment rate becomes Wicksell's *natural* rate, for in this case it may be thought of as determined by real causes' (1982, p 114).

In this explanation, income adjusts neither saving and investment nor the rate of interest and the marginal efficiency of capital so as to adjust money prices. The rate of interest is a strictly monetary phenomenon, but it has no real effects – these are determined solely by the natural rate of interest. Hicks provides no explanation of the link between the 'real' and the money rate of interest other than a reference to Wicksell's cumulative inflationary process. Indeed, what Hicks has implicitly done in giving this Wicksellian interpretation is to shift his underlying 'three market' model. Now savings and investment determine the 'real' or 'natural' rate of interest, while the supply and demand for money determines the money rate of interest; effective demand has become the check equation determining the level of income. There is only one level of effective demand compatible with stable prices, but clearly this is not what Keynes was attempting to demonstrate.

One can certainly understand that Keynes was unclear about which 'alternative' theory of interest Hicks was assuming, even though Hicks demonstrated the indifference as to which equation serves as the check equation for the equilibrium result. Keynes was thus concerned to insist that the description of the process of adjustment of the system was of fundamental importance, especially with respect to policy formation.

Economists have spent the last forty years investigating, criticising, and expounding the multiplier adjustment process in Hicks's *IS–LM* framework. This has masked the other side of the adjustment process – the role of the rate of interest in determining prices and the role of income in adjusting relative prices. One of the most important tasks of Keynesian monetary theorists must be the pursuit of Keynes's theory of the determination of money prices within the theory of liquidity preference, and his theory of price adjustment within the theory of the income adjustment process of the multiplier; both sides of the income adjustment coin should carry equal importance.

Notes

1. Keynes here refers to those who determine the rate of interest by means of physical productivity of capital, the roundaboutness of production or natural factors: e.g., Böhm Bawerk and Wicksell, cf. *CW*, VII: pp. 213ff.
2. Compare this with Tobin's (1972, p. 853) comments on Friedman: 'In terms of the Hicksian language of Friedman's two articles I thought (and I still think) ... the main issue ... was the shape of the *LM* locus.' Friedman (1972, p. 913) insists that both he and Tobin accept a positive slope, rejecting a vertical or horizontal *LM* curve.
3. Which offers a clear explanation of why post-Keynesian monetary theorists consider Tobin and Friedman's work to be similar and only tenuously linked to Keynes's theory.
4. Since there is no explicit discussion of this point in the 1937 paper it would have been impossible to criticise it directly. Yet Keynes clearly took this to be the most important point at issue, challenging Hicks to clarify and differentiate his position from that of Ohlin and Robertson, which Hicks did not feel to be necessary.
5. (*CW*, XIV: pp. 82–3) This represents an expansion of Hicks's comments in the 1936 review: cf. Hicks (1982, pp. 92–4).
6. Hicks calls this 'alternative' the 'ordinary method of economic theory' in his 1936 review (1982, p. 92). In his full explanation given in his letter to Keynes (*CW*, XIV: p. 82), Hicks's second alternative has goods prices determined by the supply and demand for money, with effective demand the check equation. Below we suggest that this was the model which finally came to characterise *IS–LM*. Hicks's first alternative was his characterisation of Keynes's approach.
7. If the supply and demand for money is the check equation, then the demand for money relative to supply determines the price level, while the supply and demand for goods determines relative prices.
8. This passage clearly indicates that Keynes did not consider liquidity preference as a new, improved explanation of the demand for money. Keynes wanted to distance his position from those who explained cyclical changes in prices by means of changes in hoarding or the velocity of circulation affecting the effective quantity of money, because such an explanation based on changes in the quantity of money demanded preserved the direct link between the quantity of money and the price level of the Quantity Theory. This intention can also be seen in the following passage from R. B. Bryce's 'Introduction to a Monetary Theory of Employment' (*CW*, XXIX: p. 142): 'It is through its effect on the rate of interest that the quantity of money actually affects investment, incomes, employment and prices. The relationship of the quantity of money to any of these latter elements is rather complex so that it is no wonder that simple directness of the quantity theory of money could shed so little light on what actually happens.'
9. As Hicks notes (*CW*, XIV: p. 82), 'Mr. Townshend seems to object against the loans theory that it leaves out the possibility of a general rise in the price of securities without any borrowing or lending.' Cf. Townshend (1937, p. 158).

10. 'I find, looking back, that it was Professor Irving Fisher who was the great-grandparent who first influenced me strongly towards regarding money as a "real" factor' (*CW*, XIV: p. 203).
11. Hicks assesses Keynes's difference from the classics as follows: 'Mr Keynes' . . . three equations . . . differ from the classical equations in two ways. On the one hand, the demand for money is conceived as depending upon the rate of interest (Liquidity Preference). On the other hand, any possible influence of the rate of interest on the amount saved out of a given income is neglected. Although it means that the third equation becomes the multiplier equation . . . this second amendment is a mere simplification and ultimately insignificant. It is the liquidity preference doctrine which is vital' (Hicks, 1982, p. 107).
12. Townshend (1937, p. 164) notes, however, that before the adjustment process comes to an end, 'in general further (similar or opposite) spontaneous changes in the liquidity premiums . . . will have taken place; obviously the physical production . . . can never take place fast enough for its effects on prices to catch up with people's purely *mental* revaluations of existing ones. Of course, in practice, the *possibility or prospect* of new production bringing down again the *money*-price . . . is present in people's minds, and operates to diminish optimism or to cause a wave of optimism to be followed by a wave of pessimism.' Thus the theory of 'shifting equilibrium' (cf. Kregel, 1976) which is constrained by short-period production factors (cf. Kregel, 1978).
13. Hicks puts it this way: 'For it is now the rate of interest, not income, which is determined by the quantity of money. The rate of interest set against the schedule of the marginal efficiency of capital determines the value of investment; that determines income by the multiplier. Then the volume of employment (at given wage-rates) is determined by the value of investment and of income which is not saved but spent upon consumption goods' (Hicks, 1982, p. 107). Thus $I = f(\text{MEC})$ and $S = f(Y)$. Taking into account the possible influence of interest on saving, and the fact that when $I = S$, $i = \text{MEC}$ the equilibrium becomes $I = S(Y, i)$ and the marginal efficiency drops out of the story, as does the adjustment of prices as Y changes in adjusting MEC to i. Support for this interpretation is also found in Hicks's later reflections. Cf. Hicks (1977, p. 66).

    It is interesting to compare this summary quotation from Hicks with the very similar one produced by Harrod (*CW*, XIII: p. 553) to convince Keynes of his full understanding of the theory. This did not prevent Harrod from producing (Harrod, 1937) a summary of the *General Theory* based on three 'market equations' which fails to consider what Keynes called the essential point of difference from the classicals and which completely ignored effective demand!

References

Friedman, M. (1972) 'Comments on the Critics', *Journal of Political Economy*, vol. 80 (Sept/Oct).

Harrod, R. F. (1937) 'Keynes and Traditional Theory', *Econometrica*, vol. 5 (Jan).

Hicks, J. R. (1932) *Theory of Wages*, 2nd edn. 1965 (London: Macmillan).

——(1936) 'Review of the General Theory', in Hicks (1982) pp. 83–99.

——(1937) 'Mr Keynes and the Classics', in Hicks (1982) pp. 100–15.

——(1977) *Economic Perspectives* (Oxford: Clarendon Press).

——(1980–1) 'IS–LM – An Explanation', in Hicks (1982) pp. 318–31.

——(1935) 'Wages and Interest: the Dynamic Problem', in Hicks (1982) pp. 64–79.

——(1982) *Collected Essays*, volume II (Oxford: Blackwell).

Keynes, J. M. (VII) *The General Theory of Employment, Interest and Money*, 1971.

——(XIII) *The General Theory and After: Part I*, 1973.

——(XIV) *The General Theory and After: Part II*, 1973.

——(XXIX) *The General Theory and After: A Supplement*, 1979. All volumes from *Collected Writings of John Maynard Keynes* (London: Macmillan).

Kregel, J. A. (1976) 'Economic Methodology in the Face of Uncertainty', *Economic Journal*, vol. 36 (June).

——(1978) 'La teoria keynesiana della domanda effettiva e la teoria classica', *Economia Internazionale*, vol. XXXI (Feb.–May).

——(1982a) 'Money, Expectations and Relative Prices in Keynes' Monetary Equilibrium', *Economie Appliquée*, vol. XXXV, no. 3.

——(1982b) 'Microfoundations and Hicksian Monetary Theory', *de Economist*, vol. 130, no. 4.

——(1983) 'Effective Demand: Origins and Development of the Notion', in *Distribution, Effective Demand and International Economic Relations* (London: Macmillan).

Parrinello, S. (1980) 'The Price Level in Keynes' Effective Demand', *Journal of Post Keynesian Economics*, vol. III (Fall).

Sraffa, P. (1932) 'Dr Hayek on Money and Capital', *Economic Journal*, vol. XLII (March).

Tobin, J. (1972) 'Friedman's Theoretical Framework', *Journal of Political Economy*, vol. 80 (Sept./Oct).

Townshend, H. (1937) 'Liquidity-premium and the Theory of Value', *Economic Journal*, vol. XLVII (March).

12 Reflections on the Microeconomic Foundations of the Keynesian Aggregate Supply Function

Rodolphe Dos Santos Ferreira
and Philippe Michel

The theoretical goal of the *General Theory* has two main components: a negative one and a positive one. The negative component is a critique of classical theory in general and in particular of Say's law, which Keynes sees as its core. The positive one is first of all an attempt to replace the false dichotomy between value theory and monetary theory by the proper dichotomy between the theory of the individual firm or industry and the theory of output and employment as a whole. We do not introduce here the shorter expressions 'microeconomic theory' and 'macroeconomic theory' which might cause confusion by bringing in yet a third distinction which could be taken to refer to two different modes rather than to two distinct objects of analysis.

These two components are closely connected. Indeed, Keynes essentially reproaches the classical economists for discarding the conceptual framework of supply and demand when they leave the domain of value theory to broach monetary theory, and, through monetary theory, the analysis of the economy as a whole. Keynes's plan is to adapt this conceptual framework, designed by classical (Marshallian) economists for the study of partial equilibria, to analysis of the determination of output, employment, and prices in the economy as a whole. And it is this adapted conceptual framework which enables him to direct a central attack on Say's law through the principle of effective demand.

Keynes's adaptation of the conceptual apparatus of supply and demand to new use corresponds to the second term in his dichotomy, but it is not simply an analogical transposition from the level of the individual firm or industry to the level of the economy as a whole. On the contrary, Keynes has built a new theoretical construction of the foundations provided by Marshallian microeconomics.

For over two decades, mainstream Keynesian economists have generally ignored these microeconomic foundations and also neglected one blade of Marshall's scissors to concentrate exclusively on the demand side. This is true not only of the orthodox school represented by the neoclassical synthesis, but also of several more heterodox groups. It is, however, well known that a group of post-Keynesian economists, inspired by Sidney Weintraub's work, have remedied this twofold neglect of both the microeconomic foundations and the supply side. In addition, Don Patinkin's successive contributions, which have created some controversy, particularly in the field of Keynesian exegesis, have also paid great attention to these two aspects of Keynes's theory that have been so often neglected.

The heart of the controversy lies in Patinkin's assimilation of the Keynesian aggregate supply function to a total variable cost function; this position contradicts the traditional interpretation laid out by Dennis Robertson and popularised by Sidney Weintraub, which holds that this function is simply an extension of the Marshallian supply function. In our opinion, the traditional interpretation and a revised version of Patinkin's interpretation both have their roles to play within a dual understanding of the effective demand principle and of the conceptual framework that underlies this principle. In this chapter, we shall start by laying out this dual interpretation of the principle of effective demand. We shall then argue that this interpretation leads us to disclose two stages in the corresponding conceptual apparatus, not only on the demand side, where this duality has already been recongnised by Robertson, but also on the supply side, where this duality is not yet acknowledged and is only revealed by the coexistence of two conflicting interpretations. This understanding of the Keynesian conceptual framework suggests that Keynes was more respectful of Marshallian orthodoxy than is usually thought. It also shows that Keynes is definitely a more rigorous theorist than is ordinarily recognised.

I A DUAL INTERPRETATION OF THE PRINCIPLE OF EFFECTIVE DEMAND

The principle of effective demand, which is formulated in the third chapter of the *General Theory*, in fact contains two distinct propositions.

The first is simply that the level of employment, and therefore also the corresponding volume of output, are determined on a 'daily' basis through the decisions of individual entrepreneurs who try to maximise their profits on the basis of their short- and long-term expectations. In the short term, where technology and capital equipment do not change and where the money wage rate is predetermined, expectations about demand conditions are the ruling factor in the decision-making process. Thus it is (expected) demand which determines employment and output levels, this idea being conveyed by the term 'effective demand'.

This proposition, and all its underlying ideas, follow directly from Marshall's teaching, and in fact echo chapters 3 and 5 in book V of Marshall's *Principles*. So this proposition is not at all revolutionary, and can only appear unorthodox from the point of view of the Walrasian tradition, which is completely foreign to Keynes. In the Marshallian universe, where there is no auctioneer, and given the existence of a production lag, entrepreneurs must try to foresee demand prices or, more generally, foresee the demand curve that awaits them.

However, the effective demand principle cannot be reduced to this first proposition. Keynes does not stop at the instantaneous determination of the actual level of employment corresponding to a given set of expectations; otherwise he would have to give up the attempt to explain the persistence of (involuntary) unemployment, which is in fact the central goal of the *General Theory*. For this reason, he examines the *equilibrium* level of employment, once more in a very Marshallian way. Following Marshall's definition of equilibrium, he considers the equilibrium level of employment to be that level at which there is no tendency towards change.

This brings us to the second proposition contained in the principle of effective demand: there exists an equilibrium level of employment which is, by definition, the level where producers' expectations are confirmed by the market, so that producers have no incentive to revise their expectations. Moreover, under certain conditions this equilibrium is unique and stable. The fact that the equilibrium level of employment can be one of under-employment contradicts Say's law, according to which supply creates its own demand, or, to put it more precisely, the market will confirm producers' expectations at any level of employment.

The second proposition contained in the principle of effective demand is based on what Keynes calls the fundamental psychological law, and also on an analysis of portfolio decisions which leads him to deny the existence of an automatic mechanism for adjusting investment plans to consumers' decisions to save. Our goal here is not to discuss whether or not Keynes's positions on these points are correct, but to show the link between the duality of the effective demand principle and the duality of the associated conceptual apparatus of supply and demand.

II THE FIRST STAGE OF THE CONCEPTUAL APPARATUS OF AGGREGATE SUPPLY AND DEMAND: THE DETERMINATION OF THE ACTUAL LEVEL OF EMPLOYMENT

We will now examine the first of the two propositions that make up the principle of effective demand. This proposition concerns the determination of the actual level of employment and refers to a unique given state of entrepreneur's expectations. To simplify matters, we will assume that all entrepreneurs are perfectly competitive, even though the *General Theory* only supposes a given, non-specified degree of competition which makes the Keynesian analysis applicable to certain kinds of imperfect competition. Hence, producers' expectations concern a demand price which does not depend on the level of employment or on the volume of output.

We will now examine the decision-making process of an individual producer, r, keeping in mind that entrepreneurs' *individual* decisions determine the overall level of employment in the economy. Our producer maximises his expected profits, that is, the difference between his expected sales proceeds, $\overline{p}_r \psi_r(N_r)$, at each possible level of employment and his expected cost of production, WN_r, where $\overline{p}_r$ represents expected demand price, ψ_r the production function, N_r the level of employment, and W the money wage rate. In order to simplify the analysis further, we ignore user cost and limit factor cost to wage cost. We also assume that labour is homogeneous and that there is a uniform wage rate. Keynes's theoretical constructs do not require such simplifications, which are not introduced in the *General Theory*. However, the reason for introducing them here is to focus attention on what is essential for our argument within the framework of a brief presentation.

If we suppose that the production function is differentiable, the necessary condition for maximisation of profits, $\overline{p}_r \psi_r(N_r) - WN_r$, with a positive level of employment N_r^* is: $\overline{p}_r \psi_r'(N_r^*) = W$. This formula expresses the equality of the marginal productivity of labour, measured in value, and the wage rate, an equality which Keynes calls the first fundamental postulate of the classical theory of employment. Naturally, if we measure value in terms of wage units, noting $\overline{p}_{wr} = \overline{p}_r / W$, the

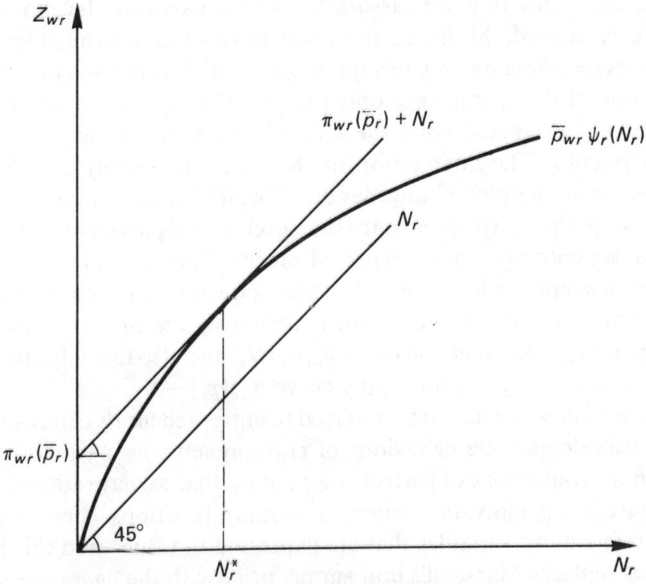

Figure 12.1

preceding condition may also be written as: $\bar{p}_{wr}\psi_r'(N_r^*) = 1$. Figure 12.1 is a graphic representation of our producer's maximisation procedure.

The curve $\bar{p}_{wr}\psi_r(N_r)$ represents entrepreneur r's total *expected* proceeds. In our interpretation, this corresponds to the entrepreneur's aggregate demand function, which is associated with his short-term expectations represented by $\bar{p}_r$. The 45° line passing through the origin represents total wage cost, evaluated in wage units. Given our simplifying assumptions, this total wage cost is equivalent to total variable costs. In Patinkin's interpretation, this corresponds to entrepreneur r's aggregate supply function. Finally, the 45° line tangent to the total expected proceeds curve represents total proceeds *required* by entrepreneur r in order for him to create the corresponding level of employment, given his short-term expectations. This line shows the sales proceeds which would just cover variable costs at each possible level of employment, and would guarantee the entrepreneur the profits he actually hopes to obtain thanks to his maximising behaviour and given his expectations about demand conditions.

This same 45° line intersects the ordinate axis at a point which represents maximum expected profits, $\pi_{wr}(\bar{p}_r)$, a function of short-term expectations. In our interpretation, it is the graph of entrepreneur r's aggregate supply function, associated with a particular level of expectations $\bar{p}_r$. Indeed, this is a relation between each employment level and the corresponding aggregate supply price which conforms to Keynes's definition of the aggregate supply price as 'the expectation of proceeds which will just make it worth the while of [the entrepreneur] to give that employment'.[1] The intersection of the aggregate supply and demand curves – in fact a point of tangency here – which Keynes calls the effective demand point, corresponds to the level of employment N_r^* which maximises entrepreneur r's expected profits. Thus our interpretation is indeed in keeping with the way Keynes characterises effective demand.[2] In the present context, this point is obviously the only optimal point along the aggregate demand curve $\bar{p}_{wr}\psi_r(N_r)$ and also the only attainable point along the aggregate supply curve $\pi_{wr}(\bar{p}_r)+N_r$.

Up until now, we have only referred to entrepreneur r's behaviour. We can easily deduce the behaviour of entrepreneurs as a whole, at least within the framework of perfect competition that we have adopted here, by aggregating individual aggregate supply functions. Since we have been referring to variables that are expressed in value – and this is why Keynes replaces Marshall's unit supply price with the *aggregate* supply price – we need only to add them. We obtain the following expression of the aggregate supply function for the economy as whole (expressed in wage-units):

$$\Phi(N) = \sum_r \pi_{wr}(\bar{p}_r) + N, \qquad \text{where} \quad N = \sum_r N_r.$$

This interpretation of Keynes's aggregate supply function is borne out by a footnote in chapter 6 of the *General Theory*, which authors have not much heeded, with the exception of Patinkin:

> For example, let us take $Z_w = \Phi(N)$, or alternatively $Z = W \cdot \Phi(N)$ as the aggregate supply function (where W is the wage-unit and $W \cdot Z_w = Z$). Then, since the proceeds of the marginal product is equal to the marginal factor-cost at every point on the aggregate supply curve, we have
>
> $$\Delta N = \ldots = \Delta Z_w = \Delta\Phi(N),$$
>
> that is to say $\Phi'(N) = 1$; provided that factor cost bears a constant ratio to wage cost, and that the aggregate supply function for each firm (the number of which is assumed to be constant) is independent of the number of men employed in other industries, so that the terms of the above equation, which hold good for each individual entrepreneur, can be summed for the entrepreneurs as a whole.[3]

According to this note, Keynes clearly attributes a constant slope equal to one (when aggregate supply is expressed in wage-units) to the aggregate supply function, at least in one of its meanings. However, contrary to Patinkin's implicit supposition, this 45° line does not necessarily pass through the origin.

III THE SECOND STAGE OF THE CONCEPTUAL APPARATUS OF SUPPLY AND DEMAND: THE DETERMINATION OF THE EQUILIBRIUM LEVEL OF EMPLOYMENT AND THE CRITIQUE OF SAY'S LAW

We will now examine the second stage of the Keynesian conceptual apparatus, which corresponds to the second proposition contained in the effective demand principle. The proposition refers to equilibrium states where entrepreneurs' short-term expectations, which concern essentially demand conditions, are fulfilled. We must now consider the behaviour of the agents on the demand side, that is of consumers and entrepreneurs, the latter acting as investors and no longer as producers.

This behaviour cannot be considered exogeneous to the determination of the equilibrium level of employment. Indeed, Keynes introduces an important distinction between an autonomous component of demand and a component which depends on financing income and hence also on the level of employment. This second, induced component, depends not only on the employment created by enterprises to which demand is directly addressed, but, above all, on the employment created by other enterprises, in other industries. We now have a causal feedback sequence: (expected) demand → distributed income → (actual) demand (which is to be compared to expected demand) which shatters the framework of Marshall's partial equilibrium analysis of the individual firm or industry. Keynes uses macroeconomic analysis to introduce interdependence between factor markets and goods markets, which is lacking in Marshallian analysis. He thereby avoids having to construct an explicit general equilibrium system. At this stage, the aggregation of behavioural relationships is therefore a crucial device and no longer a sterile exercise used to round off an analysis whose main results have already been reached.

What are the aggregate supply and demand functions now? The aggregate demand function is no longer the result of a simple operation of aggregation of individual entrepreneurs' aggregate demand functions; these functions translate sellers' expectations, while at this stage we want to consider buyers' plans. This duality in concepts of the aggregate demand function has already been recognised by Robertson and subsequently emphasised by other authors, particularly by Vandenborre and Casarosa. Our goal here is not to study the foundations of this new incarnation of the aggregate demand function. All we need remember here is that, according to Keynes's fundamental psychological law, which states that the marginal propensity to consume is always less than 1, the derivative of the aggregate demand function is smaller than the derivative of the aggregate supply function at any level of employment. However, we must determine precisely what aggregate supply function we are referring to.

In fact, demand is induced by actual income, which in this context includes wages and *realised* profits; these profits are necessarily associated with an equilibrium state, at least within a framework such as the one in the *General Theory*, which excludes any assumption about the way the economic system operates in disequilibrium. But we may still choose between two distinct concepts of the aggregate supply function.

We may use an aggregate supply function which is an extension of the Marshallian supply function. In this case, we will no longer consider only one given state of expectations but the set of all admissible states of producers' short-term expectations represented within the simplified framework of perfect competition by the prices that are possible *a priori*. Since our final goal is to analyse equilibrium states, we can immediately eliminate states of expectations where the prices foreseen by different producers within the same industry are not identical. We will then associate with each possible level of employment not the level of proceeds required by entrepreneurs given the particular state of their expectations, as we did before, but the effective demand that generates that level of employment. This means we must consider all possible states of short-term expectations. We thereby obtain the Keynesian aggregate supply function as depicted in Robertson and Weintraub's traditional interpretation. As an illustration, we will re-examine the situation of entrepreneur r (see Figure 12.2).

To two different states of short-term expectations, represented by the expected prices $\bar{p}$ and $\bar{\bar{p}}$, there correspond two expected proceeds curves $\bar{\bar{p}}_w \psi_r(N_r)$ and $\bar{\bar{p}}_w \psi_r(N_r)$, two optimal expected levels of profits, $\pi_{wr}(\bar{p})$ and $\pi_{wr}(\bar{p})$ and therefore two straight lines representing required proceeds, and of course two effective demand points corresponding to two distinct levels of employment N_r^* and N_r^{**}. The Robertson–Weintraub aggregate supply curve passes through these two points. This curve is simply a projection on the (N_r, Z_{wr}) plane of the

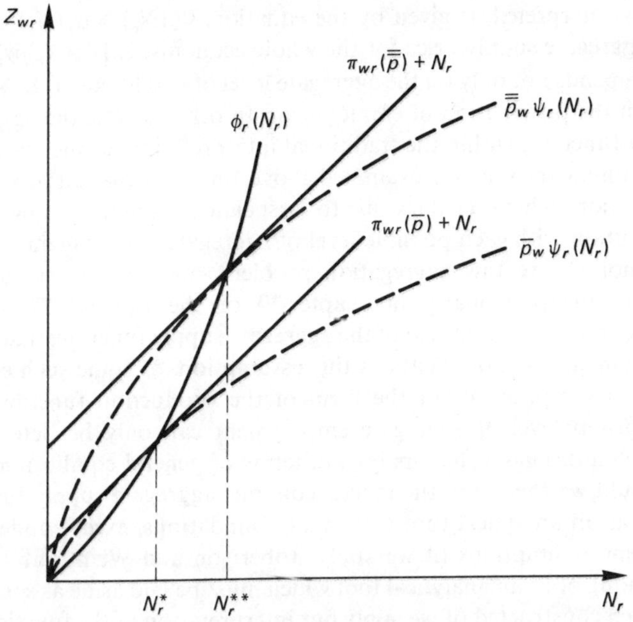

Figure 12.2

locus of potential effective demand points, that is to say, of the intersection of the expected proceeds plane and the required proceeds plane which lie in the (N_r, Z_{wr}, p) space where the third dimension corresponds to the expected price p.

Keynes's repeated statements that his aggregate supply function is merely an extension of the Marshallian supply function, along with certain passages in the *General Theory*, clearly place this function, as traditionally interpreted, at the heart of the Keynesian conceptual framework. We might logically conclude that the *equilibrium* level of effective demand (and the corresponding level of employment) is determined by the intersection of the aggregate supply curve and the aggregate demand curve as *planned on the demand side* (this second curve depending itself on the first). Things are in fact not quite so simple. According to the first fundamental postulate of classical theory, that is, according to the condition of profit maximisation, N_r is the level of employment associated with the expected price $\bar{p}$ only if: $\bar{p}_w \psi'_r(N_r) = 1$. The Marshallian supply price in wage units is therefore equal to $1/\psi'_r(N_r)$. It follows from this that entrepreneur r's aggregate supply function, as usually interpreted, is given by the equation: $\Phi_r(N_r) = \psi_r(N_r)/\psi'_r(N_r)$. The aggregate supply price for the whole economy, $\Sigma_r[\psi_r(N_r)/\psi'_r(N_r)]$, thus depends not only on the aggregate level of employment $\Sigma_r N_r$, but also on the distribution of employment. In other words, the aggregate supply function, within the traditional interpretation, cannot be aggregated, unlike the function examined above, unless we make a very strong assumption which enables us to associate a unique employment distribution with each possible level of aggregate employment. Keynes does not ignore this aggregation problem, and introduces such an assumption (particularly in chapter 20 of the *General Theory*) in connection with the inverse of the aggregate supply function, that is, the employment function. Without this assumption, or some such equally strong assumption about the form of the production functions, the equilibrium level of aggregate employment can only be determined through a disaggregated analysis in terms of general equilibrium.

Should we then view the macroeconomic aggregate supply function either as an analytical tool with weak foundations, except under very stringent assumptions (if we apply Robertson and Weintraub's interpretation), or as an analytical tool which must be laid aside as soon as it has been constructed (if we apply our interpretation of the function as a required proceeds function associated with a given state of short-term expectations)? In fact, since either one of these two forms of the aggregate supply function is sufficient for a critique of Say's law, the second one is preferable in this context in that it can be easily aggregated without further assumptions.

To illustrate this idea, we will now consider a given state of producers' short-term expectations. Furthermore, we will suppose that this is an equilibrium state: that is, that the point of effective demand that corresponds to this state is a point of intersection, not only of the expected proceeds and required proceeds curves – as it is by definition – but also of the demand curve as planned by consumers and investors; so that producers' expectations are fulfilled. We want to know if an increase in aggregate employment can be generated by a self-fulfilling increase in producers' price expectations. Of course, Say's law would answer in the affirmative. If, on the contrary, we apply the fundamental psychological law and assume that there is no automatic mechanism to adjust autonomous demand to the savings induced by changes in income, the answer is negative. The aggregate demand curve as planned by consumers and investors has a slope that is smaller than the slope of the 45° aggregate supply line, which corresponds to a fixed level of profits (and hence smaller than that of the traditional aggregate supply curve, along which profits increase). Thus, the 45° aggregate supply line is perfectly adequate for the attack on Say's law, which may explain why, within the Keynesian framework, it exists alongside another aggregate supply curve which is simply an extension of the Marshallian supply curve.

If our interpretation is correct, the use of identical terminology unfortunately hides the duality of the effective demand principle and even more so the duality of the underlying conceptual framework. In spite of confusing terminology and in spite of some possible weaknesses in conceptual precision or analytical rigour, we cannot deny that Keynes pays a great deal of attention to the microeconomic foundations of his analysis and to the aggregation procedure which enables him to make a transition to macroeconomic statements. It cannot be denied, either, that the Keynesian revolution is indeed an offshoot of the Marshallian tradition in which Keynes's theoretical thinking is firmly rooted.

Notes

1. Keynes, John Maynard, *The General Theory of Employment, Interest and Money* (London: Macmillan, 1973) p. 24.
2. Ibid, p. 25.
3. Ibid, pp. 55–6, footnote 2.

References

Casarosa, Carlo (1981) 'The Microfoundations of Keynes's Aggregate Supply and Expected Demand Analysis', *Economic Journal*, 91 (March) pp. 188–94.

Keynes, John Maynard (1936) *The General Theory of Employment, Interest and Money* (London: Macmillan).

Marshall, Alfred (1920) *Principles of Economics*, eighth edn (London: Macmillan).

Patinkin, Don (1949) 'Involuntary Unemployment and the Keynesian Supply Function', *Economic Journal*, 59 (Sept) pp. 360–83. Reprinted, with an originally unpublished mathematical appendix, in Patinkin, *Essays On and In the Chicago Tradition* (Durham, N.C.: Duke University Press, 1981) pp. 155–79.

—— (1976) *Keynes' Monetary Thought, A Study of its Development* (Durham, N.C.: Duke University Press).

—— (1982) 'A Critique of Keynes' Theory of Effective Demand', ch. 5 of *Anticipations of the General Theory*? (Oxford: Blackwell) pp. 123–62.

Robertson, Dennis H. (1936) 'Some Notes on Mr. Keynes' General Theory of Employment', *Quarterly Journal of Economics*, 51 (Nov) pp. 168–91.

—— (1955) 'Keynes and Supply Functions', *Economic Journal*, 65 (Sept) pp. 474–7.

Vandenborre, H. (1958) 'An Integration of Employment Economics Within the Keynesian Theory of Money Flows', *Oxford Economic Papers*, 10 (June) pp. 205–19.

Weintraub, Sidney (1957) 'The Microfoundations of Aggregate Demand and Supply', *Economic Journal*, 67 (Sept) pp. 455–70.

Some Remarks

Henri Guitton

We are celebrating the centenary of the Keynes's birth (5 June 1883). If he had lived longer, even if not to his hundredth year, or if he were still among us, I sometimes wonder if he would not had revised his *General Theory*, above all considering the unpredictable nature of the impact of his innovations. Alain Barrère has used the expression 'second reading'. Why should an author not be permitted a 'second writing'? It has been brought to our attention that Townshend asked Keynes a question to which Keynes could not respond. A book such as this gives the opportunity to provide the answer that each of us believes to be closest to the spirit of the Keynes's thought.

It is in this context that I ask myself a question that may appear scandalous. How long are we going to continue to preserve the distinction between microeconomics and macroeconomics? How long are we going to continue debating which of the two provides the foundation for the other, which of the two must be used to provide the foundation of our analysis?

I have come to be persuaded that it is not by means of aggregation that the real nature of macroeconomics can be best understood. It is not by means of 'space' that we can gain this understanding, but rather by 'time'; or better, by means of what I shall call the 'duration' of time.

What we have become accustomed to calling microeconomics takes place in a succession of continuous instants which give rise to the encounters in a form that we call the market and where equilibrium is established.

Under the much less elegant classification of macroeconomics, it is no longer a question of equilibrium, but rather it is the idea of the circuit which opens and closes in the duration of time – time which expresses a consistency such that it cannot be sliced into separate instants. Our theoretical efforts must from now on be consecrated towards defining those relations which exist between continuous time and indivisible time, and thus between the notion of the market and that of the circuit.

In this line of thought I admit to being impressed by the idea of the identity of aggregate supply and demand over time. Indeed, how can one be but convinced that supply and demand cannot be distinguished, and thus measured, except when they are identical, that is, at the point of intersection of the two curves that represent them.

From this perspective, reading Keynes with attention, it is easy to see that the identity which he himself recognised eliminates any idea of adjustment processes which have been the subject of unending analysis. Aggregate supply and aggregate demand never adjust one to the other, for by their very nature they are identical. Is it even reasonable to retain the expression of effective demand, given that Keynes himself expressly defines it as an inseparable supply–demand?

When Lord Kaldor tells us that the English economists never accepted the possibility of equilibrium for the long duration, that the notion of equilibrium only has value in the short duration, it seems to me that this represents a confirmation of what I believe to be the nature of macroeconomics.

Habits are so well ingrained that it seems impossible to give up the expression 'macroeconomics'. In any case, the prefix 'macro' is used in a number of other disciplines. In all of these (physics, zoology) it is intended to express a dimension of the things being analysed, what is heavy and large, the term 'micro' having been first employed for things which are small. All the same, this is a very superficial way of looking at things. When one wants to go deeper, to understand them from the inside, rather than from the outside, I am more and more convinced that some other word is necessary. Unfortunately there is no ready prefix to translate the concept of the duration of time.

Index